ROOSEVELT'S
NAVY

ROOSEVELT'S NAVY

THE EDUCATION OF A WARRIOR PRESIDENT, 1882–1920

James Tertius de Kay

PEGASUS BOOKS

NEW YORK

ROOSEVELT'S NAVY

Pegasus Books LLC
80 Broad Street, 5th Floor
New York, NY 10004

Copyright © 2012 by James Tertius de Kay

First Pegasus Books cloth edition 2012

Interior design by Maria Fernandez

Library of Congress Cataloging-in-Publication Data is available.

ISBN: 978-1-60598-285-4

10 9 8 7 6 5 4 3 2 1

Printed in the United States of America
Distributed by W. W. Norton & Company, Inc.

For
Al Zuckerman
who makes things happen

PROLOGUE

T he call came in from Paris shortly before three in the morning on September 1, 1939. Despite the early hour, the White House duty officer, following instructions, routed it directly through to the president's bedroom. Franklin Roosevelt, awakened from a fitful sleep, reached for the bedside phone with a sense of foreboding.

The caller was William Bullitt, his ambassador in France, relaying a grim but long-expected message from the American embassy in Warsaw: Hitler had invaded Poland. If Britain and France fulfilled their pledges to Poland—and Roosevelt was sure they would—World War II had just begun.

Roosevelt knew it was likely to be a long and particularly brutal war. In the coming years millions of innocent people would die before their time, killed in ugly, sickening ways. Millions more would be maimed and crippled and otherwise have their lives destroyed.

"It's come at last," he said resignedly. "God help us all."

viii | JAMES TERTIUS de KAY

Ever since taking office in 1933, Roosevelt had watched with increasing frustration and despair as the leaders of the European democracies, anxious to avert another war so soon after their countries had been devastated by the horrors of 1914–1918, humiliated themselves in their efforts to accommodate Hitler, caving in to his every threat, emboldening him to constantly raise his demands.

Year after year, as another war grew increasingly likely, isolationists in Congress and elsewhere did everything in their power to keep America out of it. Their arguments were cogent, and to many Americans, persuasive. The United States had sacrificed its blood and treasure to save Europe in 1917, they argued, and had received nothing in return. Now the Europeans were up to their old tricks again. Why should America help prop up countries that couldn't manage their own survival?

But Roosevelt was convinced the isolationists were shortsighted. All his life, he had been able to see the future more clearly than most, and what he saw convinced him that World War II posed a far greater threat to the United States than World War I had. If Hitler managed to subdue the European powers, his Japanese allies on the other side of the globe would gobble up Europe's undefended colonial empires and incorporate them into their "Greater East Asia Co-Prosperity Sphere." America would be left to stand alone, surrounded by a very powerful and hostile world.

One way or another, Americans would be drawn into the coming war. Roosevelt was sure of that. And it was up to him to lead them in that war. He was sure of that, too. He was the right man for the job. He had the training. He had the experience. Circumstances had made the President of the United States the most powerful man on the planet and because Roosevelt had that streak of arrogance that every competent leader must have, he was convinced that he knew best how to wield that power. He knew how to mobilize the nation, and he knew how to fight wars.

For months now, he had wondered if he should break with tradition and run for an unprecedented third term. Now the late-night telephone call gave him the answer. He would run. And he would win. And then he would win the war. It seemed he had been preparing his whole life for this challenge.

After a few last words with William Bullitt in Paris, the president hung up and put in calls to his secretary of state, then his secretary of war and a few other subordinates, to tell them the news. Then he replaced the phone in its cradle and picked up a pencil and wrote on a pad that he kept at bedside:

> *The President received
> word at 2:50 A.M. by telephone from
> Ambas. Biddle through
> Ambas. Bullitt that
> Germany has invaded
> Poland and that their
> cities are being bombed.
> The Pres. directed that
> all Navy ships and army
> commands be notified by radio at
> once.*
>
> > *In bed*
> > *3:05 A.M.*
> > *Sept. 1 39*

He initialed the note, then turned out the light and went back to sleep.

The hastily scribbled note has been carefully preserved, and today it holds a place of honor in the collection of the Franklin Delano Roosevelt Library in Hyde Park, New York. It is an interesting note, simultaneously self-revealing and detached. He refers to himself—twice—as "The President," as if he were making reference to some distant historical figure. It is a curious use of the third person for a master politician whose famous Fireside Chats relied so heavily on his skillful use of the first person singular.

Just as interestingly, he capitalizes the word "Navy," but not "army."

CHAPTER ONE

A boy sits alone, quietly reading a book.

Elsewhere in the house, the familiar sounds of servants going about their daily chores are punctuated now and then by the calm, authoritative voice of his mother or father supervising their activities. But the boy is oblivious to everything except the book in his hands.

The time is somewhere in the early 1890s, and the boy is Franklin Delano Roosevelt.

He is about ten or eleven years old, and the book he is reading represents something of a challenge. It is filled with unfamiliar technical terms, complicated charts, and curious diagrams; but because it is also filled with the clash of combat and the smell of gunpowder, and is crowded with thrilling accounts of derring-do in the age of fighting sail, the boy is enraptured and reads with the focused intensity of youth, totally lost in its pages.

He is sitting in the library of Springwood, his family's country home in the village of Hyde Park, overlooking the Hudson River about seventy miles north of New York City. We cannot be precisely sure when he first read the book he is holding, but we know he read it at an early age—certainly before his teens—and we know that it was to have a powerful influence upon him throughout his life. It is almost certainly the single most important book he will ever read.

The book that has so captured his attention is *The Naval War of 1812*. From early childhood, Franklin has been fascinated with the sea and things maritime. He is an avid sailor, and under his father's watchful tutelage he has learned his seamanship in knockabouts and ice boats and other small craft, and has served as crew on his father's 51-foot sailing yacht *Half Moon*, during summers on Campobello Island in the Bay of Fundy, where the family keeps a cottage.

But it is not the subject matter that has drawn him to *The Naval War of 1812* so much as it is the fact that the book is written by his distant cousin Theodore Roosevelt, of the Oyster Bay branch of the family. Young Franklin knows and greatly admires his ebullient, fun-loving 35-year-old Cousin Ted, who enjoys inventing strenuous games for children, and who, after a day of running and shouting, likes nothing better than to gather everyone around the fire and tell them ripping tales of his adventures as a cowboy in the Dakota Territory. At this point in his life, Theodore has already made a considerable name for himself as a writer but has not yet progressed as far as he would like in his other chosen interest, politics. At the moment, he is still a relatively obscure Washington functionary in the Civil Service Commission. World fame still lies in the future. But to those who already know him, his dynamism and boisterous energy already define his character. Throughout his life, Franklin will habitually refer to his fifth cousin Theodore with genuine awe as "the most wonderful man I ever knew."

The Naval War of 1812 is filled with Theodore's infectious patriotism and his delight in the exploits of the gallant and glamorous commodores who led America's early Navy—Stephen Decatur, Oliver Hazard Perry, David Porter and the rest. But Theodore Roosevelt has not limited his narrative to heroes alone. Woven into his celebration of their adventures are broader points on the strategic value of navies in general, and of the unique role they play in shaping and carrying out national policy. He explains how warships can reach across the globe to enforce the national resolve thousands of miles from home, as even the tiny American Navy managed to do in the War of 1812, when Yankee frigates engaged the enemy off the coast of Africa and as far away as the waters of Brazil and the Marquesas.

Cousin Ted points out that when navies are large enough to be organized into fleets, they can wield devastating power in combat, much as Nelson did at Trafalgar, or, in equally effective manner, choke off an enemy's supply lines by blockading his coast. And he makes it clear that navies are just as important in peacetime as they are in war. Unlike armies, which are apt to become expensive nuisances in times of peace, navies continue to serve the nation long after the battles are over. Properly deployed, they can foster and protect a country's foreign trade, and their very existence will tend to discourage an attack by any potential enemy.

Again and again, Cousin Ted hammers home his basic message, that navies are vital to a maritime nation's welfare, and young Franklin hungrily and uncritically absorbs it all. Cousin Ted's enthusiasm and his tightly organized arguments will form the foundation for his personal philosophy and provide the boy with a matrix with which to define the world around him.

Over the years to come, Franklin D. Roosevelt will read voraciously; but that one book, *The Naval War of 1812*, will always remain of singular importance to him. Fifty years onward, when fate and circumstances put him in command of the most powerful military force in history, it will be to his distant relative Theodore that he turns for inspiration and guidance. And Cousin Ted's book will never be far away, its lessons never ignored. Throughout his presidential years, FDR kept two copies in his personal library—one for the White House, the other for his boyhood home in Hyde Park.

CHAPTER TWO

T he Roosevelts were old money. By American standards, very old money. Like the Schuylers and Schermerhorns and Van Rensselears and other early Dutch settlers who arrived in New Amsterdam in the seventeenth century, Claes Martenzen van Rosenvelt and his descendants put down deep roots and quietly prospered.

At the time of Franklin Delano Roosevelt's birth in 1882, his family maintained a lifestyle somewhere between well-to-do and rich. He was born into the post–Civil War era known as the Gilded Age, a time when immense new fortunes were being created, and while his family could not boast the prodigious wealth of such neighbors as the Vanderbilts, they could take for granted the security and comfort of the moneyed classes. But it was not so much money as it was social prominence that contributed to the Roosevelts' sense of entitlement. The family held a position as close to that of nobility as it is possible to get in a democratic republic, replete with all the trappings of landed estates, carefully researched genealogies, and a family coat of arms centered around a decorous display of roses topped by three feathers, just like the Prince of Wales.

All that social prominence was not due solely to the Roosevelt side of the family. Franklin's young mother Sara was a Delano heir, who could trace her New World lineage back as far as her husband's, and who liked to point out that "Franklin is as much a Delano as he is a Roosevelt." Her son learned that lesson early, and throughout his life always included his middle name, or at least its initial, when signing papers.

Both parents taught the boy to take pride in his family heritage, and the combination of wealth and social position helped breed in him a certain confidence, a fearlessness, that served him well throughout his career. He was an only child and profited from the highly focused attention of two adoring parents.

His father, James Roosevelt, was considerably older than his mother, and had been a widower when he first met the vivacious, high-spirited Sara Delano at a party at Theodore Roosevelt's home in New York City. James was something of an entrepreneur. He managed the family's investments and served on various corporate boards and enjoyed playing the role of country squire. He encouraged young Franklin's interests in natural history, and, along with sailing, taught him the gentlemanly skills of horseback riding and hunting.

His young mother Sara watched over him solicitously, and while some have accused her of being *overly* solicitous at times, she did not pamper him. He was assigned household duties—he had to take care of his pony, Debby, and his red setter puppy, Marksman—and she made sure he performed his duties responsibly and on time.

The Roosevelts moved comfortably in high circles. One time in Washington, when Franklin was just five years old, his father took him to the White House to meet his old friend President Grover Cleveland. At the end of the visit, Cleveland, a Democrat who was having difficulties with Congress at the time, put his hand on Franklin's head and said with great earnestness, "My little man, I am making a strange wish for you. It is that you may never be President of the United States." The adult Franklin loved to repeat that story, particularly in those years after he had moved into the White House. He always followed the retelling with a loud burst of laughter.

By any measure Franklin was a well-educated boy. He had a solid grounding in English literature, was well read in history, had a good grasp of geography, knew his sums, and was conversant in both French and German, thanks to a succession of teachers and governesses imported to instruct him. And because the Roosevelts regularly toured through Europe, Franklin was well traveled, and by the age of twelve was a veteran of half a dozen Atlantic crossings.

But for all his travel and learning, there were important deficiencies in his education that would take him years to fully overcome. The most significant of these was the fact that he was taught almost exclusively at home: he did not actually go to school until he was fourteen. While academic lessons can be taught anywhere, some of the most important lessons of childhood can only be learned in the rough-and-tumble of school. Such lessons include the complex and sometimes painful ones involved with learning how to get along with one's peers—the sometimes exhilarating, sometimes humiliating competition of the classroom, with its rivalry for attention and good grades; the cut and thrust of the schoolyard, where students are sorted out in ways that are often unfair and undemocratic, but always realistic; the problem of dealing with bullies; the agonizing and delicate compromises that must be learned in order to make friends, and the further compromises needed to keep them; the bargaining and lies—black and white—required to hold your position in the crowd. These were the life lessons that Franklin Roosevelt missed as a young boy, and which would later take him decades to master. Although he was neither spoiled nor pampered, his sheltered life would leave him at a certain social disadvantage for many years.

Although home-educated, Franklin was not a recluse. There were always the children of his parents' employees to play with, augmented on occasion by other kids imported from the village for the afternoon.

There is a famous story that his mother liked to tell about her son. "Franklin had a great habit of ordering his playmates around," she remembered in her book, *My Boy Franklin*, "and for reasons I have never been able to fathom, [he] was generally permitted to have his way. I know that I, overhearing him one day with a little boy on the place, with whom he was digging a fort, said to him:

"'My son, don't give the orders all the time; let the other boys give them some time.'

"'Mummie,' he said, without guile, 'if I don't give the orders, nothing would happen!'"

The story is sometimes cited as an indication of the inherent leadership skills FDR would exhibit throughout his public life, but it is just as likely that it indicates his early grasp of basic social realities. The simple fact was that he was demonstrably superior to his playmates. They were, for the most part, the children of people who worked on the estate, and they did what his mother and father wanted them to do. By extension, it was Franklin's right to govern the activities of the servants' children. They were never his equals in any sense. He knew it and they knew it.

Years later, Mike Reilly, who as chief of the White House Secret Service detail knew FDR from a particularly intimate perspective, put it bluntly. "He never was 'one of the boys,'" he observed. "[He] was raised alone and he had just about everything he wanted throughout his youth, so it would be just a little too much to expect him to be 'one of the boys.'"

CHAPTER THREE

Although Sara Roosevelt enjoyed personally supervising her son's education at home, and was anxious to keep him under her roof as long as possible, both she and her husband were fully aware that the day would eventually come when he would have to go off to school; and when that time came, they knew precisely where they would send him. That decision had been made many years earlier, shortly after Franklin's birth, when his parents had put his name down for a place at the Groton School, a new institution thirty-five miles north of Boston that was still in the process of formation, and was the inspiration of a remarkable young Episcopal minister named Endicott Peabody.

Peabody, of old New England stock, had been educated in England when his father, a Morgan partner, had moved to London to manage the bank's British operations. After attending Cheltenham College and graduating from Cambridge University, he returned to America, and after ordination at the Episcopal Theological School he had made it his life's ambition to reproduce in the United States the English public (i.e., private) school system, which had been responsible for educating most of Britain's leaders for centuries. It was his goal to create a school for the sons of the rich and powerful, for boys who would have no need to go into trade or otherwise earn a living, and to inculcate in them a sense of service and leadership so as to encourage them to find their way into government, philanthropy, or the ministry.

As his model for the Groton School he chose Rugby, with its vigorous sports program and emphasis on the classics. The prospectus for his school proclaimed that "Every endeavor will be made to cultivate manly Christian character, having regard to moral and physical as well as intellectual development." Peabody made no secret of the fact that in his scheme of things the moral and physical aspects of the curriculum far outweighed any serious intellectual development. There would be time enough for that sort of thing when the boys reached the universities for which Groton was preparing them.

Even in the years before the school opened, Peabody's zeal had attracted the attention of many of the leaders of eastern seaboard society, including both the Hyde Park and Oyster Bay branches of the Roosevelt family (Theodore was one of his earliest supporters), and his school was quickly oversubscribed.

Peabody's students, in keeping with the standard English practice, were expected to attend Groton for six years, which meant enrolling in the first form at age twelve, and continuing on through the sixth form at age eighteen. But when the time came to send Franklin off, Sara could not bear to part with him, and held him back for two years. As a result, he did not enter Groton until the third form, when he was fourteen, in the autumn of 1896. Unfortunately for him, by that time all his classmates had long since established the friendships, cliques, rivalries, and other social strategies of adolescent males, and young Franklin was once again not "one of the boys." His classmates might have forgiven him had he been a star football player, but, as he was not particularly talented along those lines, he was generally shunned, and ridiculed for his speech mannerisms—the same plummy nasality that would in time become familiar to millions—which were perceived as an affectation.

But for all its drawbacks, time would confirm that Groton was an inspired choice for young Franklin, and his allegiance to the place, and to its founder, would last a lifetime. He always kept in close contact with Dr. Peabody, and as late as 1941 wrote to him from the White House, "I count it among the blessings of my life that it was given to me in formative years to have the privilege of your guiding hand and the benefit of your inspiring example."

It was a novel and challenging world that Franklin Roosevelt entered into when he arrived at Groton, and even though he was no longer the center of attention, and was in fact something of an odd man out, it seemed to suit him, and he settled in with little fuss.

Sept. 18, 1896

Dear Mommerr & Popperr

I am getting on finely both mentally and physically. I sit next a boy named A. Gracie King at meals, he is from Garrisons and knows the Pells and Morgans. Do you know about him? . . . I am all right in Latin, Greek, Science and French; a little rusty in Algebra, but not more so than the others. . . . We have just had Latin and Algebra, and we study French tonight. We went to Mrs. Peabody's parlor last night for half an hour and played games. . . . We are off to dinner now, so I cannot write more but I will write you Sunday. With lots of love to Pa & yourself

F.D.R.

Life at Groton was built around a deliberately Spartan regime. The daily routine consisted of a cold shower on rising, followed by breakfast at 7:30, chapel services at 8:15, classes from 8:30 to noon, and two afternoon school periods of forty-five minutes each, followed by athletics. In the evening, when the boys were required to dress in starched white collars and properly shined shoes (blue suits were required on Sundays), there was another chapel service after supper, then a study period in the schoolroom, after which the director and Mrs. Peabody shook hands with each and every boy as they filed out to their dormitories. The rules were clearly defined and inviolable. There were punishments for every infraction. Tardiness was a particularly serious offense. Sleeping arrangements were minimal. Each boy had his own cubicle, about six feet wide and nine or ten feet deep, with walls that were about seven feet high and did not reach the ceiling. Each cubicle was furnished with a bed, a bureau, a chair, and a small rug. There were no doors, only a cloth curtain that could be drawn for privacy.

Peabody spoke regularly at chapel services, repeatedly returning to the character-building theme of service: service to the community, service to the nation, service to the world. He was a man of simple religion but profound and unquestioning faith. A steady stream of distinguished guest speakers challenged the boys to go forth and make the world a better place, whether it be the joss houses of China, the slums of New York, or the halls of Congress. Occasionally, as a special treat, Peabody was able to snare his friend Theodore Roosevelt, one of the boys' favorites, as a speaker.

By the end of his first year at Groton, in the spring of 1897, an interesting new streak of independence, not previously notable in Franklin's character, began to make itself evident. His parents were out of the country, having sailed for Germany in their annual search for cures for his aging father's ailments. They would not return until the school year was over, and in their absence Franklin accepted an invitation from Anna Roosevelt Cowles, Theodore's sister and a close friend of Franklin's mother, to spend the Fourth of July with her family. He was greatly upset when his mother wrote from Europe, declining the invitation. In response, he wrote angrily to her, "I am very sorry to hear that you refused Cousin Bammie's invitation for the 4th and as you told me that I *cd* make my own plans, and as Helen [Roosevelt] writes me there is to be a large party and lots of fun on the 4th, I shall try to arrange it with Cousin B next Wednesday."

He closed on a caustic note of sarcasm that must have come as something of a shock to his mother: "Please don't make any more arrangements for my future happiness."

Further complications regarding Independence Day developed a few days later when Theodore Roosevelt, recently Police Commissioner in New York and newly appointed assistant secretary of the Navy, arrived in Groton to give one of his talks. "After supper tonight, Cousin Theodore gave us a splendid talk on his adventures when he was on the Police Board," he reported to his parents. "He kept the whole room in an uproar for over an hour, by telling us killing stories about policemen and their doings in New York." After his talk, Theodore repeated the invitation to Franklin for the holiday, and Franklin quickly accepted. But this did not end the controversy. On June 8, 1897, he wrote his mother: "I am going to Oyster Bay to stay with the Theodore Roosevelt's on Friday, July 2, and shall stay there all Monday." He added on June 11: "I am sorry you didn't want me to go to Oyster Bay for the 4th but I had already accepted Cousin Theodore's invitation & I shall enjoy it very much . . . I am so sorry you have refused Cousin Bammie's invitation and I wish you had let me make my own plans as you said. As it is, I have accepted Theodore's invitation. And I hope you will not refuse that too."

Franklin's relationship with his mother would remain notably close for the rest of her long life, but there is no question that his stubborn intransigence in the spring of 1897 helped redefine it and make it a little less one-sided.

CHAPTER FOUR

I n 1932, many years after Franklin Roosevelt was graduated from Groton, Endicott Peabody remembered him as "a quiet, satisfactory boy . . . but not brilliant." Throughout Roosevelt's life, a surprising number of people who worked closely with him and knew him at first hand tended to agree with the headmaster's less-than-flattering assessment of Roosevelt's intelligence. A co-worker at the law firm where he began his career remembered him as "a harmless bust. He had a sanguine temperament almost adolescent in its buoyancy." In Washington, the venerable Senator Henry Cabot Lodge characterized him as "a well-meaning, nice young man—but light," while Supreme Court Justice Oliver Wendell Holmes judged him "a second class intellect," and the highly regarded political commentator Walter Lippmann described him as "a perfectly estimable person with no discernable qualifications for the burdens of the presidency."

If we are to accept the word of these men and others, we must assume that the breezy, casual style that Franklin Roosevelt developed as an adult defined a man of only average understanding, and that his astonishing achievements over the years were either the result of blind luck or the efforts of other, brighter minds. But there is abundant evidence that behind his distinctive upper-class accent and ready laugh, there lay a remarkably shrewd and perceptive mind. Examples of this precisely focused intelligence can be found time and again in his personal papers. One particularly notable example dates back to his Groton years, in the form of a penciled set of notes that he prepared for a debate on January 19, 1898 during his fourth-term year, when he was fifteen years old.

The subject to be debated was "Resolved: that Hawaii be promptly annexed." The issue was very much in the news at the time, having been seriously discussed since at least 1893 and being desired by many people in both the Republic of Hawaii and the United States, and a bill providing for such a step had recently been introduced in Congress. The case for the affirmative was to be presented by headmaster Endicott Peabody himself, after which young Roosevelt was to respond with the rebuttal.

Reading his notes today, and making allowances for the occasional grammatical awkwardness, it is abundantly evident that young Franklin understood his subject in truly remarkable depth and managed to present it with uncommon clarity and conviction, demonstrating an impressive grasp of geopolitical issues, naval strategy, and relative national strengths. The notes reveal just how sophisticated an intellect he was developing, and how deeply Cousin Ted's naval precepts had helped define his own understanding of his country and the world in general. The entire text is included below, and even a casual skimming presents a fascinating look into a mind that was just beginning to understand its capabilities.

After Mr. Peabody had presented his case in favor of annexing Hawaii, his youthful opponent opened with a formal acknowledgement of his audience, which included not only the headmaster and the entire student body, but Mrs. Peabody as well. He then began his rebuttal with a sweeping generalization that let his listeners understand that the day's subject was of global significance, and immediately established its naval importance.

> *Mr. President, Lady and Gentlemen,*
> *Of all the great powers of the world, the United States and Russia are the only ones which have no colonies to defend. All our territory is on this continent and all of it except Alaska is continuous.*
>
> *Therefore the United States and Russia are the only two countries no part of whose territory can be cut off by a naval enemy. At present we have no really vulnerable point. Now, the annexation of Hawaii by us would affect the feelings of the European powers in two ways: first it would anger them because Hawaii is a common stopping point, secondly it would embolden them because we should for the first time in our history have a vulnerable point.*
>
> *Mr. Peabody has told us that our country cannot be safe without Hawaii. I shall try to disprove this: now if we own the islands it means that we must protect them, and to do that we should have not only to fortify the Islands themselves but also maintain a much larger navy. Now to do this we should have to spend at least $100,000,000., every year on our navy besides a large sum on erecting forts and maintaining soldiers on the Islands.*

To put his argument in context, it is worth remembering that Roosevelt was describing a world in which there were as yet no aircraft, no radio, no Panama Canal, a world in which oil had not yet replaced coal as the standard fuel for navies, and a world in which a hundred million dollars was worth billions in today's currency.

> *Let us remember that the islands are over 2,000 miles from the nearest point of the U.S. and so are too far away to be of any*

service to our Western coast in time of war. For the same reason
they would not help to defend the Nicaraguan canal should we
ever built it. And also, as California is nearer Nicaragua than
Hawaii it would be quicker to send warships from the former
place.

His citing of the "Nicaraguan canal" is a reference to a proposed
isthmus canal project with which his father was prominently connected, and which would eventually be abandoned in favor of the
passage through Panama.

Another argument of Mr. Peabody's that we need a coaling-
station for our ships. Now it is not generally known that Pearl
Harbor, a port in one of the islands belongs to the United States.
All that is needed is a little inexpensive dredging and we shall
have a coaling-station without annexation.
    If we must have another coaling station in mid-Pacific why
not fix up one of the Aleutian Islands in the North.
    But before we bother about foreign coaling-stations and for-
tifications we should look to the defense of our own coasts. New
York, Boston and S. Francisco are still at the mercy of an enemy
and why should we spend the millions needed to fortify these cities
on those worthless Islands in the middle of the Pacific. Captain
Mahan himself says it is nonsense to think of annexation unless
we decide to spend an enormous sum for fortifications. Now is it
worthwhile to do this? In what way will it advantage us?

Young Franklin could speak with authority concerning Admiral
Alfred Thayer Mahan, U.S. Navy, who was the leading naval theorist
of his day. Mahan was the author of *The Influence of Sea Power Upon*
History, which FDR had received as a Christmas gift a few weeks
prior to the debate and had just finished reading. Mahan was also the
author of *The Interest of America in Sea Power*, which FDR was about

to receive on his upcoming sixteenth birthday less than a fortnight after the debate.

Having covered the naval situation, Roosevelt then turned to the question of other nations that might have an interest in Hawaii.

> *Mr. Peabody says that if we do not take the islands, some other power will, but let us look at the question. England might have had Hawaii years & years ago if she had wanted it. She has also disclaimed any intention of taking Hawaii, but supposing [she] does take it. In what way would it harm us? We should have free trade with the Islands, for England stands for free trade. England would not use the group for a base of supplies against us in case of war, for she has a veritable Gibraltar at Esquimalt a port in British Columbia within sight of our own shores.*
>
> *Now about Japan's interfering. She also has disclaimed any intention of seizing the Islands, and it would indeed be a foolish enterprise for her, for any armies in Hawaii would be as lonely as Robinson Crusoe. Besides all this Hawaii is entirely out of the Japan–America sailing-route. No country outside of the U.S. wants to have Hawaii and. . . .*

He then follows with a dismissive attack on Senator Cushman Kellogg Davis, chairman of the Committee on Foreign Relations, who was using every argument he could think of to support annexation, and who had featured prominently in news reports on the day of the debate.

> *Some foolish senator has argued that if after annexation for any reason we should wish to abandon the Islands, we could easily turn them over to Japan, England or Germany. Now the United States has never been in the habit of giving up territory once acquired, and I am sure the people of this country would never consent to have the Stars and Stripes hauled down from*

a country over which they had once waved. Therefore if we once annex Hawaii we shall always be obliged to keep the wretched Islands whether we wish to or no.

Throughout the nineteenth century—and well into the twentieth—the central pillar of American foreign policy was the Monroe Doctrine, which specifically precluded European powers from acquiring any new territories in the Western Hemisphere. Although the Monroe Doctrine had no direct relation to the question of the Hawaiian Islands, it was important, and Roosevelt wanted to bring it into his argument.

There is no more reason for the U.S. to annex Hawaii than to annex Nicaragua and it is ridiculous to say we should hand over that country to a foreign power for that would be contrary to the Monroe Doctrine. We do not want to own any of these tropical countries or to go there ourselves. By the Monroe Doctrine we are only supposed to keep foreign powers from these countries but not to govern them or own them. Now if we once go in for foreign colonies we must stick to that policy and not only are foreign colonies expensive, but they are dangerous children and may bring political difficulties upon the mother country at any moment.

What we want is a favorable trade treaty with the Islands, and this we have already, for everything of commercial value is provided for in it.

Finally he turns to domestic politics and proudly supports his father's Democratic Party in front of an audience whose sympathies, we can assume, were virtually 100% Republican.

The Bill for annexation before the Senate now comes straight from the White House. It is significant to note that if the treaty

were not pressed by [President William] McKinley himself
there is no doubt that it would be beaten, for not one of the
older Republican Senators are in favor of it. All the goods
[sic] Democrats in both the House and Senate are against the
treaty, while the only support comes from the White House and
McKinley is only trying to make his administration popular
with the masses.

Why can we not leave Hawaii alone, or else establish a sound
Republic in which all Hawaiians shall be represented [,] not a
government such as they have at present, under the influence
of Americans. As I have shown no power would take Hawaii
now as a gift, but supposing some Power should in the remote
future should wish to have it. Then the expression of the feel-
ings of the United States would be enough to stop it, just as the
feeling of America led Louis Napoleon to withdraw his troops
from Mexico, a number of years ago.

His reference to Mexico relates to the time in 1862 when the
Emperor Napoleon III took advantage of America's preoccupation
with the Civil War to invade Mexico and set up a puppet government
in defiance of the Monroe Doctrine. The French were eventually
forced to abandon their Mexican adventure, due in part to America's
support of the Mexican leader, Benito Juarez.

Several nations of modern times ruled upon the monarchic
plan, have seized territory for commercial reasons and because
of sympathy with the people residents, but we have no such plea
for seizing Hawaii as W [Wendell Blagden, a fellow student]
shows. Why should we soil our hands with colonies? See how
Italy's colonial system has utterly failed, then ask yourself what
good France's colonies do her.

As Mr ——— has so ably shown the inhabitants are not
ignorant folk. Why then does the government shrink from

submitting the treaty to a general vote of the inhabitants. The answer is obvious: they would vote against it to a man. Why then annex them without their consent? Why take away the nationality of a free people? Why meddle with this land thousands of miles away whose inhabitants are so different from us in every way? Why weaken our strategical position and why spend millions in a foolish cause?

He had planned to close his peroration with a simple—and somewhat simplistic—exhortation to patriotic fervor . . .

I appeal to your American common-sense, that common-sense which has never yet made a mistake and which let us pray never will

. . . but crossed it out at the last minute to take advantage of what he perceived as a weakness in the headmaster's argument:

Mr. P. says our trade will double in ten years, I do not see why this should be so as he has not proved it.

The notes for the debate on Hawaiian annexation are one of the few examples of Franklin Roosevelt's school work to be found in the FDR Library. Undoubtedly the notes survived because he was proud of them, as he had every right to be. At the age of fifteen, he had assembled the case for a position paper fit to be presented at a presidential cabinet meeting.

It was around the time of the debate on Hawaii that young Franklin began seriously contemplating the possibility of applying to the U.S. Naval Academy at Annapolis, and it would take all of his father's considerable powers of persuasion to convince him that he would be better off applying to Harvard.

CHAPTER FIVE

Neither Franklin Roosevelt nor anyone else at the Groton School on that night of the debate could have guessed that within only a few months America's place in the world would change dramatically, and that the United States would transform itself from a country with no colonies to defend into an imperial power with global holdings reaching halfway around the world, from Puerto Rico to the Philippines. As if to confirm America's radically new status, Congress would annex those same Hawaiian Islands for whose independence young Franklin had so eloquently pleaded.

The new American empire was the result of the brief but significant Spanish–American War, which was triggered by a mysterious explosion on board the American battleship *Maine*, moored in Havana Harbor on February 15, 1898. The rival press lords William Randolph Hearst and Joseph Pulitzer, caught up in a newspaper circulation war, jumped on the story and in banner headlines, each more lurid than the last, accused the Spanish colonial government in Cuba of deliberate sabotage and demanded war. The public ate it up. President McKinley tried his best to calm things down, vainly pointing out that the Spanish authorities denied responsibility and were offering every assistance to determine the cause of the mysterious explosion, but the public outcry, urged on by the yellow press, only grew louder.

Franklin Roosevelt was very much aware that one of the loudest voices calling for war was President McKinley's assistant secretary of the Navy, Theodore Roosevelt. Cousin Ted, champion of the strenuous life, and always eager to promote action, was conspicuous in his demands for a military response, but was frustrated by the fact that he had no authority to order such a response. As the public outrage continued to mount, Cousin Ted bided his time, and one day, when his superior, the secretary of the Navy, left the office to have a painful corn treated by a podiatrist, Theodore sprang into action, and under his temporary authority as Acting secretary of the Navy, sent a secret cable to Admiral George Dewey, commanding the American Asiatic Fleet:

ORDER THE SQUADRON . . . TO HONG KONG. KEEP FULL OF COAL. IN THE EVENT OF DECLARATION OF WAR YOUR DUTY WILL BE TO SEE THAT THE SPANISH SQUADRON DOES NOT LEAVE THE ASIATIC COAST, AND THEN OFFENSIVE OPERATIONS IN PHILIPPINE ISLANDS.

In the days that followed, the White House made no immediate call for further action, and Theodore complained that "McKinley has no more backbone than a chocolate éclair." But Admiral Dewey had deployed his ships as directed, and four weeks later, when war did indeed break out, he was in a position to steam into Manila Bay, wipe out the Spanish Navy, and win an almost bloodless victory. Overnight, Admiral Dewey became a national hero, and Theodore Roosevelt decided he wanted to be one too. He forthwith resigned from the Navy Department, attached himself to Army General Leonard Wood, and within weeks raised a regiment of dismounted cavalry made up for the most part of adventure-seeking cowboys. He dubbed his regiment the Rough Riders and embarked for Cuba, where he led a spectacular assault on San Juan Hill that made headlines around the country and earned him a recommendation for a Congressional Medal of Honor. With the war easily won, Colonel Roosevelt returned in triumph to America and, riding on a wave of public adulation, was swept into office as Governor of New York. The total elapsed time from the sinking of the *Maine* to his election as Governor of New York was just ten months. The startling speed of Theodore Roosevelt's rise to prominence was not lost on his young cousin in Hyde Park.

From his office in Albany, Cousin Ted continued to impose himself on the national scene. After little more than a year as governor, he had excited so much attention throughout the country that the leaders of the Republican Party, who mistrusted and detested him with a passion but grudgingly appreciated his vote-getting ability, felt compelled to put him on the national ticket as Republican candidate for vice president in McKinley's bid for reelection.

This dramatic turn of events created great excitement in Hyde Park, where Franklin was preparing to go off to Harvard for the first time. He had already made sure that university life was going to be a very different experience from Groton. No more cold showers and Spartan living. Franklin and his Groton classmate Lathrop Brown had arranged to room together at Harvard, and made a visit to Cambridge the spring before graduation and took a lease on a luxury apartment—two bedrooms, sitting room and bath—in the recently constructed Westmorly Court on Mount Auburn Street, just off campus, one of the private residences on the "Gold Coast" that catered to the upper-crust students. There they would live in comfort and style throughout their years at Harvard, protected from the noise and crowding of the university's dormitories in Harvard Yard.

One of Franklin's first moves after arriving at Harvard was to join the Harvard Republican Club, despite the fact that he was eighteen and still far too young to vote. In an excited letter to his parents he described his participation in "a grand torch-light Republican parade of Harvard & Mass. Instit. of Technology. We wore red caps & gowns and marched by classes into Boston and thro' all the principal streets, about 8 miles in all. The crowds to see it were huge all along the route & we were dead tired at the end." He was thrilled a week later when the McKinley & Roosevelt ticket handily trounced William Jennings Bryan and the Democrats, 292 electoral votes to 155.

Franklin's entry into Harvard was shadowed by the passing of his father, still another of the events that would help define his future. The death of James Roosevelt was not an entirely unexpected event. He was seventy-two years old at the time and had been in ill health. Much of his last few years had been spent in a largely fruitless search for cures for his failing health, involving travels to various European spas and other medical treatment. But in spite of his increasing frailty, he had remained as attentive to his young son as Franklin's much younger and more robust mother, the 46-year-old Sara.

James left Franklin a bequest of $120,000, which if handled prudently was enough to allow him to live a life of frugal independence, but he left the bulk of his estate to Sara, which combined with her Delano inheritance made her a millionaire and gave her the means to become an even more formidable factor in Franklin's world than previously.

Harvard—and Boston—offered plenty of opportunities for an active social life, and Franklin, after the close monitoring and strict regimentation of Groton, was eager to participate, although he was not always successful. According to the journalist John Gunther, who many years later interviewed a number of Roosevelt's college classmates, he was never particularly popular and was remembered as "a mixture of affability, marked sensitiveness, and superiority. His desire to be universally liked repelled some of his fellows, who called him 'two-faced.'" Apparently some of the awkwardness and seeming insincerity of the Groton years still clung to him.

Another biographer, Kenneth S. Davis, suggests that Roosevelt's off-campus reputation was equally equivocal: "In his own social circles there were a few who thought him immature for his age and circumstances and that his enjoyment of high society, his excessive enjoyment in their view, manifested this. There were girls, attracted by his lithe handsomeness and social prestige, who were put off by what they deemed an all-too-smug awareness of these on his part and by a personality that seemed to them shallow, trivial, timidly conventional beneath a superficial self-assurance. They told one another that he was a lightweight with many of the attributes of a prig."

Such reflections would indicate that young Roosevelt still had a considerable amount of growing up to do. But then, the same could undoubtedly be said for many of his peers as well.

Following his freshman year at Harvard, Franklin and his mother, still in mourning, spent the summer in Europe along with some family friends, where they chartered a yacht to explore the Norwegian coast. During the cruise, when they steamed into the little harbor at Molde, they found Kaiser Wilhelm's yacht *Hohenzollern* at anchor, surrounded by various German naval vessels. The Kaiser accepted their invitation and came aboard their yacht for tea, and later invited the Americans aboard the *Hohenzollern*. That European royalty would deign to mix with American tourists gives us a measure of the Roosevelts' elevated social status.

They were still on the other side of the Atlantic when they heard the shocking news that President McKinley had been shot by an assassin but was expected to recover. Days later, as they were returning home on a liner, they learned from the pilot boat that McKinley had died, and that Cousin Ted was now President of the United States. Theodore's sudden elevation to the White House would in time prove to be one of the most important turning points in Franklin Roosevelt's life, and would influence his personal philosophy, his life goals, and even his choice of a wife.

At least one more event during his Harvard years would impact significantly on Franklin's future. Harvard, at the turn of the twentieth century, had a student body of around five hundred undergraduates. The great majority—around eighty percent—lived either in the dormitories on campus or commuted from home. The remainder, including Franklin, made up the club set, the well-to-do dandies who were socially active and lived in the apartments on Mount Auburn Street or in similar digs, and who participated in the complex rituals governing the social pecking order of their peers.

The complicated process by which members were selected for the various clubs at Harvard began in the autumn of their second year, when the new sophomores first competed to be selected by the oldest and largest of the clubs, the Institute of 100. Over a period of months, the Institute offered membership to a hundred candidates who would be nominated in groups of ten, with the most desirable sophomores in the first groups, and later groups being made up of those perceived to be of lesser worth. By the time of the Christmas break, the first fifty sophomores had been selected. These included Lathrop Brown, Franklin's roommate, but not Franklin, who was forced to go home for the holidays in an agony of suspense. He was undoubtedly greatly cheered at New Year's to be invited to Washington to attend the most glamorous social event in the nation, the debut of his Cousin Alice, Theodore's eldest daughter, at the White House.

When at last he returned to Harvard he learned that he had indeed been selected by the Institute of 100, "the 1st man in the 6th ten," as he reported proudly to his mother. The immediate next step was "running for the Dickey," a club that was a shadowy remainder of what had been Delta Kappa Epsilon, the national fraternity once prominent at Harvard, but which now served as what was known as a "waiting club." After acceptance and a week of initiation rites, Franklin was duly elected to the Dickey, and was now ready for the final test, when candidates hoped to be selected to the most prestigious "final clubs."

Of these, the most socially prominent was the Porcellian, and Franklin was confident that he belonged there. He had good reason to be hopeful of selection. He was a "legacy," a candidate who deserved special consideration, because his father had been a member, as had Cousin Ted, who took great pride in the fact.

The selection process for Porcellian was secret and final. The sixteen juniors and seniors who made up the membership sat in conference, discussed each prospect in turn, and then voted for or against inviting him to join. Each member registered his choice by dropping either a white ball into the voting box, signifying a positive vote, or a black ball, signifying a negative vote. When the box was opened, a single black ball was sufficient to condemn a candidate.

No one today knows whether the vote for Franklin Roosevelt included a single black ball or more than one, and who it might have been who cast those votes. No one knows the reasons for his rejection. All that is known is that Franklin did not make it into Porcellian. Once again, he was not "one of the boys."

It was a crushing blow to him, a disproportionately devastating disappointment that is difficult for a modern observer to appreciate. And the pain continued to hurt for years. Almost twenty years later, in 1919, he admitted his rejection by Porcellian had been "the greatest disappointment of my life."

CHAPTER SIX

Weddings are by definition important ceremonies of commitment, and never was that more true than in the case of Franklin Roosevelt, who on March 17, 1905 would marry his distant cousin, Anna Eleanor Roosevelt. He was twenty-three years old and a student at Columbia Law School. She was twenty and of the Oyster Bay branch of the family. The fact that the bride and groom shared a surname was only one indication of how deeply entwined were the family ties involved. The bride, Theodore Roosevelt's favorite niece, was the daughter of the late Elliott B. Roosevelt, who was not only the brother of Theodore but the godfather of Franklin as well.

Within the cloistered walls of the two adjoining private houses at 6 and 8 East 76th Street, New York, the sliding doors had been opened to accommodate the two hundred or so guests. A small string orchestra was entertaining the assemblage with appropriate selections, and its music mixed somewhat awkwardly with the more robust brass and timpani strains of "The Wearing of the Green" seeping in through the windows from nearby Fifth Avenue, where the city's Irish were celebrating St. Patrick's Day with their annual parade.

The wedding date had been selected to fit into the busy schedule of the bride's uncle, who was in New York that day to deliver two speeches, and who would give the bride away. The drawing room where the marriage was to take place was crowded with palms, lilies, and of course a profusion of roses, the family flower. At the request of the groom, the Reverend Endicott Peabody had come down from Groton to officiate, and, as the time for the ceremony approached, he and others glanced nervously at their pocket watches as they awaited the final member of the wedding party. Eventually sounds from the front door below indicated he had at last arrived, and moments later he came energetically pounding up the stairs and expressing profuse apologies—Theodore Roosevelt himself, President of the United States.

This particular marriage was of great significance to the president, who was always conscious of his patrician heritage and took family matters seriously. On first learning of the engagement, he had written to the prospective groom from the White House:

> *Dear Franklin,*
>
> *We are greatly rejoiced over the good news. I am as fond of Eleanor as if she were my daughter, and I like you, and trust you, and believe in you. No other success in life—not the Presidency, or anything else—begins to compare with the joy and happiness that come in and from the love of the true man and the true woman, the love which never sinks lover and sweetheart in man and wife. You and Eleanor are true and brave, and I believe you love each other truly and unselfishly; and golden years open before you. May all good fortune attend you both, ever.*
>
> *Give my love to your dear mother.*
> *Your aff. Cousin,*
> *Theodore Roosevelt*

Sara had been distressed when Franklin first told her of his plans to marry Eleanor. He was too young, she insisted, and left unstated the fact that she was not yet ready to share Franklin with anyone else. She persuaded the couple to put off the announcement of their engagement for a year, during which time she did what she could to distract her darling boy, but to no avail, and when the year was up they were still determined to wed.

Many had been surprised by the news of the engagement, and more than a few—those who knew the couple best—had been frankly puzzled. Who would have dreamed of such a union? The two seemed so entirely dissimilar—the glib, handsome, outgoing Franklin, who reveled in society, and the plain, withdrawn, thoughtful Eleanor, intensely shy and quiet.

They had first met—neither remembered the occasion and had to be told about it years later—when Franklin was four and Eleanor just two years old. Her father, Franklin's godfather, had brought her up to Hyde Park, and the boy had entertained the little visitor by getting down on hands and knees on the nursery floor and carrying her about on his shoulders.

The two had experienced vastly different childhoods. Franklin's had been sunny and protected, suffused with the love of two doting parents. Eleanor's childhood, in comparison, had been little short of a nightmare. Her mother, a well known society beauty, had despaired of Eleanor's prominent teeth and receding chin, and never tired of commiserating with her daughter over her lack of beauty. She made fun of her daughter's somber manner, calling her "Granny," and saved her love for her sons, Eleanor's two younger brothers.

Eleanor's father was a drunk, constantly in and out of treatments or sent off to distant parts where his escapades would not embarrass the family. He genuinely loved Eleanor and was always sweet and openly affectionate with her. She returned his love in full measure, but his repeated absences from home, often for many months at a time, did little to brighten the misery of her days.

When Eleanor's mother died at a young age, her father reappeared in her life, but always fitfully and only on occasion. While his presence was always welcomed by his love-starved daughter, his drinking brought a new level of anxiety and unpredictability into her life. One time, when Eleanor and her father were out for a walk with the three hunting dogs he kept, he stopped in front of the Knickerbocker Club and, handing the leashes to Eleanor, asked her to mind the dogs while he stepped inside for a moment. Poor Eleanor was still standing outside the Knickerbocker several hours later when the doorman hoisted her comatose father into a cab, and then helped Eleanor and the dogs into another and sent them home.

Elliott Roosevelt did not last much longer than his wife, dying of delirium tremens when Eleanor was nine years old. She and her younger brother Hall (her other brother, Elliott, Jr., had succumbed to diphtheria) were put in the care of relatives and more or less left on their own, free to deal as best they could with a world that had done little to merit their confidence.

What attraction had brought Eleanor and Franklin together? The sad, gawky wallflower and the hearty—perhaps overly hearty— debonair swain? At the time of the wedding, there were those who wondered. Thirty years later, the couple's children still wondered. There is no question of their affection. Franklin and Eleanor were in love. Their hundreds of letters over the years—often dealing with the most ordinary and commonplace considerations: the illness of a child, the need to pay a bill—show a depth of commitment on both their parts that is unquestionable. Yet the wide disparity in their tastes and personalities never changed.

It is easy enough to understand the relationship from her point of view. It could indeed be flattering for someone weighed down by her awareness of her own awkwardness to have such an accomplished young man constantly in attendance. But she was so serious and he was so frivolous. What possible common ground could they have found? Or had she reason to believe that beneath the banter and the chat there lay something of far deeper substance, some quality that she might help draw out, a seriousness of purpose that would make their partnership a far more homogenous meeting of the minds than others might suspect?

And what of Franklin? What, if anything, did he discern in her serious demeanor and quiet acceptance? Did he sense someone who could help give direction to his ambition, who could help him to grow up? Could she help him deal with his complicated relationship with his mother?

And so this unsure waif and her optimistic groom stood on the threshold of their future, ready to move into a challenging new world, one that they could only hope was as bright as he predicted it would be.

Eleanor's cousin Alice, Theodore's eldest daughter, served as her maid of honor. She and the bridesmaids were all wearing headdresses displaying the three silver feathers of the Roosevelt crest. Franklin's best man, Lathrop Brown, and the ushers wore diamond-studded stickpins with the same motif.

The bridal gown, as a society reporter described it, "was a white satin princess robe, flounced and draped with old point lace, and with a white satin court train. The bride's point lace veil was caught with orange blossoms and a diamond crescent. She wore a pearl collar, the gift of the bridegroom's mother, and a diamond bowknot, the gift of Mrs. Warren Delano, Jr. Her bouquet was of lilies of the valley."

At the close of the ceremony, the president congratulated the couple and reflected, with a toothy grin, "There's nothing like keeping the name in the family."

At the reception following the service, the president dominated the scene, and the bride and groom were largely ignored. But Franklin was not concerned. By their marriage he and Eleanor had not only strengthened the family by bringing together the Oyster Bay and Hyde Park branches, but on a more personal level Franklin had strengthened the bonds between himself and the one man he admired most in all the world—he who had been a somewhat distant Cousin Ted was now a far more familial Uncle Ted.

CHAPTER SEVEN

At the end of Franklin's first year of law school, he and Eleanor embarked on an extended three-month honeymoon in Europe that took them through England, France, Italy, Switzerland, Germany, and then back through Scotland and England before returning home on the *Kronprinz Wilhelm* of the Norddeutscher-Lloyd Line. It was toward the end of that summer of 1905, when the couple arrived in Paris, that they consulted a famous clairvoyant, and Franklin reported to his mother that she had predicted that "E. is to inherit a fortune . . . and I am to be President of the U.S. or of the Equitable, I couldn't make out which!" His jokey offhand comment suggests that even at this early stage he had probably already given some thoughts as to his future, although we can safely assume it did not have anything to do with the Equitable Life Insurance Company.

Throughout that summer, wherever the newlyweds traveled, the European papers were filled with praise for President Theodore Roosevelt, who had brought Russian and Japanese diplomats together in Portsmouth, New Hampshire, to negotiate an end to their bitter war. In a letter home to his mother, Franklin reported: "Everyone is talking about Cousin Theodore, saying that he is the most prominent figure of present day history, and adopting towards our country in general a most respectful and almost loving tone. What a change has come over English opinion in the last few years! Even the French were quite enthusiastic, but the German tone seemed to hide a certain animosity and jealousy as usual."

As the time approached to return home, Franklin learned that he had failed two courses at Columbia—Contracts and Pleading & Practice—and would have to make them up before he would be allowed to start his second year. He was unperturbed. A hurried cable home brought the required textbooks by the next boat, and he spent most of the return crossing swotting up on the failed courses in preparation for the makeup tests, both of which he passed easily soon after returning to New York, in plenty of time before the start of his second year of study. It was another example of just how formidable his intellect could be when he chose to use it.

The following June, while he still had one more year to go in law school, FDR took the eight-hour examination for admission to the New York Bar. Eight months later, in February 1907, he received word that he had passed with flying colors, and he immediately informed Columbia that he would not return for the spring term. A law degree held no interest. The license to practice was enough for him.

Now all he needed was a job; and for someone from such a prominent family, the choice of where to look for one was not overly difficult. He applied to Carter, Ledyard & Milburn, of 54 Wall Street, one of the city's most prestigious law firms, and in due course he received a letter from one of the partners, Edmund L. Baylies, offering him a position. "I have talked over with Mr. Ledyard the question of your coming to our office," he wrote, "and I find that we can arrange to have a place for you at such time as you may wish to come here in the autumn, not later than October 1st, preferably a week or so earlier.

"In case you come to us, the arrangement will be the same as we usually make in such cases, that is to say, you will come to us the first year without salary, and after you have been with us for a year we would expect, if you remain, to pay you a salary which, however, at the outset would necessarily be rather small."

Many years later, during a presidential press conference in 1941, Roosevelt remembered his early days at Carter, Ledyard & Milburn. "Somebody . . . said 'Go up and answer the calendar call in the Supreme Court tomorrow morning. . . . We have such and such a case on.' I had never been in a court of law in my life. . . . Then the next day somebody gave me a deed of transfer of some land. He said, 'Take it up to the County Clerk's office.' I had never been in a county clerk's office. And there I was, theoretically a full-fledged lawyer!"

For the rest of the time, when he wasn't running errands, he sat behind a high roll-top desk, handling petty cases brought against the firm's major clients, including American Express and John D. Rockefeller's Standard Oil. It probably amused him that he was working on behalf of the same powerful "malefactors of great wealth" that President Theodore Roosevelt was so determined to bring down.

But with every passing day it was becoming increasingly clear to him that he was, in his own words, little more than "a full time office boy." For someone as restless and determined as Franklin Roosevelt, the pressure must have been growing to find some meaningful direction to his life, some plan of action that would feed his ambitions and take him away from the world of law, which he found so confining.

Somewhere toward the end of that first year on Wall Street, on a particularly slow day at the office, FDR and his five fellow law clerks sat at their desks casually discussing their hopes and plans for the future. When it came his turn, Franklin surprised his listeners by stating clearly that a life in the law was not for him. He would, when the opportunity presented itself, go into politics and run for the New York State Legislature. After an indeterminate stay in Albany he would, he said with no hint of irony, somehow arrange to get himself appointed assistant secretary of the Navy in Washington. From there he would run for Governor of New York, and "anyone who is Governor of New York," he explained in reasoned tones, "has a good chance to be president with any luck."

Of course, it was not lost on any of his listeners that FDR was precisely retracing the meteoric rise of Theodore Roosevelt, and the fact that the speaker carried the same name gave his prediction a certain semblance of plausibility. The most significant reaction on the part of his fellow law clerks to his amazing pronouncement was neither laughter nor derisive hooting. Instead, they heard him out quietly, apparently accepting at face value his confession of almost unparalleled hubris. Grenville Clark, one of the other law clerks that day, recalled the scene years later, remembering that Roosevelt spoke modestly enough, and with such sincerity as to convince them all that his outlined future sounded "entirely reasonable."

Even today, when we know that FDR's career path eventually fulfilled his casual daydream to the letter, one item in his litany of offices stands out in bold relief—his plan to be named assistant secretary of the Navy. Apparently not just any subcabinet office would do, only the job that TR had once held. And how was he going to manage that? It was not an office he could campaign for, in the normal sense. Someone—a president!—would have to appoint him, a difficult thing to arrange, at best. His listeners did not challenge him on the point, and it is likely that he set the question aside to be dealt with at a more appropriate time.

CHAPTER EIGHT

I t was all very well for the humble clerk at Carter, Ledyard &
Milburn to announce his grand scheme for the presidency, but
even he recognized that there were going to be numerous details
that needed attending to if he were to achieve such an oversized
ambition.

For one thing, he would have to join a political party. Should
he be a Republican or a Democrat? As an undergraduate, when
still too young to vote, he had joined the Harvard Republicans in
support of Cousin Ted; and when he finally was able to cast his
first vote, in 1904, it was for the Republican ticket, now headed by
TR. But family loyalties aside, did Franklin Roosevelt want to be
a Republican? Or, like his late father was he a Cleveland Democrat, protective of the weak while simultaneously promoting the
interests of the business class? At that particular time in political
history, Franklin Roosevelt probably considered himself neither
a true-blue Republican nor a true-blue Democrat, but something
quite distinct, a Progressive, someone who supported commercial
interests as well as such humanitarian issues as child labor laws,

limited working hours, and women's suffrage. There were Progressives in both parties.

It was not much of an oversimplification to list both Theodore Roosevelt (Republican) and Grover Cleveland (Democrat) as Progressives. Cleveland had been successful in building up the Progressive movement within the Democratic Party, but the party leaders since his time—William Jennings Bryan in the West, representing the farmers, and the urban bosses in the big cities, representing the laboring classes—had little sympathy for the factory owners and financiers that the Progressives also supported.

Theodore Roosevelt, on the other hand, openly ran his administration along Progressive lines, although he was meeting considerable resistance from the business leaders who were the dominant supporters of the GOP.

If Franklin Roosevelt were to make his party choice on sentiment alone, he would almost certainly have preferred to run as a Republican, so that he could stand shoulder to shoulder with his hero Theodore, united in affiliation as in family. But there were at least four good reasons for him not to run as a Republican, and they were the president's four sons, Theodore, Jr., Kermit, Archie, and Quentin, all of whom were politically astute and would make attractive candidates. Should any of them decide to enter politics, they would of course have first call on TR's support, and young Franklin was likely to be left out in the cold. (TR had two daughters as well, but in the days before women won the vote they were so rare in politics as to be statistically irrelevant, and would not have been seen by FDR as potential rivals.)

And so, for purely practical reasons, FDR made the decision to be a Democrat.

Having made that important first choice concerning his future career, Franklin then needed to determine from what constituency he would run and for what office. As a Wall Street lawyer, his primary residence was New York City, but he had no intention of running from the city, where the Democratic Party was largely composed of

Irish, Italian, and Jewish immigrants under the aegis of Boss Charles F. Murphy and the Tammany Hall machine. He would far prefer to enter the arena from his country home upstate at Hyde Park; and if there was no more exalted means of getting in the game, he would consider offering himself as candidate for the lowly office of Hyde Park town supervisor, a position his father had once held.

When he let it be known to those in charge of upstate Democratic circles that he might be interested in running for office, things began to move forward of their own accord, particularly after he made it clear that he understood that his main attraction to the Dutchess County politicos was his wealth, and that he would be expected to finance his own campaign and perhaps even to contribute to that of others. Judge John E. Mack, District Attorney of Poughkeepsie, promised to keep an eye open for any likely opportunity.

Meanwhile, there was more than enough to keep Franklin occupied in the city. In the first five years of their marriage, Eleanor had given birth to four children—three of whom survived—and to help house them, his mother had commissioned the construction of a large and comfortable new private home for them at 47 East 65th Street. It was part of a double house, with adjoining interior doors, and Sara moved in beside them at 49 East 65th Street. In a professional move, Franklin left Carter, Ledyard & Milburn and set up shop with two other attorneys in the partnership of Marvin, Hooker & Roosevelt.

Early in 1910, Judge Mack journeyed down from upstate and dropped into FDR's office on some business relating to the Astor estate. When that was quickly settled, their discussion got around to FDR's political ambitions, and in particular to the local seat in the State Assembly. Mack told Roosevelt that the Democratic incumbent, Lewis Stuyvesant Chanler, was signaling that he might not choose to run again, and if that were to be the case, would Franklin be interested in running? There was no guaranteeing victory, he cautioned, but the seat represented the Poughkeepsie area, and its urban constituency gave the edge to the Democrats. FDR leaped at the chance, making it abundantly clear that he would be very interested indeed.

All proceeded smoothly until the summer, when FDR arranged to have lunch with Assemblyman Chanler, the man he was scheduled to replace. Chanler had disappointing news. He told Roosevelt that on reflection, he had decided that he was very comfortable in his seat in the Assembly and had no intention of giving it up. Outwardly Roosevelt took the news with good grace, but inwardly he seethed, and he stormed furiously into a meeting with Judge Mack, demanding satisfaction and vowing that if he could not have the Democratic nomination for the Assembly, he would run as an independent if necessary. He might not win, but he would almost certainly throw the election to the Republicans. The threat was a real one. Given Roosevelt's financial resources and the strength of the Roosevelt name, Judge Mack knew he had to come up with a counterproposal. He offered to support Roosevelt in a run for the State Senate for the 26th District, composed of Dutchess, Putnam, and Columbia counties. The Senate seat was a far more prestigious office than the Assembly seat, but it had a major drawback: the constituency included, along with the Democratic-leaning city of Poughkeepsie, large numbers of farmers, who traditionally voted Republican. The incumbent senator, Republican John F. Schlesser, of Fishkill Landing, had every reason to be confident of reelection. Even Judge Mack, anxious to put as good a face as possible on the proposal, had to admit that he thought FDR's chance of winning the election was no better than one in five. Was he interested?

It was a critical decision the young would-be politician was being asked to make. His mother, who would be asked to finance his campaign, had already opposed his run for the Assembly, and that was for a seat that he had a good chance of winning. What would be her response to this far more risky undertaking?

And what of Theodore Roosevelt? By 1910, he was no longer president, but he remained the undisputed head of the Roosevelt clan, and was still a major power in New York State Republican politics. How would he take young Franklin's entry into politics as a Democrat? Once campaigning began, TR was likely to give speeches all over the state, and as a practical matter if he had any plans to campaign in the 26th Senatorial District, his mere appearance there could scuttle all of Franklin's hopes.

Franklin asked Theodore's older sister, Auntie Bye Cowles, to sound out the great man. When she raised the question with her younger brother, he replied, "Franklin ought to go into politics without the least regard as to where I speak or don't speak." He added, "He is a fine fellow," but he wished Franklin held Republican views. (Geoffrey Ward, one of FDR's most perceptive biographers, pointed out that "party loyalty was never more than a technical matter for either of the Roosevelts; each saw his party primarily as a vehicle for personal power.")

In one of the most fateful decisions of his young life, FDR decided to accept the offer to run for the New York State Senate.

The campaign was brief but intense. It consisted of five weeks of constant campaigning, crisscrossing a large geographical area, giving as many as ten speeches a day, wherever he could pull together an audience. FDR paid almost no attention to the urban vote, leaving Poughkeepsie to the party machine. He would concentrate on the farmers, at least some of whom he would have to win over if he had any chance of beating the incumbent. He would have to venture deep into the rural countryside to reach the audience he was after, and a horse and buggy was hardly suitable for such an undertaking, so he rented a bright red two-cylinder Maxwell automobile, decorated it with patriotic banners, and used it to get him over the unpaved country roads he would have to cover. Because he did not know how to drive a car, he hired the owner to act as his chauffeur.

FDR quickly discovered that he delighted in campaigning. It brought him together with disparate people he would ordinarily never have had a chance to meet in his normal rarefied society, and it seemed to touch some heretofore hidden part of his psyche. He was able to speak on matters of real concern to his listeners, common-sense matters that really made a difference in their lives, like the need for better roads to get produce to market, new laws to protect farmers from unscrupulous dealers, and establishing safeguards in the marketplace.

He learned quickly that his noisy bright-red Maxwell could frighten horses and in the process lose him the vote of their owners. He made it a rule to slow down or even stop whenever horses approached from the opposite direction; and, as the wary horse owner passed, Franklin made it a point to let him know the name of the polite young man in charge of the car, and that he was running for office. Advertising, he was learning, pays.

There were occasional misadventures. In those early days of horse-less carriages, there were few road signs or maps to guide the traveler. One afternoon, campaigning in the eastern edge of the district, they came to a small town and stopped in front of a hotel. Roosevelt went into the bar, and when he saw there were enough gathered there to constitute an audience, he ordered a round of drinks for everybody. As the bartender filled the glasses, Roosevelt asked the name of the town.

"Sharon, Connecticut," came the answer. A chagrined Roosevelt surveyed a room full of non-voters, burst out laughing, and paid up. He enjoyed retelling the story for the rest of his life.

One time, his car ran over a puppy and killed it. Roosevelt sought out the puppy's owner, apologized, and paid him five dollars for his loss. The gratified owner told FDR he had had three other puppies killed by automobiles on the same stretch of road, but no one had ever before bothered to search him out to apologize—or pay him, for that matter. This became another story Roosevelt enjoyed retelling over the years. According to him, the dog owner promised to vote Democratic and persuaded fifteen of his friends and neighbors to do so as well.

At the end of five weeks, Roosevelt's energy and enthusiasm, and his obvious interest in the voters' concerns, won over enough Republicans to win him the election on November 8, 1910, and to win it big. He defeated Schlesser by 15,708 to 14,568 and ran ahead of his ticket not only in Democratic Poughkeepsie but in the Republican rural areas as well.

Franklin Delano Roosevelt was on his way.

CHAPTER NINE

W e have a vivid description of Franklin Roosevelt as he was seen by one of his contemporaries in the weeks immediately following his first political victory in November 1910. The witness was Frances Perkins, a crusading young social worker who would, years later, become one of Franklin Roosevelt's most loyal adherents (she would serve as his secretary of labor throughout his entire time in the White House)—but her initial reaction to him was decidedly skeptical.

"I first saw Franklin Roosevelt in 1910 at a tea dance in the house of Mrs. Walston Brown in Gramercy Park, New York City," she wrote in her 1946 memoir, *The Roosevelt I Knew*. "Mrs. Brown was a pleasant lady who delighted to entertain serious-minded young people who were not too serious to dance and relax, strictly on tea, for such was the innocent habit of late afternoon parties of the pre-World War I period."

At the time of their meeting, Frances Perkins was studying for her master's degree at Columbia University and was already deeply involved in the cause of social justice, working to abolish child labor and the dangerous and unhealthful working conditions and brutal labor practices that were then still common.

"Roosevelt had just entered politics with a Dutchess County campaign, which was not taken too seriously either by Roosevelt himself, his supporters, or his friends. The Republicans and farmers had voted for him as state senator largely because of his name. . . .

"There was nothing particularly interesting about the tall, thin young man with the high collar and pince-nez; and I should not later have remembered this meeting except for the fact that in an interval between dances someone in the group that I joined mentioned Theodore Roosevelt, speaking with some scorn of his 'progressive' ideas. The tall young man named Roosevelt, I didn't catch his first name on introduction, made a spirited defense of Theodore Roosevelt."

It was that spirited defense that caught Perkins's attention. Like many young people at the time, she was an ardent admirer of Theodore Roosevelt, and had in fact chosen her career on the strength of his speeches. "I had read [his] inaugural address of 1905, and had straightaway felt that the pursuit of social justice would be my vocation. Therefore this tall young man who was one of Theodore Roosevelt's admirers made a slight impression on me. We did not become well acquainted, but occasionally I saw him at purely social functions."

She noted that the young Franklin Roosevelt had "an unfortunate habit—so natural that he was unaware of it—of throwing his head up. This, combined with his pince-nez and great height, gave him the appearance of looking down on people."

FDR's social awkwardness, which had dogged him at Groton and again at Harvard, seems to have remained a problem into his adult life, although to a lessening degree over the years. His acute political instincts—which were about to be put to the test in Albany— undoubtedly convinced him of the need to address this failure.

Frances Perkins, already committed to the cause of social justice, quickly recognized that she and the tall young man with the pince-nez did not seem to share much in the way of core values. "I was not much impressed by him. I knew innumerable young men who had been educated in private schools and had gone to Harvard. He did not seem different except that he had political rather than professional or scholarly interests.

"I believe that at that time Franklin Roosevelt had little, if any, concern about specific social reforms. Nothing in his conversation or action would have indicated it. . . . I think he started that way not because he was born with a silver spoon in his mouth and had a good education . . . but because he really didn't like people very much and because he had a youthful lack of humility, a streak of self-righteousness, and a deafness to the hopes, fears, and aspirations which are the common lot.

"The marvel is that these handicaps were washed out of him by life, experience, punishment, and his capacity to grow. He never wholly ignored these youthful traits himself. He once said to me when he was president, 'You know, I was an awfully mean cuss when I first went into politics.'"

CHAPTER TEN

O n January 1, 1911, Roosevelt arrived in Albany and, literally within days, established his reputation as "an awfully mean cuss." It was an amazing performance that caught everyone's attention. He came into town as an obscure new state senator representing three equally obscure upstate New York counties, and three months later he would emerge as a nationally recognized leader of the liberal wing of the Democratic Party, recognized across the country for his dedication to honest politics and good government. How he managed this remarkable evolution says a great deal about lessons he had already learned from Uncle Ted, as well as his ability to think on his feet.

One of the first orders of business for the new Legislature that January was the election of a new U.S. senator to represent New York in Washington. (The 17th Amendment, which would mandate public election of senators, would not be ratified until 1913.)

Chauncey M. Depew, a Republican, was up for reelection; but since the voters had returned Democratic majorities to both houses of the Legislature, it was recognized by all that Depew would not be sent back to Washington, and that he would be replaced by a Democrat. Boss Charles F. Murphy, leader of Tammany Hall, the powerful political club that ran the downstate Democratic Party, had decided that his crony William F. "Blue Eyed Billy" Sheehan was the right man for the job, but other names had been put up as well. Franklin D. Roosevelt decided that Edward M. Shepherd of Brooklyn, a counsel for the Pennsylvania Railroad, who had long been an advocate of clean government, was the man he favored. FDR wrote in his diary on January 1: "Shepherd is without question the most competent to fill the position, but the Tammany crowd seems unable to forgive him his occasional independence, and Sheehan looks like their choice at this stage of the game. May the result prove that I am wrong! There is no question in my mind that the Democratic Party is on trial, and having been given control of the government chiefly through up-State votes, cannot afford to surrender its control to the organization in New York City."

As Franklin quickly learned, the process of electing a new U.S. senator had as much to do with arithmetic as it did with party loyalty. There were a total of 200 state legislators, of which 114 were Democrats, giving that party a clear majority. Each party met separately in a caucus to select a candidate. Roosevelt learned that the rules allowed him to vote for whoever he wanted to in the caucus, but once the party had selected a candidate, he was obliged to vote for that candidate when the vote came up before the Legislature *if he had attended the caucus.* On the other hand, if he had not attended the caucus, he was still free to vote for the candidate of his choice in the final legislative election.

FDR was not alone in his opposition to Sheehan. Several other Democratic legislators were against Murphy's choice. One of them was an assemblyman named Edward R. Terry of Brooklyn, who had worked out some interesting mathematics. He calculated that if all 114 of the Democrats showed up at the caucus, Murphy would only have to arrange for 58 of them—a bare majority—to vote for Sheehan in order to guarantee that all 114 of them would have to vote for "Blue Eyed Billy" in the legislative election. Since Murphy controlled more than 58 Democratic votes, he had the power to personally appoint the next U.S. senator from New York. Sheehan's election appeared a sure thing.

But Terry calculated that if only 18 Democratic legislators refused to attend their party caucus, and thereby retained their freedom to vote against Sheehan, they could deny Murphy the votes he needed. They could even threaten to combine with the Republicans to reelect Depew, which of course Murphy could not allow to happen. Given the right arithmetic, Terry pointed out, Tammany would be forced to withdraw Sheehan's name. By January 12, he had persuaded 18 other disaffected Democrats to join him in boycotting the caucus. Four days later, on the day of the caucus, Franklin Roosevelt joined the insurgents and signed a manifesto declaring that he would not be bound to vote for Sheehan. It may have been Terry and the other insurgents who put together the plan and worked out the details, but their newest recruit was the one with the famous name, and they all recognized it was that simple fact that made Roosevelt their de facto leader.

That evening, when the caucus convened, so many insurgents failed to show up that Tammany was only able to put together 91 Democratic votes for Sheehan, ten shy of the number they would need to elect him in the Legislature. Murphy was stymied, and the New York *Times* took immediate notice:

"It is marvelous how quickly interest in the Senate contest here has shifted from Charles F. Murphy and his lieutenants and William F. Sheehan, who up to the time of the Democratic joint caucus last night were the central figures in the game of politics which is now being played at the Capitol," the paper reported the following morning in its dispatch from Albany. "Tonight the little group of insurgents who, under the leadership of Senator Franklin D. Roosevelt of Dutchess, have dared to resist the domination of the Tammany boss, are the center of attention. They are the talk of the capital to-night, and the politicians crowding the hotel lobbies are craning their necks to catch a glimpse of them as they are pointed out. . . . The action they have taken, to the wonder of men who are older than they in political life, is evidence of their independence. And yet they are not radicals. They speak with moderation, and have made it clear that while they will resist to the last any attempt at coercion, they are amenable to real leadership and keenly alive to the necessary processes of government by parties."

Two days later, on January 18, the embattled Sheehan met privately with Roosevelt in the Ten Eyck Hotel in an effort to find some means of rescuing his cause. Sheehan was determined to badger the young aristocrat from the Hudson Valley into submission, as FDR's note to himself on the meeting suggests: "He said in substance: 'Having a majority of the Democratic Caucus which according to all precedence should elect me, this action against me is assassination[.] I will give up my law practice and will devote my time to the vindication of my character, and I will go into the counties where these men live and show up their characters—the character in which they have accomplished this thing.'"

As newspaper accounts of the insurgency spread, Franklin Roosevelt was rapidly turning into a folk hero, battling for good government. "I am delighted with your action," wrote William Grosvenor, a prominent clergyman, "& told Woodrow Wilson today of how he & you are serving your country."

A stringer from the New York *Herald* named Louis Howe put his own spin on the story. "Never in the history of Albany," he wrote, "have 21 men threatened such ruin of machine plans. It is the most humanly interesting political fight in many years."

When a New York *Times* reporter asked Roosevelt what pressure had been brought on him and the other insurgents in order to get them to change their vote, FDR told him, "Every conceivable form of pressure, that's all I can say—now."

State senators were paid only $1,500 a year, and had to commute home between legislative sessions in order to earn a living. Very few could afford to stay in Albany for extended periods, and even fewer maintained a residence there. In contrast, Franklin and Eleanor had rented, at $400 a month, a commodious three-story house at 248 State Street, large enough for their growing family and their servants. This spacious dwelling quickly became headquarters for the insurgents, giving further support to the idea that FDR was their leader.

The battle over Sheehan continued to make headlines, and toward the end of the month Franklin received the one communication that he would have most cherished. It was from Oyster Bay:

> *Dear Franklin,*
> *Just a line to say that we are all really proud of the way you have handled yourself. Good luck to you! Give my love to dear Eleanor.*
> *Always yours,*
> *Theodore Roosevelt*

W. Axel Warn, writing in the New York *Times* under the headline SENATOR F. D. ROOSEVELT, CHIEF INSURGENT AT ALBANY, burnished FDR's image, describing his subject as "a young man with a finely chiseled face of a Roman patrician, only with a ruddier glow of health on it," and then went on to rhapsodize: "Senator Roosevelt is . . . tall and lithe. With his handsome face and his form of supple strength he could make a fortune on the stage and set the matinée girl's heart throbbing with subtle and happy emotion. But no one would suspect behind that highly polished exterior the quiet force and determination that now are sending cold shivers down the spine of Tammany's striped mascot." (Tammany's symbol was a tiger.)

Virginia Tyler Hudson, writing in the New York *Globe*, went even further than W. Axel Warn in her gushing account of the young Lochinvar: "He is 30 years old [actually, FDR had just celebrated his 29th birthday on January 30, 1911], but only when you are close enough to see the lines about his mouth that a strenuous fight may have made can one believe him even that age. Tall, with a well set up figure[,] he is physically fit to command. His face is a bit long but the features are well modeled, the nose is Grecian in its contour, and there is the glow of country health in his cheeks. His light brown hair, closely cut and crisply curling at the top, is parted on the side over a high forehead. His eyes are deep set and gray, and he wears glasses. It is the chin, though, aggressive and somewhat prominent, that shows what a task the leaders in Albany have if they have thought of making this particular young man change his mind. His lips are firm and part often in a smile over even teeth—the Roosevelt teeth."

At the end of January, with no resolution to the impasse in sight, Murphy sent word that he wanted to see Roosevelt. The two met at the Ten Eyck, and years later FDR described the scene: "We talked about the weather for five or 10 minutes. Then, with a delightful smile, Murphy said, 'I know I can't make you change your mind unless you want to change it. Is there any chance of you and the other 20 men coming around to vote for Sheehan?' 'No, Mr. Murphy,' I replied, 'the opposition is not one against Sheehan personally. In the first place, we believe a great many of our Democratic constituents don't want him to be the United States senator, and in the second place, he is altogether too closely connected with the traction trust in New York City.' Murphy said, 'Yes, I am entirely convinced your opposition is a perfectly honest one. If at any time you change your minds, let me know.'"

After the meeting, Murphy was ready to move on. He instructed his people to try to persuade "Blue Eyed Billy" to step down, but Sheehan refused to go quietly. He was determined to claim the Senate seat he had paid for. Eventually, after weeks of repeated votes proved to every-body's satisfaction that the Legislature was deadlocked, Boss Murphy ignored Sheehan's objections and selected a new candidate—New York Supreme Court Justice James A. O'Gorman, another Tammany stalwart. By any objective measure, O'Gorman was little different than Sheehan and therefore no more deserving of the insurgents' votes. But Roosevelt realized that it would be dangerous to defy Tammany so soon again and bowed to the inevitable. After O'Gorman won the caucus vote, FDR rose in the Senate chamber and announced: "Two months ago, a number of Democrats felt that it was our duty to dissent from certain of our party associates in the matter of selecting a United States Senator. . . . We have followed the dictates of our consciences and have done our duty as we saw it. I believe that as a result, the Democratic Party has taken an upward step. We are Democrats— not irregulars, but regulars. I take pleasure in casting my vote for the Honorable James A. O'Gorman."

Nothing much had really changed in Albany. Roosevelt and his fellow insurgents had won no great political victory. Tammany still ruled the party. But a legend of steadfast idealism had been born, and word of it was beginning to spread. Franklin Delano Roosevelt was now nationally recognized as a crusader for good government, and beyond New York State, other likeminded advocates of Democratic Party reform took note. One of them was the recently elected governor of New Jersey, Woodrow Wilson.

CHAPTER ELEVEN

F ranklin Roosevelt's highly publicized stand against Sheehan did not come without a price. While it made him popular in Progressive circles, it caused nothing but anger and suspicion among most of his fellow Democratic legislators. Boss Murphy and the Tammany faction recognized that his vote for O'Gorman, which many outsiders perceived as a victory for clean government, was in fact a capitulation to political reality. Thereafter, he was tolerated by the Democratic leadership because they needed his vote, but he was never accepted. Once again, he was not "one of the boys."

Frances Perkins, who had moved up to Albany during the legislative session to lobby for laws to protect female laborers, remembered Roosevelt in operation. "I have a vivid picture of him operating on the floor of the Senate: tall and slender, very active and alert, moving around the floor, going in and out of committee rooms, rarely talking with the members, who were more or less avoiding him, not particularly charming (that would come later), artificially serious of face, rarely smiling. . . . Many staunch old Tammany Democrats in those days felt that he did look down his nose at them. I remember old Tim

Sullivan, himself the acme of personal amiability, saying after a bout with Roosevelt, 'Awfully arrogant fellow, that Roosevelt.'"

As the legislative session played out, Franklin found plenty of reason to continue being arrogant. Tammany was taking advantage of the party's control of both houses and the governorship to advance any number of dubious legislative initiatives calculated to line the pockets of supporters, and Roosevelt stubbornly fought them all. His anti-Tammany activities were warmly welcomed by his constituency back home—the Republican farmers and Democratic urban voters of the Twenty-Sixth Senatorial District—but they were doing him no good whatsoever in Albany, where it counted most.

When the Legislature finally recessed on July 22, Roosevelt was relieved to rejoin his wife and children, who had already decamped for Campobello, and to cruise down the Maine coast in the *Half Moon II*, the 60-foot luxury schooner he had inherited from his father.

The summer break provided an ample opportunity to assess his immediate future, and it would have been all too clear that while his dramatic entry into politics had been a resounding success, the fact that he remained at odds with those who ran his party strongly suggested he would have to look elsewhere within the Democratic Party if he hoped to live up to the ambitious career path he had so boldly proclaimed in the offices of Carter, Ledyard & Milburn.

One answer to his problem might lie with Governor Woodrow Wilson of New Jersey. Wilson, who until recently had been president of Princeton University, had been elected governor the same year FDR entered politics, and within four short months of his inauguration he had pushed through a spectacular series of reform measures, including a corrupt practices law, an employers' liability law, a primary and direct election law, and a law establishing a strong public utilities commission with rate-setting powers. As a result, Wilson had attracted a lot of attention and was the frontrunner in the early odds for the Democratic nomination for president in 1912. Many Progressive Democrats from around the country were eager to connect with this rising star, and one of them was Franklin Delano Roosevelt.

Early in October 1911, he arranged an appointment with Wilson at the governor's office in Trenton. That first meeting between those two men, each destined to become a giant of American politics, was to prove crucial to the 29-year-old Roosevelt. In the way of political trade-offs, he had very little to offer Wilson other than his famous name and his new reputation as an anti-Tammany crusader. But that turned out to be sufficient. The national convention was scheduled for the following June in Baltimore, and the governor asked him how much support he could expect from the New York delegation. Roosevelt told him that he estimated that about a third of the New York delegates might be expected to favor a Wilson candidacy, but that figure meant little since they could not vote for him. The delegation would be bound by the unit rule, he explained, which meant they were already pledged to vote for whoever Charles Murphy told them to vote for, and both men were well aware that Murphy did not favor Wilson.

Roosevelt had further to admit that because he himself was personally out of favor with Murphy, he did not expect to be named a delegate or even an alternate. Wilson was intrigued by Roosevelt's grasp of the situation and by his obvious energy and enthusiasm. There was one other critical issue that undoubtedly came up, although there is no record either of Wilson's question or Roosevelt's response. It concerned FDR's Uncle Ted. In those closing months of 1911, Theodore Roosevelt was making it increasingly clear that he was frustrated by the way his hand-picked successor William Howard Taft was running the country, and it seemed increasingly likely to many observers that he might try to recapture the Republican nomination at the GOP convention. If TR became the Republican candidate, Woodrow Wilson wanted to know, where would Franklin Roosevelt stand? Would he cross the aisle and support his dynamic cousin, or would he remain loyal to his party?

FDR must have recognized that the question would arise, and he would have long since decided on an answer. In all likelihood, he promised to remain loyal to Wilson if Wilson managed to get the nomination, but if someone else was named the Democratic nominee he would have to reassess his allegiances. Whatever his answer was—and he left no record of it—it apparently satisfied Wilson, for after their meeting the two men left the governor's office together and continued their conversation on the Pennsylvania Railroad's short run from Trenton to Princeton Junction, where Wilson still made his home on the university campus.

That first meeting between Roosevelt and Wilson marks the moment when the younger man had to make a critical shift in the twin loyalties that formed his psychological center, gently loosening his ties to family and strengthening them to party. The fact that he was able to do this as easily as he did suggests his growing political skill and self-confidence.

CHAPTER TWELVE

I n April 1912, with the Baltimore convention not scheduled to convene until late June, Roosevelt took the opportunity to head south to the Caribbean to soak up some sunshine and visit what had become the most fashionable new tourist attraction for well-to-do Americans, the still-unfinished Panama Canal. The trip would prove to be another important learning experience for the fledgling politico.

The Panama Canal had been the single most spectacular achievement of Theodore Roosevelt's administration, an elaborate engineering marvel now nearing completion. Everyone knew the tortured history of the canal. Since the days of the conquistadors, men had dreamed of a cross-isthmus waterway connecting the Atlantic and Pacific. In the nineteenth century, the French visionary Ferdinand de Lesseps, following up on his immense success digging the Suez Canal, had determined to repeat that success by building a canal across the Isthmus of Panama. He negotiated an agreement with the government of Colombia, which controlled the isthmus, only to fall victim to insurmountable obstacles, yellow fever, corruption, and financial ruin, when work began on the canal. Over twenty thousand men died in the attempt before the project was finally abandoned.

Theodore Roosevelt was sure he could succeed where de Lesseps had failed. Like his much younger Cousin Franklin, Theodore was heavily influenced by the strategic theories of Admiral Alfred Thayer Mahan. Basic to Mahan's philosophy was that in times of national danger, the U.S. Navy must act as a single unit. While it was reasonable under normal peacetime conditions to deploy ships of the Navy to both coasts and even scatter them to various distant parts of the globe, if the country was threatened, it was imperative that the fleet be united to face the enemy as a single, concentrated unit for maximum effectiveness. A Panama Canal would make such a swift gathering of the fleet practical. Without a Panama Canal, the theory went, America would be forced to build and maintain two entire fleets, one for each ocean, to protect its thousands of miles of coastline.

TR lobbied Congress into authorizing a takeover of the failed de Lesseps holdings. When the Colombian Senate threatened to hold up the project by refusing to agree to America's less-than-generous offer of a $250,000 annual rental fee, TR was not deterred. He subsidized a group of Panamanians to stage a revolution in the name of the "Republic of Panama" and stationed a squadron of U.S. Naval vessels near the Isthmus "in the event of any disorders there." He then ordered troops landed to "protect life and property," and finally, with the help of the American businessmen who controlled the Isthmus Railroad, saw to it that the newly born Republic of Panama seceded from Colombia on November 4, 1903, and was immediately recognized as a sovereign nation by the United States. This was, after all, the Age of Empires, and it was the way that people like Theodore Roosevelt got things done. Two weeks later, it was TR who pushed through the Hay–Bunau-Varilla Treaty, which gave the United States de facto sovereignty over a ten-mile-wide swath of land from ocean to ocean, wherein to build the canal.

Having built a new country, it was time to build a new canal to run through it. Originally the Americans had hoped to adapt the French plan, which was to build the canal all at sea level, but the chief engineer convinced the president that it would be necessary to discard the French plan and build a far more ambitious and expensive canal with dams and locks.

As work progressed, so did the costs, partly because the needs of the United States Navy took precedence. The locks at Gatun had originally been designed to accommodate ships as wide as 94 feet, but in 1908, when the admirals in Washington realized that the new dreadnought designs on the drawing boards were going to mean wider battleships, the locks were redesigned to a width of 110 feet.

Ostensibly, Franklin's trip to Panama had been planned for the benefit of Eleanor's younger brother, Hall Roosevelt, who was due to graduate from Harvard and enter engineering school. "I am taking the trip chiefly on Hall's account," Franklin wrote in a letter to Theodore Roosevelt, angling for an introduction to General George Washington Goethals, TR's handpicked chief engineer of the canal, "and feel that it will help his [Hall's] future engineering career if he could see the Isthmus intelligently."

It was of course equally true that Franklin, as a lifelong naval student and an adherent of Mahan's theories, was eager to see the Canal as well. So on April 20, 1912, he stood on the deck of the S.S. *Carillo* and watched as the little port city of Colon, soon to become the Atlantic terminus of the Panama Canal, came slowly into sight over the horizon. Standing alongside him and watching the approaching landmass of Central America were his two traveling companions, his young brother-in-law Hall Roosevelt and a Republican colleague in the State Senate, J. Mayhew Wainwright. "Hall is I think having a very good time," Roosevelt reported in a letter home. "Mayhew Wainwright is one of the most delightful travelling companions I have known, and he is always in good spirits and ready to do things."

The trip, which had already touched at Cuba and Jamaica, was proceeding under pleasant conditions: "weather perfect, sea like the much overworked millpond, boat roomy and cool, food and all appointments excellent."

Roosevelt's connections to the Canal ran deep. Uncle Ted was not the only family member involved. Franklin's own father had been an investor in an earlier scheme for a trans-isthmus canal through Nicaragua that had not worked out. And the original name for the town of Colon that the ship was approaching had been Aspinwall, named after its founder, the railroad entrepreneur William H. Aspinwall, who was Franklin's great-uncle.

The three travelers spent the afternoon of their arrival touring the town of Colon, which was under the control of the Panamanian authorities, before crossing into the newly created adjoining town of Cristobal, administered by the Isthmian Canal Commission, an American agency. Cristobal was to form the Atlantic terminus of the Canal, and Franklin was duly impressed with the new construction. "The American quarters were a revelation, spotless and comfortable, yet with an air of absolute efficiency," Franklin wrote to his mother. "Here are located the Commissary headquarters, cold storage plant for the whole Zone, etc. The ice cream factory alone is the largest in the world!"

Later they boarded the train for the fifty-mile journey to the Pacific coast, getting "splendid glimpses of the Canal" from the observation car. The Canal Zone was under American control and administered by the YMCA, and was strictly alcohol-free. The three tourists were not to be denied their cocktails, and arranged to spend the evening exploring neighboring Panama City, which was under local control and satisfactorily wet. The following morning, after a night on the town, they drove out to Balboa, where they inspected what would become the Pacific terminus and the site of the future docks and harbor. "Tremendous operations now in progress," FDR reported. Later that afternoon they had "a nice long talk" with General Goethals. When they expressed their admiration for the Canal, he told them, "We like to have Americans come down, because they all say it makes them better Americans."

The enormous size and vast ambitions of the Canal did not become truly evident until the next morning at Culebra, where the three were taken on a guided tour of the great Cut, nearly nine miles in length. It was here, where most of the sixty-five thousand men in Goethals's workforce were literally moving mountains, that the battle for the Canal would be won or lost. Gigantic steam shovels, purpose-built for the unprecedented work, towered over the landscape, loading six-ton boulders onto flatcars, which were then sent to the coasts where the huge rocks were turned into breakwaters for the terminals. Years later, a still-awed Franklin would describe the scene from the mountaintop, looking down on a huge rift in the earth's crust, at the base of which pygmy engines and ant-like forms were rushing to and fro seemingly without plan or reason. The constant noise was deafening. The strident clink, clink of the drills eating their way into the rock; the shrill whistles of the locomotives; the constant and uninterrupted rumble of the dirt trains plying the crowded tracks; the clanking of chains and the creaking of machinery, all punctuated by the shouts of the workmen.

That afternoon they inspected the great locks of Pedro Miguel and Miraflores, designed to raise the vessels 85 feet to the level of the Cut. "I can't begin to describe it," Franklin wrote breathlessly, positively bubbling over with enthusiasm. "The two things that impress the most are the Culebra cut, because of the colossal hole made in the ground, and the locks because of the engineering problems and size. Imagine an intricate concrete structure nearly a mile long and three or four hundred feet wide, with double gates of steel weighing 700 tons apiece!"

After two more days of sightseeing, Franklin and his companions boarded the S.S. *Abangarez* for the trip home. Deeply impressed by the scale and promise of what he had witnessed, he closed another letter to his mother, "I wish you could see this wonder of the world, greater than the Tower of Babel or the Pyramids."

For the rest of his life, Franklin Roosevelt would draw inspiration from his brief visit to the Canal. Here, he recognized, was political boldness of a very high order, a vision that dared to change the world. Ever afterwards, somewhere in his memories of the trip, would lie his new understanding of presidential power, an understanding that in later years would time and again generate visionary concepts that would always astonish, sometimes baffle, and on occasion infuriate the world with its daring: grand, far-reaching projects like the North Sea Barrage, the New Deal, the Tennessee Valley Authority, the Lend-Lease Act, the Manhattan Project. With the Canal, Theodore had provided Franklin with his last great gift—he had shown his young cousin how to think like a Roosevelt.

CHAPTER THIRTEEN

P olitical tides can be fickle, and by the time Roosevelt returned to New York, he had reason to wonder if he had been wise to commit himself so definitely to the Wilson candidacy. By that time, Wilson's financial backing, which had come chiefly from Wall Street, had largely evaporated. Roosevelt was still convinced that of all the potential Democratic nominees, Wilson had the best chance of beating the Republican candidate—the GOP had not yet decided whether to renominate Taft or to once again go with Uncle Ted—but Wilson was no longer the frontrunner, and FDR predicted that the same Wall Street faction that had originally supported Wilson's campaign would force Tammany to back Governor Judson Harmon of Ohio, and if he did not make it, Senator Oscar Underwood of Alabama, or Speaker Champ Clark of Missouri. The still formidable William Jennings Bryan, the Great Commoner who had three times led the Democrats to defeat in national elections, remained a shadowy prospect waiting in the wings, but the Wall Street people so detested him that his nomination was not taken seriously even by his most loyal supporters, although they thought he might still have enough clout to tip the scales for one of the other candidates.

American politics has its unique rituals, and probably the best known and least understood are the presidential conventions. Every four years, some of the best and brightest, most ambitious and most idealistic Americans—along with an assortment of mountebanks and frauds—gather together in convention halls to select the candidate they hope will be the next President of the United States. To an outsider the process looks chaotic—a boisterous, clownish, messy exhibition of loyalties and dreams carried out by sweating delegates waving banners and shouting slogans, catch-phrases, and anthems, the whole process suffused with insincerity and subject to rumors, panic, last-minute hysteria, and the machinations of dealmakers holed up in airless hotel rooms quietly trading promises. In recent years, the increase in the number of primary elections has transferred much of this noisy ritual to the hustings and spread the process over a period of months rather than days, but its seemingly disorderly and confused character remains unchanged.

The 1912 Democratic National Convention would have appeared particularly chaotic with its confusing spectrum of candidates, its arguments over the party platform, its petty and often silly disputes over credentials and protocol; but the professional politicians who made their way to Baltimore that June—including Franklin Roosevelt, who was rapidly turning himself into one of the more astute members of that group—would have known better. What appeared to be chaos was in reality a battlefield of serious ideas, with sweaty, overweight delegate-soldiers fighting a war to decide the practical issues of governance, ultimately defining the questions that would be put to the voting public the following November: where should the country be going, and who should lead it there?

Franklin and Eleanor arrived early for the convention, and rented a house with two other couples. As he predicted would be the case, Tammany had shut him out completely from the nominating process.

He was accredited neither as a delegate nor an alternate. He could justify his presence in Baltimore solely as the leader of something he called the New York State Wilson Conference, an earnest but totally powerless group of 150 anti-Tammany Democrats. On arrival, he set up quarters in Room 214 of the Munsey Building, across the street from the Wilson and Clark headquarters, and immediately issued a manifesto to the assembling delegates: "New York has a large progressive vote. Unless you give us a candidate that will get this vote, we still lose the state," it warned, pointing out that in the long history of the party, no Democrats other than Madison and Buchanan had ever been elected president without the electoral vote of New York. The message, well thought out and reasonable, was quickly drowned out by the noise and excitement of arriving delegates.

Winning the nomination required a two-thirds majority of the 1,090 delegate votes. At that point, before balloting began, Speaker Champ Clark was very much in the lead for the nomination, with 436 pledged votes in his pocket. Wilson was in second place with 248 votes, and Judson Harmon of Ohio was in third with about 150, which included Boss Murphy's 90 New York votes. Lurking in the shadows, in case no candidate could gain the necessary 726 votes required for nomination, was William Jennings Bryan, the old prairie populist of Nebraska, who still held the allegiance of many Western delegates.

In the days leading up to the opening of the convention on June 25, a further element of uncertainty was added to the political scene when the Republican convention turned its back on Theodore Roosevelt, despite his numerous victories in the primaries, and on June 22 renominated the sitting president, William Howard Taft. Theodore responded by walking out of the convention and forming the Progressive Party with himself as candidate, guaranteeing that there would be three major candidates running for president. The split in the Republican Party might have seemed to favor the Democrats' chances in the November election, but this was not at all clear as their Baltimore convention opened.

Although uncredentialed, Franklin quickly demonstrated his skills as a propagandist. Because of his famous name and his record in the "Blue Eyed Billy" Sheehan fight, he had easy access to the press, and he casually mentioned to a reporter that on his way to the convention he had run into Theodore Roosevelt's son Kermit, who had told him "Pop is praying for Clark," with the clear implication that Champ Clark would be the easiest Democrat to defeat. Franklin understood full well that such a juicy tidbit, coming from such an unimpeachable source, would spread like wildfire among the delegates, which of course it did. Within minutes, it was being discussed excitedly by everyone in the electoral cauldron of the convention. One delegate who was particularly intrigued by the story was Josephus Daniels, editor of the Raleigh (North Carolina) *News & Observer* and one of Wilson's chief advisers. He was impressed that a powerless observer of absolutely no significance to the convention could find such a brilliant way to boost the Wilson cause. Daniels, who would play a critically important role in Roosevelt's subsequent career, remembered meeting him for the first time in Baltimore: "I thought he was as handsome a figure of an attractive young man as I have ever seen. At that convention Franklin and I became friends—a case of love at first sight."

The heat and humidity of Baltimore in midsummer turned the entire city into a Turkish bath, and the climate, along with the convention itself, with its raucous humor, its garish confusion and air of blatant excess, soon became too much for Eleanor. After standing it as long as she could, she bade farewell to her husband and caught the train north, where she collected the children at Hyde Park and trundled them off to the cooler serenity of Campobello.

But if the convention was too much for Eleanor, it was catnip for Franklin. He found he loved national politics, rubbing elbows with powerful figures from across the country, conniving with backstage kingmakers, attending the ad hoc committee meetings and emergency strategy sessions, buttonholing delegates and organizing floor demonstrations, and generally whooping it up for Woodrow Wilson at every opportunity.

Here was a challenge he could appreciate: democracy in action. It had all the ingredients that would appeal to him—an inherent sense of urgency, a need to make sense out of confusion, a chance to work with others who shared his enthusiasms and tastes; all of it carried out in the raucous, undignified world of power politics, and all of it dedicated to a most solemn and worthy cause.

Once the nominations were in, the balloting went on for several days, with Clark in the lead most of the time, and at first apparently close to victory. Wilson was second, Harmon third, and Underwood fourth, clinging tenaciously to a block of Southern delegates.

As each ballot was tallied and recorded, the contest narrowed to the two leading candidates. Each gained votes, but Clark was moving inexorably into what looked like an unbeatable lead. Then, after a late-night session, the Clark team finally managed to capture half of the votes. Historically, with only one exception in the long history of the Democratic Party, getting to the halfway point had always led to the two-thirds majority necessary for the nomination. The Wilson people needed some way to stop the inevitable. Roosevelt, operating from the visitors' gallery, learned that the Clark leaders had arranged for two or three hundred Baltimore ward heelers and their henchmen to storm the floor at the evening session. A big Clark demonstration at that point was almost sure to tip the scales and give Clark the nomination. The doorkeepers had been instructed to admit all who wore Clark buttons. Roosevelt had a personal friend who was active in Baltimore politics. He agreed to lend Roosevelt about a hundred of his people. Roosevelt lined up another hundred from New York, supplied them all with Clark buttons and instructed them to enter on the heels of the Clark crowd. At the appropriate moment, the "real" Clark shouters poured into the aisles, unfurling banners and shouting "We want Clark!" In a few seconds, there arose from immediately behind them an equally excited cry, "We want

Wilson! We want Wilson!" The demonstration that had attempted to stampede the convention for Clark disintegrated into pandemonium, which threatened to turn into a riot, and both brigades were eventually thrown off the floor.

On the fourteenth ballot, Bryan, after talking quietly with his old friend Daniels, dramatically switched the Nebraska delegation's votes from Clark to Wilson. While this did not set off any landslide, it slowly became evident, as the balloting continued in almost endless monotony, that Wilson was gaining. Finally, on the forty-sixth ballot, Wilson won the nomination.

Roosevelt was ecstatic. He wired Eleanor WILSON NOMINATED THIS AFTERNOON ALL MY PLANS VAGUE STOP SPLENDID TRIUMPH. The next day, after the convention went on to nominate Thomas R. Marshall, Governor of Indiana, as Wilson's vice presidential running mate, Roosevelt joined the winning team at Sea Girt, New Jersey, where the candidate had a summer cottage and where the party's leaders now gathered to discuss the upcoming campaign. FDR quickly realized that he carried little or no weight in that setting, and he hurried back to New York to prepare his own local campaign for reelection to the state senate.

Franklin Roosevelt had every reason to be satisfied with his performance in Baltimore. While historians generally agree that his presence in Baltimore had little or nothing to do with Wilson's eventual victory, they also concede that something had changed. Somehow, this tall young man with a famous name from an obscure corner of upstate New York had come out of Baltimore as someone to be watched. Someone to be consulted. Someone to be relied upon. He had been dealt a weak hand, and he had played it with spectacular skill.

CHAPTER FOURTEEN

Toward the end of summer, as soon as he had secured his renomination for the 26th Senatorial District, Roosevelt headed north to join his family at Campobello for a brief respite before throwing himself into the campaign for reelection. Then, early in September, he and Eleanor closed up the cottage and took the steamer south. After depositing the children at Hyde Park, they took the train into the city for what they expected to be a single night at their house on East 65th Street before returning upstate to begin campaigning. But such was not to be.

Early that evening, Franklin became violently ill with a high fever and severe stomach pain. He was unable to eat or even stand up. The next day he was no better, and when Eleanor summoned help, the doctor was unable to diagnose her husband's condition. Franklin remained in bed for ten days with no improvement, nursed by Eleanor, who began showing symptoms of the same mysterious illness. Finally the malady was diagnosed as typhoid fever, and Eleanor was ordered to bed as well. No one was sure how they had contracted the disease, but Eleanor thought it might have been due to the possibility that both of them had brushed their teeth with contaminated water on board the steamer from Campobello.

Franklin was far too ill to attempt anything as physically challenging as a political campaign, and time was getting increasingly short. He needed help. He remembered a newspaper man named Louis Howe, the upstate political correspondent for the James Gordon Bennett papers, the New York *Herald* and the *Telegram*. The two men had come to know each other in Albany, and they had become friendly. Howe admired Roosevelt's dash and determination, and it was he who had written that the battle against Sheehan was "the most humanly interesting political fight in many years." His reporting had done much to enhance Roosevelt's reputation throughout the state. Their relationship had grown closer when Roosevelt hired Howe to handle the publicity for the New York Wilson Conference at Baltimore. Franklin asked Eleanor to contact Howe and ask him to come down to New York and take over the campaign.

Roosevelt's decision to seek out Howe to deal with this newest emergency must have seemed an obvious choice. But whatever the reasoning behind it, the choice was more than simply fortuitous. In terms of FDR's future career, his sickbed selection of Louis Howe was almost certainly the most important decision he made in the seminal year of 1912.

Louis McHenry Howe was a chain-smoking wizened gnome of a man who was one of the first people to recognize the young Roosevelt's enormous potential. As events would soon reveal, he was also a brilliant strategist and publicist. He was vacationing on the Massachusetts shore when he received Eleanor's telegram asking for help, and he immediately caught the next train to New York. On his arrival, the two men huddled together in the sickroom and, over the course of the next few days, put together a plan for a campaign that in all likelihood might have to be conducted without a single appearance of the candidate. Constituencies were defined, needs assessed, budgets estimated, and schedules established. Louis Howe was brought on board for $50.00 a week plus expenses.

Howe immediately moved his small family to a boardinghouse in Poughkeepsie to be closer to the action, and again leased the same red two-cylinder Maxwell that FDR had used in his first run for office and hired its owner to drive him around the district. Simultaneously, he threw himself into the preparation of something still comparatively new in American politics—an advertising campaign.

Soon subscribers to the local papers in Dutchess, Columbia, and Sullivan counties found themselves reading full-page ads—a distinct novelty at the time—trumpeting Roosevelt's agrarian progressivism, his support of women's suffrage and fair labor practices, his bipartisanship, his anti-boss credentials, and his knowledge of and concern for the specific needs of his constituents.

Howe developed "a great farmer stunt," a proposal for a bill to protect farmers from commission merchants, the middlemen who pocketed the difference between the low prices they paid to farmers and the high prices they charged consumers. A poster addressed to fruit-growers who sold their produce on a per-barrel basis and were often cheated when buyers used oversized barrels to measure the fruit, gives an idea of Louis Howe's style of targeted, specific political promises:

TO FRUIT GROWERS!

I am convinced after careful investigation that the present law making a 17⅛ inch barrel the legal standard for fruit unjust and oppressive to fruit growers.

I pledge myself to introduce and fight for the passage of an amendment to the law making a Standard Fruit Barrel of 16½ inches.

This barrel to be the legal standard for fruit and to be marked, "Standard Fruit Barrel."

The justice of this seems so plain that I feel assured of the passage of the amendment. . . .

FRANKLIN D. ROOSEVELT
Candidate for State Senator

When Franklin Roosevelt says he will fight for a thing, it means he won't quit until he wins—you know that.

In addition to running an advertising campaign and giving the occasional speech, Howe also had to recruit the army of volunteers necessary for a tri-county race, and then organize them and supervise their efforts. Shrewd, sharp-witted, and delighted with his new career, Louis Howe took to campaigning with the same alacrity Franklin had shown two years earlier. "I'm having more fun than a goat," Howe told his boss.

On Election Day, November 5, all of Louis Howe's efforts paid off handsomely. That night, he was able to telephone Roosevelt and tell him he had won big. Wilson and the Democratic candidate for governor, William Sulzer, also won; but in his district FDR had received more votes than either, and he could claim that he had helped them far more than they had helped him.

In the national campaign, Wilson won the White House with a popular vote of 6,293,019 to Uncle Ted's 4,119,507 and Taft's 3,484,956. The Electoral College tally was even more definitive: 435 for Wilson, 88 for Theodore Roosevelt, and a mere 8 for the incumbent Taft.

Franklin had won an important victory, an election that proved his vote-getting abilities to the people who would now judge him for possible inclusion in the upcoming administration in Washington. But in the process he had won something just as important—in fact, arguably *more* important: the fealty of a very smart and totally dedicated Louis Howe, who could offer him the same fierce love and loyalty he had always had from his mother, but with none of the imperious second-guessing, none of the controlling mechanisms that could on occasion try the patience and thwart the vision and ambitions of this remarkable young man.

CHAPTER FIFTEEN

W hen Roosevelt returned to Albany in January 1912, he did not bring his family with him or rent a commodious residence, as he had two years previously. It was clear to those who bothered to take notice that the young senator representing the 26th District did not expect to be spending much more time in Albany. His ambitions now lay elsewhere, and even though he immediately threw himself into the business of fulfilling the promises that Louis Howe had made on his behalf, what he was looking forward to was some indication of interest from the president-elect, who was still in his office in New Jersey.

It was not until halfway through January that a telegram finally came from Joseph Tumulty, Woodrow Wilson's private secretary, inviting him to come down to Trenton to discuss the future.

There is no historical record of the meeting between Roosevelt and Wilson, other than a couple of mentions by FDR in personal letters that it had been a "very satisfactory talk," but it is easy enough to reconstruct the main thrust of their discussion. Wilson clearly wanted Roosevelt on his team. He would have remembered FDR's prominent role in the Sheehan fight, and the effect upon the convention of his casual and well-timed quote from Cousin Kermit that "Pop is praying for Clark." In addition, Senator O'Gorman, Sheehan's Tammany-directed replacement, had been singularly helpful to Wilson in Baltimore; and although O'Gorman and Roosevelt were hardly friendly, Wilson and Tumulty kept in mind that O'Gorman's seat in the U.S. Senate was largely due to Roosevelt's leadership in the battle over Sheehan. And then there had been his impressive showing in the recent legislative election. Clearly, the young Roosevelt was someone to have on your side.

Roosevelt, with his career plan in mind, undoubtedly expressed his keen interest in the office of assistant secretary of the Navy, and would have supported his claim for the job by describing his life-long interest in the Navy, his close study of Admiral Mahan's strategic theories, and his sophisticated understanding of the new technologies that were radically changing the navies of the world. Wilson would of course have been aware of Theodore's history as assistant secretary, but it is likely that Franklin made no mention of it, knowing Wilson's visceral dislike of TR.

We know that Franklin petitioned for the job that day, and that Wilson appeared favorably inclined to grant his wish. But almost certainly the president-elect would have made no promises and would have pointed out that it would be up to whoever he selected to be secretary of the Navy to name his own assistant secretary.

We know the subject was discussed because not long after the November election, a young Philadelphia lawyer named Michael Francis Doyle, who had been a longtime supporter of William Jennings Bryan and had moved to the Wilson camp with Bryan, had expressed interest in the assistant secretaryship and had been told by Bryan that Wilson was favorably disposed to appoint him. Then a few weeks before the inauguration in March, Doyle and Bryan had met again, and Bryan had told him that Franklin Roosevelt had asked for the job, and while Wilson was ready to stand by his promise, Bryan suggested to Doyle that he should withdraw his bid, which he did.

Meanwhile Roosevelt, unsure of where he stood, but encouraged by Wilson's reaction at their meeting in Trenton, returned to Albany and once again immersed himself in the parochial issues of the Legislature, keeping a close watch on the news emerging from the office of the president-elect. He would have noted—and probably been a little puzzled by—the announcement of some of Wilson's choices for his cabinet, which included the nomination of two avowed pacifists to positions where pacifism might not have been thought to be a particularly useful attribute—William Jennings Bryan to be secretary of state, and Josephus Daniels to be secretary of the Navy. Here indeed was something to ponder. Just how would a pacifist secretary of the Navy look upon having a Roosevelt as assistant secretary?

Three days before the inauguration, Roosevelt took the train down to Washington on the assumption that whether his bid for the assistant secretaryship proved successful or not, Washington was the place for any office-seeker to be at that moment. Also on the train was William Gibbs McAdoo, the designated new secretary of the treasury and a member of Wilson's inner circle. McAdoo offered Roosevelt two very tempting appointments, one as assistant secretary of the treasury, and the other as collector of the Port of New York. The first would put him in almost daily contact with the White House, in one of the most sensitive positions in the new administration. The second would put him in control of one of the most lucrative patronage bankrolls in the country and provide him with an unparalleled opportunity to build an anti-Tammany machine in New York. Roosevelt recognized that these were both political plums of the highest grade, and the fact that they had been offered to him gave proof of McAdoo's (and therefore Wilson's) high opinion of him; but he turned down both positions with thanks.

On the morning of the inauguration, Roosevelt ran into Josephus Daniels in the lobby of the Willard Hotel. In Daniels's account of the meeting, Roosevelt "was bubbling over with enthusiasm at the incoming of a Democratic administration, and keen as a boy to take in the inauguration ceremonies. He greeted me cordially and said, 'Your appointment as Secretary of the Navy made me happy. I congratulate you and the president and the country.' I responded by asking him, 'How would you like to come to Washington as assistant secretary of the Navy?' His face beamed with pleasure. He replied, 'How would I like it? I'd like it bully well. It would please me better than anything in the world. I'd be glad to be connected with the new administration. All my life I have loved ships and have been a student of the Navy, and the assistant secretaryship is the one place, above all others, I would love to hold.'"

Daniels always insisted that his offer was no sudden impulse. "It was in fulfillment of what I had told my wife on the day I received a letter from President Wilson asking me to be a member of his cabinet. As I finished reading the letter . . . I said, 'I will ask the president to appoint Franklin Roosevelt as assistant secretary.'"

Daniels went on to describe a conversation he had with Wilson two days after his encounter with FDR at the Willard Hotel. "I asked him if he had anyone in view for the position [of assistant secretary of the Navy]. He said he had not given it consideration. I then said, 'If you have no one for the position, I would like to make a recommendation.' 'You are quick on the trigger,' he said. 'Whom have you in mind?' I told him I would like him to appoint Franklin D. Roosevelt, and the reason I was quick on the trigger was I knew that there would be a number of applicants and that by filling the position at once, we would not be under the necessity of rejecting any applicant. Moreover, I felt that the sooner the new organization was effected, the better. I added, 'As I am from the South, I think the assistant secretary should come from another section, preferably from New York or New England.'

"'How well do you know Mr. Roosevelt?' he asked, 'and how well is he equipped?' 'I never met him until the Baltimore convention,' I replied, 'but I was strongly drawn to him then and more so as I met him during the campaign when I was in New York. I have admired him since the courageous fight he made in the New York State Senate, which resulted in the election of a liberal who had favored your nomination in Baltimore. Besides, I know he has been a naval enthusiast from his boyhood.' I expressed the convention that he was one of our kind of liberal. 'Very well,' he said, 'send the nomination over.'"

As a courtesy, since Roosevelt's appointment would have to be confirmed by the Senate, Daniels sounded out the two New York senators on the proposed nomination. "Senator O'Gorman... said the appointment was agreeable to him, and the Senate would confirm it promptly. I expected him to show enthusiasm for the appointment of the young man chiefly responsible for his election to the Senate. The most I gathered was that it was agreeable."

When Daniels told Elihu Root, a Republican, that the president had in mind naming Franklin Roosevelt as assistant secretary, "a queer look came over his face. 'You know the Roosevelts, don't you?' he asked. 'Whenever a Roosevelt rides, he wishes to ride in front.'" Then he added, "I know the young man very slightly . . . but all I know about him is credible, and his appointment will be satisfactory so far as I'm concerned, though, of course, being a Republican, I have no right to make any suggestions. I appreciate your courtesy in consulting me."

Such is the generally accepted account of how Franklin Delano Roosevelt came to be named Woodrow Wilson's assistant secretary of the Navy, his first important step toward national and eventually international power. Virtually identical versions of the story are found in almost all of FDR's biographies. But there is something suspiciously pat about Daniels's account.

In an effort to claim full credit for the selection of FDR to be assistant secretary, Daniels builds up an unlikely "chance meeting" at the Willard Hotel, and a president who seems to have given no thought to the appointment, neither of which quite rings true. It is likely that Daniels was not aware of Roosevelt's discussion with

Wilson in January, and of course he had never heard of Roosevelt's citing the assistant secretaryship as a key step in his career plan in the offices of Carter, Ledyard & Milburn all those years ago, both of which incidents speak volumes about Roosevelt's ambition, his vision, and his cunning.

There is no harm in accepting Daniels's account at face value. It does not materially distort the essential truth, which is that FDR wanted very much to become assistant secretary of the Navy, and got the job in March 1913. But it obscures an understanding of just how focused, just how determined, just how skillful this young politician had already become at making things happen in accordance with his own game plan.

When the news of Franklin Roosevelt's appointment was announced, a Syracuse newspaper, recalling his pitched battles in Albany, headlined the story WATCH OUT JOSEPHUS.

CHAPTER SIXTEEN

F ranklin Roosevelt was sworn in as assistant secretary of the Navy on Monday, March 17, 1913, his eighth wedding anniversary and a little less than five years after he had declared that office to be his goal. At age thirty-one, he was the youngest man ever to hold the office, and he would serve in it until August 1920, a total of seven years and five months, the longest tenure of any assistant secretary of the Navy.

On his first day in office, Josephus Daniels, who had expressed such unreserved enthusiasm for Roosevelt, was still a little shaky about some of the personal details about his new assistant, and noted in his diary that "Mr. Frederick D. Roosevelt arrived today."

The Navy Department was staffed with competent personnel well prepared to help Roosevelt learn his new duties, and, as was his wont, he dived energetically into his new responsibilities, as he reported to his mother on his first day on the job.

Dearest Mama

I am baptized, confirmed, sworn in, vaccinated—and some-
what at sea! For over an hour I have been signing papers which
had to be accepted on faith—but I hope luck will keep me out
of jail.

All well, but I will have to work like a new turbine to master
this job—but it will be done even if it takes all summer.
Your affec. son
Franklin D. Roosevelt.

He had apparently signed so many official papers that day that
out of habit he signed his letter to his mother with the same formal
signature. She took the opportunity to offer some advice in her
response. "My dearest Franklin—You can't imagine the happiness
you gave me by writing to me yesterday. I just *knew* it was a *very* big
job, and everything so new that it will take time to fit *into* it. Try
not to write your signature too small, so it gets a cramped look and
is not distinct. So many public men have such awful signatures,
and so unreadable. . . ."

The Reverend Endicott Peabody, who had started his school
specifically to encourage the sons of the rich to enter public service,
was quick to express his approbation of Franklin's new position.
"Your friends at Groton—and they are numerous—are delighted
over your appointment to High Office. It is a great triumph of
Honesty & Loyalty over the lower powers which are trying to best
the Country. . . ."

But it was another letter that must have been a source of particular
satisfaction.

Dear Franklin:

I was very much pleased that you were appointed as Assistant
Secretary of the Navy. It is interesting to see that you are in
another place which I myself once held. I am sure you will enjoy

yourself to the full as Assistant Secretary of the Navy, and that
you will do capital work. When I see Eleanor I shall say to her
that I do hope that she will be particularly nice to the naval
officers' wives. They have a pretty hard time, with very little
money to get along on, and yet a position to keep up, and every-
thing that can properly be done to make things pleasant for them
should be done. When I see you and Eleanor I will speak to you
more at length about this.
Yours aff,
Theodore Roosevelt

Franklin was fortunate to inherit as private secretary Charles H. McCarthy, who had served several of his predecessors, and who proved invaluable in winnowing through the endless waves of paperwork that went with the job. But Roosevelt knew he would need another, even more private, secretary to handle his more personal agenda, and straightaway sent out a summons to Louis Howe, the man he would come to trust above all others in the years to come. "Dear Ludwig," he wrote, "Here is the dope. Secretary—$2,000—expect you April 1, with a new uniform."

Howe wired back, "I am game but it's going to break me . . . L. M. Howe." Roosevelt, concerned that Howe seemed to be taking a pay cut to come to Washington, began looking for ways to improve his salary, and eventually managed to have him promoted to special assistant at an additional thousand dollars a year.

There were many in Washington who considered the office of assistant secretary of the Navy more important than some cabinet-level jobs, and with good reason. While the secretary of the Navy was responsible for overall Navy policy, and worked with the White House on the disposition of the fleet and with the Congress on naval bills and appropriations, the assistant secretary—there was only one— was responsible for the administration of the Navy's $143,497,000 annual budget—representing 20% of the entire federal government's outlay—as well as the welfare of the sixty-five thousand officers and enlisted men of the Navy and Marine Corps, plus all civilian personnel. In addition, he was responsible for the administration of the Navy bureaus and the negotiation of contracts for coal, steel, oil, naval stores, and the thousands of other goods and services the Navy required to carry out its functions. He had primary responsibility for docks and yards, and therefore labor relations, and was required to fill in as acting secretary in the absence of his boss.

The job carried a salary of $5,000 a year, which was a substantial income in its day, although nowhere near enough to support Franklin and Eleanor in the style to which they were accustomed. But for all that, it was everything that Franklin Roosevelt could have wished for. In a letter to a friend he wrote, "I now find my vocation combined with my avocation in a delightful way."

The day after his swearing in, FDR was bantering with some newspapermen and announced jocularly, "There's a Roosevelt on the job today. . . . You remember what happened the last time a Roosevelt occupied a similar position?" Of course the newspapermen were familiar with the famous story of TR's overstepping his authority by sending an unauthorized cable to Admiral Dewey commanding an attack on Manila in case of war with Spain.

Everyone had a good laugh.

CHAPTER SEVENTEEN

For all the shining idealism ushered into Washington by the new administration, it brought with it a cheerless, Puritan quality that threatened to take all the fun out of the city's social life. Woodrow Wilson set the tone by refusing to hold an inaugural ball, and Secretary of State Bryan added to the sense of joyless seriousness by forbidding the serving of alcohol at diplomatic functions.

Franklin Roosevelt, who enjoyed his cocktails and the gaiety and laughter they encouraged, paid no heed to the glum solemnity of his superiors. One of his first steps on arriving at the capital was to join the Chevy Chase Club, where he golfed regularly, and he then joined the even more exclusive Metropolitan Club, where he met with the capital's movers and shakers several times a week.

During his first months in office, he lived a bachelor life, first at the Willard Hotel and later at the Powhatan, while Eleanor and the children remained in New York and eventually migrated to Campobello when the weather turned hot. Franklin would join them for weekends or longer when he could get away, but between inspection tours, conferences, and the normal press of works he spent most of the time on the job.

It was part of his responsibilities to mix with those in the capital whose work touched on his own, and he made much use of his club memberships to entertain the admirals, diplomats, business leaders, cabinet officers, and members of Congress he needed to know. He was also a frequent guest of these same leaders, so his social schedule was busy.

Within the Navy Department, Franklin's famous name guaranteed him a particularly warm reception. Theodore Roosevelt had done more to promote the United States Navy than any president in history, and throughout his administration he constantly strove to improve the fleet and glorify its status. He had pushed the construction of the Panama Canal, which vastly increased the Navy's ability to respond to any potential threat, he had encouraged the development of new naval technologies, including aerial and underwater branches of service, and capped his presidency by organizing the Great White Fleet, the Navy's highly publicized round-the-world tour that announced America's arrival as a global power and thrilled the public, ensuring support for ever larger naval appropriation bills for years to come.

With the arrival of Theodore's nephew-in-law, the admirals saw another champion and welcomed him with open arms.

Franklin further endeared himself to the brass with a speech he gave in New York in April, before the Navy League, a civilian lobby made up of "big navy" enthusiasts, supported for the most part by business interests that would profit from any increase in the size of the U.S. Navy. In his speech, the new assistant secretary pleaded eloquently for the need of an expanded Navy to meet the requirements of America's growing responsibilities, and his audience ate it up. The president of the League was Colonel Robert M. Thompson, chairman of the board of the International Nickel Corporation, and one of the vice presidents was Herbert Sattertee, son-in-law of J. P. Morgan. These were the kind of people FDR had grown up with, the men who would support him if he supported them.

If the Navy officer corps looked with favor upon the new assistant secretary, their opinion of his boss was considerably less sanguine. Almost to a man, the senior officers detested Josephus Daniels with a passion. They considered him a country bumpkin. They were outraged when he appointed a civilian professor to head the English department at the Naval Academy, and apoplectic when he banned alcohol from the officers' mess. They cringed when he called battleships "boats," and despaired of naval traditions when he ordered that sailors be trained to refer to "left and right" rather than "port and starboard." He was determined to make the Navy officer corps more democratic by reserving a number of places in each Annapolis class specifically for qualified enlisted men, and sought to turn warships into "floating universities," with classes for all who cared to attend.

At times, Franklin Roosevelt tended to share the admirals' low opinion of Daniels. In private conversations, he would describe him as "the funniest little hillbilly you ever saw" and mock his Southern accent. One time, when he spoke disparagingly of Daniels during a dinner with his friend Secretary of the Interior Franklin K. Lane, Lane admonished him. "You should be ashamed of yourself," he told him sternly. "Mr. Daniels is your superior, and you should show him loyalty or you should resign your office."

If the officer corps did not take kindly to their new secretary of the Navy, there were plenty of others in Washington who defended him. FDR's earliest biographer, Ernest K. Lindley, cites one supporter who defined Josephus Daniels as "one of the few living men who had the exact combination of qualities needed to grapple with the Navy as it was in 1913. He had no personal friends in the Navy, and he had the Puritan's conscience and stubbornness. He entered the department with a profound suspicion that whatever an admiral told him was wrong and that every corporation with a capitalization of more than $100,000 was inherently evil. In nine cases out of ten his formula was correct; the Navy was packed at the top with deadwood, and with politics all the way through, and the steel, coal, and other big industries were accustomed to dealing with it on their own terms. With all that[,] he had sound judgment of men."

Daniels's sound judgment of men included a good understanding of his assistant. Not long after the two men had moved into their adjoining offices in the State, War, and Navy Building, photographers wanted a picture of the two of them. As Daniels remembered in his memoirs, "It was taken as we stood on the eastern portico . . . looking down on the White House. It was about the best picture taken during our service. Roosevelt was just turned thirty-two—was tall, athletic, handsome, happy in his new work. When the photographers brought the proof of the picture for approval, I asked:

"'Franklin, why are you grinning from ear to ear, looking as pleased as if the world were yours, while I, satisfied and happy, have no such smile on my face?'

"He said he did not know of any particular reason, only that he was trying to look his best.

"'I will tell you,' I answered. 'We are both looking down on the White House and you are saying to yourself, being a New Yorker, "someday I will be living in that house"—while I, being from the South, know I must be satisfied with no such ambition.'"

Roosevelt was not always contemptuous of his boss. He strongly supported many of Daniels's ideas for turning naval vessels into "floating universities" and contributed ideas in support of the program. One of the most successful was the "Assistant Secretary's Swimming Cup." There had been a number of needless drownings on board U.S. fighting ships because a large proportion of American sailors did not know how to swim. With Daniels's enthusiastic support, Roosevelt ordered that every new recruit would have to qualify in swimming before going to sea, and that every Annapolis midshipman would have to do so before receiving his commission. He also instituted an annual competition among warships to determine which could qualify the highest percentage of its crew in a test involving a dive of 18 feet or more followed by a 100-yard swim. The winning ship would be awarded a cup donated by the assistant secretary.

In that first year in office, Franklin Roosevelt came to admire and even to emulate the unfailingly polite but stubbornly unyielding way in which Daniels sometimes dealt with certain defense contractors. The secretary had been only briefly in office before he advertised for bids for armor plate to be used in construction of a new battleship that would eventually be christened the USS *Arizona*, but at the time was still known only as Battleship No. 39. Only three American companies had the ability to make armor plate—US Steel, Bethlehem Steel, and Midvale Steel—and when their bids were submitted to Daniels's office, they turned out to be identical, right down to the penny: $454.00 per ton. Old hands at the Navy Department were not surprised. This was in keeping with standard practice. But Daniels would have none of it. He promptly summoned the responsible officers of the three companies to his office. He pointed out to each that all had sworn under oath not to confer, much less agree with one another, while in the process of determining their bids. And yet each had come up with precisely the same bid. He charged the three with illegal collusion. They denied the charge, yet at the same time cited as precedent for their procedure the department's policy in the past of dividing each armor-plate purchase equally among the three companies at whichever price was the lowest bid, a procedure that destroyed the reason for competitive bidding. The steel companies insisted that the production of armor plate was not a significant part of their business, and that they only maintained their armor-plate mills at the government's specific request, and therefore were within their rights in submitting high bids. Daniels pointed out that at least one of the three, Bethlehem, was in the habit of selling armor plate to foreign governments at prices markedly below those charged their own government. ("In 1894, the Bethlehem Company sold armor plate to Russia at $240 per ton and charged the United States Navy $616.14 per ton," Daniels would recall. "In 1911, they sold to Italy at $395 and charged Uncle Sam $420. Later they sold to Japan at $406.35 and to the United States at prices ranging from $440 to $540 a ton.") He then refused to accept the bids as submitted and ordered the men to reconsider their costs and resubmit them on a genuinely competitive basis. He ordered in vain: the second bids were also identical, again to the penny, whereupon Daniels sent Roosevelt to New York City to consult with a British steel magnate who had just arrived in America. Roosevelt took the train the next day and explained the situation to the Englishman, who said he would be happy to bid on the job and could guarantee prompt delivery. Roosevelt explained that the Navy Department would welcome his bid, but warned that if the American companies came anywhere close to matching his price the Navy would feel obligated to let them have the contracts. With great fanfare the British bidder came to Washington to see Daniels, who had arranged that the representatives of the American steel companies should all be waiting in the Navy secretary's anteroom. After a lengthy conference with the British steel man, Daniels called in the American representatives and told them he would send the entire contract abroad if they did not reduce their bids. The Americans dropped their prices substantially.

"I loved his words," FDR recalled later, remembering the steel men's glum expression as they left.

Later Daniels was able to tell Congress that the enforced foreign competition had reduced the *Arizona*'s armor-plate costs by $1,110,084.

Franklin took great pleasure in the honors and ceremonies that were due him in accordance with Navy tradition. As assistant secretary, he was accorded a booming seventeen-gun salute (the same as for a four-star admiral) whenever he inspected a naval vessel, along with four drum ruffles and a personal honor guard. When he learned that both the president and the secretary of the Navy each had a special flag that was to be hoisted to the main whenever they were on board, he decided the assistant secretary should have one as well, and forthwith designed one and had it run up by a seamstress. He arranged to have it on hand on July 4, 1913, when by his orders one of the Navy's newest and largest battleships, the massive USS *North Dakota*, sailed into tiny little Eastport, Maine and anchored across the water from Campobello. When the assistant secretary came on board, his personal flag was duly hoist to the main and he was greeted by his seventeen-gun salute and four drum ruffles. The local folks were duly impressed.

In the autumn of 1913, when Eleanor and the children finally arrived in Washington, the family moved into 1733 N Street N.W., a comfortable old-fashioned home which they rented from Eleanor's Aunt Bamie, the older sister of Theodore. The house was known as the Little White House because Theodore had lived there when he first became president, in order to give the widowed Mrs. McKinley ample time to depart the White House after the death of her husband. It was located just a short walk down Connecticut Avenue from Franklin's office.

At that time, the Roosevelt household consisted of three children, a governess and a nurse to watch over them, a chauffeur, a cook, and three live-in servants to clean and do laundry.

Managing this small army fell to Eleanor, who soon discovered that her household responsibilities represented only a fraction of her duties. As the wife of a prominent officeholder, there were luncheons, teas, and large formal dinners to be presided over, and, as her Aunt Bamie explained, there were the house calls. Eleanor was obliged to spend her afternoons calling on the wives of other prominent officeholders, including the wives of Supreme Court justices, congressmen, cabinet members, diplomats, and admirals. The ritual required that she make as many as twenty or thirty calls a day on Mondays, Tuesdays, Thursdays and Fridays. If Eleanor was lucky, Bamie explained, the lady of the house would be absent, and Eleanor was then required only to leave her card; but if the lady was at home, Eleanor was to introduce herself and make polite chat for about six minutes before departing on her next call.

On Wednesdays it was Eleanor's turn to receive callers, and she would remain "at home," never knowing how many callers she might or might not expect.

"I am trying to keep up with my calls," she reported to Aunt Bamie six weeks after her arrival in Washington, "but it is quite strenuous. I've done all the Cabinet, Pres. & V. Pres., justices, Speaker, NY Senators, & some others, also some Congressmen. All Embassies, Counselors, Naval Attaches, & there are only a few less important Ministers & the Military Attaches left. Besides, I've paid dozens of calls on people who've called on me."

The social responsibilities became increasingly burdensome and difficult to handle. In desperation, she turned again to her aunt. Could she recommend someone who could help her? Aunt Bamie thought she had just the answer—a young woman of impeccable breeding who was intimately familiar with the Washington social scene, and whose family had fallen upon hard times and therefore needed money. Her name was Lucy Mercer.

Eleanor invited Lucy to come for an interview, and at their first meeting the two women got along easily and quickly came to an agreement. Lucy would come in three mornings a week to serve as Eleanor's social secretary at a salary of thirty dollars a week. As the holiday season approached, with its inevitable quickening of social obligations, Eleanor Roosevelt could count herself fortunate in finding a means of easing the very real pressures of life in Washington.

That Christmas, Franklin took it upon himself to heal any possible breach with Secretary Daniels that might have been caused by his boss learning of any of his indiscrete comments about him. For a Christmas present, he commissioned a photograph of a nineteenth-century watercolor of the USS *North Carolina*, a famous ship of the line from the age of fighting sail. Daniels was deeply appreciative.

My dear Mr. Roosevelt:
You cannot know how much I value the beautiful picture of the
North Carolina which you sent me. Nothing could have given
me more pleasure. I will keep it and transmit it to one of my
sons and also transmit to all of them the affection and regard I
bear to you. When I came to Washington one of the anticipated
pleasures was the close association with you. As yoke-fellows
this association has been both helpful and delightful. I wish you
to know my regard and appreciation of you as a man and as a
fellow worker.

In his personal diary, Daniels called the gift "my most prized
Christmas present."

CHAPTER EIGHTEEN

G etting a grasp of the size and dimension of the Navy of which he was now an integral part was a daunting assignment, even for a very bright, very focused young man in a hurry like Franklin Roosevelt. He was the assistant secretary of the third largest navy in the world, smaller than that of Britain (the largest) and Germany (second largest), but still considerably larger than the navies of Japan, France, Russia, and Italy. In 1913, all the naval powers were busy upgrading their fleets to keep abreast of the important technical advances that were under way in warship design. One of the most important developments was the shift in fuel from coal to oil. Coal was abundant in many parts of the world, but oil was a superior power source not only because it could increase a fleet's speed by as much as twenty percent, but because it extended a warship's cruising range. With the discovery of the huge Spindletop Oil Field in Texas in 1901, the United States was the only world naval power with a secure domestic oil supply, and it was in a particularly advantageous position to capitalize on the shift.

But by far the single most important change in warships had come about in 1906, when Britain launched HMS *Dreadnought*, the first battleship in the world with no secondary battery. Typical battleships of the day carried four big 12-inch guns (which fired a projectile 12 inches in diameter at a maximum range of around ten miles), eight 8-inch guns for use at intermediary range, and twelve 6-inch guns for close range. The dreadnought design dispensed with all the smaller guns, and instead carried ten 12-inch guns, which gave the ship enormous advantage in firepower over ships with a mixed battery. Naval officers around the world instantly recognized the revolutionary implications of the new design, and began laying plans for fleets of dreadnoughts of their own.

When Germany, under Kaiser Wilhelm II, announced a plan to build fifty-eight dreadnoughts for its High Seas Fleet to challenge Britain's Royal Navy, a full-scale arms race began which would ultimately affect the size and nature of the U.S. Navy. Britain, faced with a rival on her doorstep, withdrew her fleet from global commitments and consolidated it in home waters, virtually abandoning her presence in the Pacific to Japan. This shift was formalized by an Anglo-Japanese naval treaty, and when the Japanese Navy astonished the world by destroying the Russian Baltic Fleet at the Battle of Tsushima in 1905, Japan became the dominant power in the western Pacific. This in turn forced the United States, with its newly acquired Asian island territories, to look nervously out from her West Coast and perhaps for the first time ponder the responsibilities of empire.

The new developments among the naval powers, with Germany challenging Britain's centuries-old supremacy of the seas and Japan emerging as a global presence, had important foreign-policy consequences in Washington. For a century, since the close of the War of 1812, America had maintained generally cordial relations with Britain, and the U.S. Navy, because of its small size, had come to rely on the Royal Navy to help enforce the Monroe Doctrine, which barred European incursions into the Western Hemisphere. The British were happy to help, since it was in their interest to discourage other nations from building empires that could challenge theirs. But the United States had no such cordial relations with the other naval powers, and the emergence of the German and Japanese navies and the possibility that they might someday combine their fleets for an attack on the United States became a major concern of American naval strategists.

Nor were their anxieties unreasonable. Both potential enemies had in recent years demonstrated aggressive tendencies and had shown that they were willing to take considerable risks in pursuit of their national interests. What concerned the American admirals most was the fact that the United States had an Achilles' heel—the republic of Mexico—that made America a particularly tempting target. Ever since the fall of the Diaz government in 1910, Mexico had been in a state of revolt, with no government capable of holding the country together for very long, and different factions warring with each other for control. With Mexico in turmoil, and with scant ability to defend itself, the long, unfortified border she shared with the United States represented a tempting target for any adventurous foreign power with a decent-sized navy, or so the admirals feared.

They were right to worry. Just prior to Wilson's election in 1912, the United States had been caught up in a diplomatic standoff known as the Magdalena Bay affair, relating to precisely such a scenario.

Magdalena Bay is a large, well-sheltered inlet about halfway up the Pacific coast of Baja California, in one of the most remote, inaccessible areas of North America. Sometime after the Civil War, a syndicate of American entrepreneurs had purchased the entire bay and its surrounding land—a total of some four million acres—with the goal of turning it into a huge dye works, with the area's abundant shellfish providing the raw material. The scheme never took off, and by the end of the nineteenth century the project had been abandoned. The syndicate attempted to sell the property, but its remote location and its bleak, infertile nature discouraged any potential buyer. There was a flurry of excitement in 1902 when Kaiser Wilhelm II expressed an interest in purchasing the property, but nothing came of it, and another flurry in 1908 when there were rumors of Japanese interest, but again nothing materialized.

Then, early in 1912, a group of Japanese businessmen made an offer on the property. This was not a rumor. They explained that they wanted to build a seafood-processing facility at Magdalena Bay so that Japanese fishing boats operating in the eastern Pacific could land their catches without having to return all the way to Japan. Negotiations for the sale began, and it almost certainly would have been satisfactorily concluded had not the U.S. Navy raised the alarm.

The Japanese syndicate's story sounded plausible enough, the admirals said; but once they held title to the property, what was to stop them from turning it over to the Imperial Japanese Navy, which would then send swarms of engineers to Baja California to build an impregnable naval base within striking distance of San Diego and San Francisco? A powerful bloc of politicians, led by Republican Senator John Cabot Lodge of Massachusetts and enthusiastically supported by his close friend, former president Theodore Roosevelt, rose up in protest. Lodge declared: "Magdalena Bay can have no value whatever at the present time, except as a military and strategic value. Its military and strategic value, however, is very great indeed."

Under Lodge's direction, an amendment to the Monroe Doctrine, in the form of a Senate resolution, was passed by an overwhelming vote of fifty-one to four: "Resolved, that when any harbor or other place in the American continents is so situated that the occupation thereof for naval or military purposes might threaten the communications or the safety of the United States, the Government of the United States could not see, without grave concern, the actual or potential possession of such harbor or other place by any government, not American, as to give that government practical power of control for naval or military purposes."

The Japanese "seafood consortium" withdrew its offer.

The whole matter had only taken a few weeks once the admirals had raised the alarm, but it had left behind a deep sense of suspicion of Japan in Washington, particularly in the Navy Department, a suspicion that Franklin Roosevelt shared.

The year after the Magdalena Bay affair, the lingering distrust between Japan and the United States sparked another angry confrontation, only weeks after the Wilson administration took office. Early in May 1913, the California Legislature, alarmed by suspicions that the Japanese government was organizing and subsidizing the migration of its excess population from its overcrowded islands, passed a bill making it illegal for Japanese nationals to purchase land in the state. The Japanese government immediately lodged a formal complaint, charging that the action was "prejudicial to the existing rights of Japanese subjects" and "opposed to the spirit and fundamental principles of amity and good understanding upon which the conventional relations of the two countries depend." There were angry anti-American demonstrations in Japanese cities and calls for war in the Japanese press.

Theodore Roosevelt, always alert to threats from overseas, immediately wrote to his young cousin:

> *Dear Franklin:*
> *It is not my place to advise, but there is one matter so vital that I want to call your attention to it. I do not anticipate trouble with Japan, but it may come, and if it does it will come suddenly. In that case we shall be in an unpardonable position if we permit ourselves to be caught with our fleet separated. There ought not to be a battleship or any formidable fighting craft in the Pacific unless our entire fleet is in the Pacific. Russia's fate ought to be a warning for all time as to the criminal folly of dividing the fleet if there is even the remotest chance of war.*
> *Give my love to Eleanor. . . .*
> *Always yours,*
> *Theodore Roosevelt.*

Other high-ranking officials were equally suspicious of Japan. At a meeting of the Joint Board of the Army and Navy in Washington, General Leonard Wood, Theodore Roosevelt's old comrade in arms from the Spanish–American War, warned that war with Japan was imminent and probably inevitable, and as a precaution called for the Navy to move five of its cruisers from their vulnerable position on the Yangtze River to Manila to protect the Philippines. Rear Admiral Bradley A. Fiske, aide for operations, agreed with Wood and laid out his reasons for fearing a war with Japan in a memorandum to Josephus Daniels:

> *The islands of Japan are not at all fertile; the climate is very trying; the people have a hard time to subsist on the Islands. The Philippine Islands, which lie to the southwest of Japan, are extremely fertile, are very sparsely inhabited, and would be an extremely desirable possession for Japan as an outlet for their surplus population. . . . The Hawaiian Islands also are very fertile, and would be an extremely desirable possession for Japan. Japanese people are already on the Islands in great numbers, and it has frequently been stated that Japan declared just previous to the Spanish War that she did not desire the United States to take possession of the Hawaiian Islands. It is not impossible that Japan, in spite of her poverty, may decide that it is worth her while to go to war with the United States in order to secure possession of the Philippine Islands and the Hawaiian Islands. Should she decide to go to war, she could at once occupy the Philippine Islands and the Hawaiian Islands, and hoist the flag of Japan on those Islands. . . . It is possible that Japan may believe that there is so large a number of people in the United States who would be glad to get rid of the Philippine Islands, that they would easily come to terms with Japan after an inglorious and expensive war that lasted, say, two years. In other words, it is conceivable that Japan may conclude—may have already*

concluded—that if she should go to war with the United States,
she could, by enduring a period of privation and distress lasting
about two years, acquire possession of both the Philippine Islands
and the Hawaiian Islands. Her war against China supplies a
precedent for such a procedure.

The following day, Fiske added a whole new level of urgency to his argument. He warned "that war is not only possible, but even probable," and then capped his case by noting that Lindley M. Garrison, the secretary of war, agreed with the Joint Board and approved its recommendations.

Fiske's two memos were enough to convince Franklin Roosevelt of the Japanese threat. Already mindful of TR's admonitions, always respectful of General Wood's wisdom, and stirred by Admiral Fiske's dark vision, he was prepared to follow their lead and support the recommendation to withdraw the cruisers from the Yangtze, but was brought up short by Josephus Daniels's sharp and vehement disagreement.

An angry Daniels told Fiske he did not think there was the remotest likelihood that the Japanese would attack, and reminded him that "if there was any movement of naval ships[,] it could not be done without the order of the Secretary of the Navy or the Commander in Chief." He worried that the movement of the cruisers from the Yangtze River to Manila might be interpreted by the Japanese as a provocative act, and then, in a move that must have surprised Roosevelt, the Secretary, the supposedly wooly-headed pacifist with little interest in nuts-and-bolts issues, criticized the Board's recommendations on technical grounds. He asserted that the cruisers in the Yangtze were "of an old type with guns of short range," and all five of them would easily be sunk by a single dreadnought "if the Japanese were so minded."

Daniels repeated his arguments later in a cabinet meeting, and despite Secretary of War Garrison's counterarguments in support of the Board, the president agreed that the Navy should take no action.

Within a fortnight, the crisis was over, but not before Franklin Roosevelt had learned an important lesson about civilian control of the military.

Franklin Roosevelt's suspicions concerning the Japanese lingered, and his distrust of their motives became even more pronounced only days after the crisis over the Yangtze-squadron crisis blew over, when an incident came to light that clearly demonstrated that the Japanese government was still determined to gain control of Magdalena Bay and had concocted an ingenious plan to circumvent the Lodge resolution by playing on America's racial prejudices.

Washington in 1913 was very much a Southern town, with all the Jim Crow laws on its books common throughout the old Confederacy. Segregated schools, separate public accommodations, and strictly enforced racial restrictions of every kind were the norm. Even President Wilson, a native of Virginia, found it easy to be openly racist, and whenever possible he used his office to further encourage the separation of whites and blacks.

Yet for all the racial prejudice that permeated Washington, the U.S. government was one of the few places in America where it was possible for blacks to find employment above the level of unskilled labor, and as a result many blacks were drawn to the city. One such jobholder was an African American named Ralph W. Tyler, an auditor for the Navy Department. His story, which Roosevelt learned of from a memorandum from the chief of the Justice Department's Bureau of Investigation (precursor of the FBI), revealed a complex Japanese scheme to evade America's Monroe Doctrine.

According to the Justice Department memo, one morning in April 1913, Ralph W. Tyler was on his way to his office when, around Eighth and P Streets N.W., he encountered, apparently by chance, a Japanese stranger "whom he describes as very genteelly dressed in citizen's clothes, about thirty-five years of age, as near as he can tell the age of a Japanese, a slight moustache, about five feet, six, and fairly well built, although he thinks it very doubtful whether or not he could identify the man should he see him again." At that first meeting, the Japanese simply asked Tyler for a match and exchanged a few brief words with him. But the next morning, Tyler was met once again by the same man, and this time, as he walked along with Tyler, he made him a remarkable proposal. He told Tyler that the Japanese government was eager to pay a high price to "some colored person of prominence . . . to get colored persons to migrate to Mexico in numbers and that persons so migrating could be offered money and land." In short, the Japanese wanted to subsidize a large African American colony in Mexico. It would have been obvious to Franklin Roosevelt and others in the Navy Department who read the memorandum that the colony would almost certainly be located in the Magdalena Bay area, and that, because the colonists were American citizens, they would not be subject to the restrictions of the newly revised Monroe Doctrine. The U.S. State Department could not interfere, even if it became known that the colonists were being liberally subsidized by Japan. It would have been equally obvious that at some later date, the Japanese would buy back or otherwise regain possession of the land from its black American owners and build the military base the admirals so feared.

As it turned out, the Japanese agent who proposed the plan had approached the wrong man. Ralph Tyler was a patriotic citizen. He had no interest in the Japanese offer and turned it down on the spot, even when the agent remonstrated "that members of the colored race have less protection at the hands of the [American] Government than do foreigners here, and intimated that there was no reason why they should follow the flag of this country." Tyler responded that "this was the only country that the colored men knew; that he regarded himself as an American citizen, and that he believed that the colored people would be found in the future, as in the past, fighting for the United States in any war she might have."

Ralph Tyler was almost certainly not the only African American approached by the Japanese representative. Undoubtedly the same agent or group of agents working in different cities tried to interest other "colored persons of prominence" in the scheme to establish a subsidized black American colony in Mexico; but for whatever reasons, the subtle and ingenious scheme—which must have looked brilliant in Tokyo—never played out. But the message left with Franklin Roosevelt was that the Japanese were highly ingenious and would go to any lengths to gain an advantage against the United States, and they were not to be trusted. For the most part, that opinion lasted his lifetime.

CHAPTER NINETEEN

E arly in his tenure in the Navy Department, Roosevelt installed a large map of the world on his office wall, displaying the location of every ship in the fleet. Using pins to indicate each vessel and changing their locations in accordance with the ships' movements, FDR had a clear picture of the size and scope of the fleet, its activities, and its relative strengths and shortcomings, and graphically saw what the sixty-five thousand officers and enlisted men of the U.S. Navy and Marine Corps were up to on any given day.

Taken together, the pins also provided him a precise overview of America's national and international ambitions as they were perceived by the Wilson administration in the last few months before the chaos of World War I changed everything.

As it happened, when he had cause to examine the map on February 12, 1914, the pins were in a relatively circumscribed area. All the Navy's ships were located between the longitudes of Haiti in the east and Canton, China in the west, with the exception of one small gunboat used as a station ship at Constantinople.

Reading from west to east—that is, from left to right—and starting with the Asiatic Fleet, the Navy was operating five light-draft river gunboats on the Yangtze River, as well as two others near Canton. (American gunboats had been in place on the Yangtze since the nineteenth century, maintaining a friendly patrol to protect American interests in the area and to discourage the activities of local warlords and river pirates. These were not the cruisers that General Leonard Wood had wanted shifted to Manila in 1913.)

To the south, concentrated in the Philippines, lay the main body of the Asiatic Fleet, a total of twenty-one vessels including the cruisers *Saratoga, Cincinnati,* and *Galveston,* the monitors *Monterey* and *Monadnock,* one gunboat, five torpedo-boat destroyers, six submarines, and four auxiliaries. These vessels were deemed sufficient to guard the various American interests in the Far East, but Roosevelt knew that in time of war they would be all but useless against an attack by a modern battle fleet such as the Imperial Japanese Navy.

Moving eastward, a single gunboat "protected" the island of Guam, and another gunboat "protected" Tutuila, or American Samoa. There were no naval vessels whatsoever in the Hawaiian Islands, but Roosevelt knew this was only a temporary situation, because ongoing construction at Pearl Harbor would soon make it an important strategic base.

On the American mainland, the Pacific Reserve Fleet was stationed at Puget Sound and consisted of the predreadnought battleship *Oregon;* the armored cruisers *South Dakota, West Virginia* and *Colorado;* the cruisers *Albany, Charleston, Chattanooga, St. Louis,* and *Milwaukee;* two submarines; and five auxiliaries. These vessels, like those in the Philippines, were outdated. They were manned by skeleton crews, and Roosevelt thought of them as place-savers for the modern fleet he was hoping Wilson—and Congress—would authorize.

In San Francisco Bay, the cruisers *Cleveland* and *Marblehead* were held in reserve and would require refitting and manning before they could be sent to sea. Also in reserve were four torpedo-boat destroyers and two torpedo boats. Those vessels actually fit for sea duty included only one gunboat, four submarines, and two auxiliaries.

On that particular day, off the California coast between Santa Barbara and San Diego, five torpedo-boat destroyers and a mother ship were engaged in their annual maneuvers; two submarines and a monitor were undergoing practice drills; and the armored cruisers *Maryland* and *California* were holding winter target practice.

South of the border, on the Pacific coast below San Diego, the armored cruiser *Pittsburgh* was patrolling the troubled waters off the Mexican coast, along with the cruisers *Raleigh* and *New Orleans*, one gunboat, and one auxiliary.

Still farther south, the cruiser *Denver* was proceeding to relieve the transport *Buffalo* at Corinto, Nicaragua, where, Roosevelt explained somewhat opaquely to a visitor, "the State Department has considered the presence of an American warship desirable."

It was on the Atlantic side of North America that the Navy maintained its chief strength. Far to the north, in the Gulf of St. Lawrence, the fleet tug *Potomac*, bound on an errand of mercy to rescue the crews of American fishing boats caught in the ice floes, had herself been caught and was in danger of destruction.

At Portsmouth, New Hampshire, the cruiser *Tacoma* was undergoing repairs. At Boston, the predreadnought battleship *New Jersey*, recently returned from Mexico, was being overhauled. The armored cruiser *North Carolina* and the cruiser *Chicago* were in reserve, and a new submarine was in the process of being commissioned. At Newport, Rhode Island, four old torpedo boats were in reserve and a submarine was being fitted out.

At New York, the dreadnought battleship *North Dakota*, which FDR had so triumphantly inspected at Campobello the previous July 4, was under repair; the dreadnought *Arkansas* was in quarantine, with a few cases of illness aboard; the armored cruiser *Washington* was being used as a receiving ship; one gunboat was in reserve; and a monitor and a submarine were preparing for the formation of a new submarine division.

At the Philadelphia Navy Yard, the cruiser *Montgomery* and two destroyers were in reserve, and a submarine was fitting out. Here also were stationed the ships of the Atlantic Reserve Fleet, consisting of the predreadnought battleships *Idaho, Maine, Missouri, Alabama, Illinois, Kearsarge, Kentucky, Wisconsin, Indiana, Iowa,* and *Massachusetts,* the armored cruiser *Tennessee,* the cruiser *Salem,* and the repair ship *Panther.*

Five torpedo boats were stationed at the Naval Academy in Annapolis, and two converted yachts at Washington. At the Norfolk Navy Yard in Virginia, the predreadnought battleship *Vermont* was undergoing repairs and the monitor *Tallahassee* was being used for ordnance experiments. Off Cape Hatteras, the dreadnought battleship *Michigan* was proceeding south to join the other ships of the second division at Guantanamo.

Charleston, South Carolina was the regular base for the torpedo boats and destroyers in reserve, but only five of the former and three of the latter, together with one submarine, were there on February 12, 1914. The other six reserve destroyers were engaged in their annual practice cruise off the coast of Florida, manned by half-crews.

At Key West, three new destroyers, recently placed in commission, were in shakedown trials and undergoing torpedo practice prior to joining the Atlantic Fleet. In Pensacola Bay, the predreadnought battleship *Mississippi* was being used in experimental aeronautic work. At New Orleans, the monitor *Tonapah* and the second submarine group of five vessels were engaged in the annual practice cruise.

Off the north coast of Cuba, the transports *Prairie* and *Hancock* were returning with two regiments of Marines from a month of "advance base" maneuvers on the island of Culebra, just east of Puerto Rico, another American possession acquired in the war with Spain.

To the south of Cuba, all the ships of the Atlantic Fleet, except those in Mexican and Haitian waters, were engaged in fleet and division drills, torpedo and target practice, boat drills, etc. At Guantanamo were the following ships: predreadnought battleships *Louisiana, Kansas,* and *New Hampshire,* cruiser *Birmingham,* one gunboat, and twelve torpedo boat destroyers. To the west, near Guacanayabo Bay, Cuba, were the rest of the ships of the Atlantic Fleet, engaged in similar practice—the dreadnought battleships *Wyoming, Delaware, Florida,* and *Utah,* plus six torpedo-boat destroyers and one destroyer tender.

At Santo Domingo, on the island of Hispaniola, lay the gunboat *Petrel.* Off the coast of Haiti were the battleship *South Carolina,* the armored cruiser *Montana,* the gunboat *Nashville,* the mine-layer *San Francisco,* and the surveying ship *Eagle.* Both the *Montana* and the *San Francisco* had been "hurried to Haiti on the outbreak of the revolution there."

Off the coast of Honduras, the auxiliary *Hannibal* was engaged in hydrographic surveying; and at Cristobal, the Atlantic end of the soon-to-be-opened Panama Canal, were five submarines and their mother ship, the submarine tender *Severn.*

And finally, on the east coast of Mexico "performing an obvious duty" were: at Tampico, predreadnought battleships *Rhode Island, Georgia, Nebraska,* and *Virginia,* cruiser *Des Moines,* and one gunboat; and at Vera Cruz, predreadnought battleships *Connecticut, Ohio,* and *Minnesota,* and the cruiser *Chester.*

In short, the single greatest concentration of United States naval power in the late winter of 1913–1914 was either off the east coast of Mexico or within easy reach of it. The ships were there because Woodrow Wilson wanted them there. Why he wanted them there, and the inherent instability their presence created in the area, would soon teach Franklin Roosevelt an important lesson in the need to maintain close control of naval vessels in foreign waters, the difficulty in doing so, and the limits of presidential hubris.

CHAPTER TWENTY

M exico, throughout the latter part of the nineteenth century and into the twentieth, had been a land of opportunity for American businessmen, so long as the dictator Porfirio Díaz remained in power. For decades, Díaz, supported by the Catholic Church, a few hundred immensely wealthy land owners, and the U.S. State Department, ruled the country with an iron fist, until finally, in 1911, he was driven into exile by an insurgency made up of Mexico's tiny middle class backed by millions of land-hungry peons, rallying behind the revolutionary leader Francisco Madero.

The American government, and the military in particular, grew increasingly nervous as the Mexican revolution threw the country into bloody confusion, with one warring faction after another competing for dominance, making Mexico an increasingly tempting target for any ambitious power that might want to take advantage of the chaos to gain control of America's most strategically vulnerable neighbor.

In February 1913, just weeks before Woodrow Wilson's inauguration, General Victoriano Huerta, with the active support of Henry Lane Wilson, American ambassador to Mexico, drove President

Madero from office, proclaimed himself provisional president, and then, just days later, arranged to have Madero murdered in cold blood. American business interests in Mexico looked on, unconcerned. At the time, they owned 78% of Mexico's mines, 68% of its rubber plantations, 68% of its railroads, 72% of its smelters, and 58% of its oil, and, as long as they were allowed to operate with a free hand, they were content to let the revolution take any course it had a mind to. But Woodrow Wilson, the Calvinist idealist, was incensed, and was determined to remove Huerta from office. He began a passionate but ineffective campaign to force his resignation, using every tool he could muster—diplomatic, commercial, and military. The United States Navy was central to his anti-Huerta campaign, and both Josephus Daniels and Franklin Roosevelt were deeply involved. But all of Wilson's attempts at intimidation proved ineffective, and the Mexican leader remained defiant.

By 1914, Wilson had established powerful naval squadrons off Mexico's east coast, at both Tampico and Veracruz. Ostensibly, they were on station solely to protect American lives and property. Wilson characterized their presence as "watchful waiting." But all those American warships were also an unsubtle reminder of American power and a constant irritant to the local officials of both ports. A sense of smoldering resentment permeated the dockside atmosphere.

On April 9, 1914, the USS *Dolphin*, a 240-foot Navy dispatch boat which lay at anchor in the Pánuco River at Tampico, sent in a whaleboat bearing the paymaster and seven crew members to pick up supplies at a warehouse dock. At the dock, the paymaster and two of the crewmen were arrested on the orders of a Mexican Army colonel acting on his own initiative. When the colonel's superiors learned of his action, they recognized the potential diplomatic problem, and the Americans were immediately released. The Mexicans apologized profusely to the Navy men and the local American consul, and requested that their apologies by relayed to Rear Admiral Henry T. Mayo, the American commander off Tampico.

But Mayo was in no mood to be conciliatory. As he saw it, a simple apology was nowhere near an adequate response to make up for such a grave breach of national honor. He insisted that the colonel responsible for the arrest be severely punished, that officers of the Mexican Navy be dispatched to the *Dolphin* to present formal apologies, and that the local Mexican army commander, within twenty-four hours, "publicly hoist the American flag in a prominent position on shore and salute it with twenty-one guns."

When the news of Admiral Mayo's demands reached Washington, both Secretary of State Bryan and Josephus Daniels were furious. They considered Mayo's reaction excessive, and, given the fact that he was within easy reach of Washington by radio and telegraph, they felt that he should have checked with Daniels before issuing such humiliating demands. But President Wilson's reaction to the news was quite the opposite. Obsessed as he was in his determination to unseat Huerta, he saw the Tampico Affair as an opportunity to further that aim. He upped the ante by personally issuing a demand to Huerta that Mayo's orders were to be immediately obeyed, warning of "the gravest consequences" if they were not.

Huerta's reply was guarded but apologetic enough to satisfy Bryan and Daniels, but not the president, who insisted that Mayo's demand for a flag-raising and 21-gun salute be carried out immediately and to the letter. This was too much for Huerta, who angrily refused, whereupon Wilson ordered the North American battleship fleet to sail for Tampico and the Pacific fleet to sail for Mexico's west coast, and petitioned Congress for a resolution justifying the use of armed force against the Huerta government. Congress immediately complied by a vote of 337 to 37, and Wilson ordered the Navy to plan for a blockade of Mexico and the Army to prepare to seize Tampico and Veracruz and to march on Mexico City.

Throughout this sequence of high-tension confrontations, Franklin Roosevelt was out of Washington on an inspection tour of West Coast naval facilities, and had to rely on Louis Howe for details of the events.

"I understand the State Department is yelling blue murder because Mayo on his own initiative commanded a salute," Howe reported. "I am afraid Mayo is not a good 'watchful waiter.'"

As the tensions escalated, sparked by Wilson's determination to force Huerta's abdication, Roosevelt, who was undoubtedly reminded of Uncle Ted's meteoric political rise under similar circumstances, feverishly monitored the Navy's West Coast activities and gave bellicose interviews to the press. At Portland, he told reporters: "We're not looking for trouble, but we're ready for anything."

On April 21, Washington learned that a German cargo ship, the *Ypiranga*, had reached Veracruz with two hundred machine guns and fifteen million rounds of ammunition for Huerta's army. Secretary Daniels, on Wilson's order, wired Admiral Frank F. Fletcher to SEIZE CUSTOM HOUSE. DO NOT PERMIT WAR SUPPLIES TO BE DELIVERED TO HUERTA GOVERNMENT OR TO ANY OTHER PARTY. American sailors and Marines were immediately landed and seized the custom house, while other naval units impounded the German ship. But it was not to be a neat, antiseptic incursion. The Mexican troops fought back, and before Fletcher finally secured Veracruz the next day, 19 Americans had been killed and 71 wounded, while the Mexicans had lost 126 dead and 195 wounded.

Roosevelt was thrilled by the news and anticipated further hostilities, but Wilson, shocked by the results of his own recklessness, started looking for a way out of the situation he had brought on, and Admiral Fletcher, acting on the orders of State Department lawyers, was forced to apologize to the *Ypiranga*'s captain, and to permit the vessel to sail with her cargo intact. She eventually docked at Puerto Mexico, where her cargo was delivered into Mexican hands, presumably those loyal to Huerta, but possibly those allied with the insurgent army in the north, led by General Venustiano Carranza and his chief lieutenant, Pancho Villa.

Roosevelt, still only vaguely aware of the dramatic shift in Wilson's thinking, boarded a train for the East, prepared to rattle his saber at every stop along the way. Asked by a reporter in Minneapolis what the crisis meant, he answered, "War! And we're ready!" The next morning in Milwaukee, he said, "I do not want war, but I do not see how we can avoid it. Sooner or later, it seems, the United States must go down there and clean up the Mexican political mess. I believe that the best time is right now."

By the time his train reached Chicago, he had become fully aware of Wilson's change of heart, and knew that the president had gratefully accepted the offer of Argentina, Brazil, and Chile to mediate the situation. The likelihood of an armed conflict was now remote, but Franklin was still in a very Theodore Roosevelt mood and was spoiling for a fight. He told a reporter almost wistfully, "The war spirit is sweeping the West like a prairie fire. The general opinion is that since the United States has finally started military activities they should be carried through to a finish with no compromise. Many persons and newspapers are openly advocating annexation as the only solution of the Mexican problem. This sentiment seems to be growing."

When he finally got back to his office in Washington and had a chance to talk with Josephus Daniels, he could see clearly that whatever war spirit might be sweeping the West, it was not igniting the White House, and his comments to reporters on the Mexican situation abruptly stopped.

It was not lost on Franklin Roosevelt that those members of the Wilson cabinet more inclined to finding a peaceful resolution could at times see things more clearly than those who favored confrontation. The other, more complex lesson related to the limits of presidential power. Woodrow Wilson's determination to depose Huerta might be morally sound and politically rational—after all, an unpredictable and untrustworthy leader just south of the border posed a legitimate threat to America's defense—but any attempt to address that threat had to be carefully calculated. The president's precipitous response to the events of April 1914 had brought on a needless loss of life, aroused worldwide outrage, and sparked angry anti-American demonstrations throughout Latin America.

Reverberations from the incident would directly shape President Franklin Delano Roosevelt's "Good Neighbor Policy," a quarter century later.

CHAPTER TWENTY-ONE

I n June 1914, Roosevelt was busy negotiating with Congress for the sale to the Greek Navy of two undersized and obsolete battle-ships, the USS *Idaho* and the USS *Mississippi*. Relations with Congress were usually handled by Josephus Daniels, who was particularly good at it and enjoyed the genial give-and-take that was such an important part of getting along with senators and representatives; but there were numerous technical questions involved in the battleship sale, and Roosevelt, who understood the naval specifics much better than Daniels, was kept busy putting together an appropriate bill for submission to Congress.

The sale of the two battleships raised important diplomatic considerations. Turkey, which at the time was involved in a bitter dispute with Greece over the ownership of certain Aegean islands, protested the sale, and Roosevelt had to assure the Congress that the transfer of the two battleships was not likely to ignite still another Balkan war similar to the back-to-back conflicts of 1912 and 1913 that had caused the weary diplomatic community to coin the catchphrase "trouble in the Balkans" to define those fierce, brief, and generally inconsequential wars that seemed to erupt every year or so in remote corners of eastern Europe.

The sale of the battleships was approved by Congress as a rider to the Naval Appropriations Act on June 30, 1914; and as soon as Daniels had accepted the check for $12,535,275.96 from the Greeks, Roosevelt had only to arrange for the delivery of the two ships. It is safe to say that with his attention focused on the details of the battle-ship deal, Roosevelt was paying little attention to reports from Sarajevo concerning the assassination of Austrian Archduke Ferdinand and his wife by a Serbian nationalist. That incident, which would soon erupt into the most terrible war in history and eventually touch the lives of virtually all people on the face of the earth, went largely unnoticed by the rest of the world and was shrugged off as just another example of "trouble in the Balkans."

There were other, more pressing, issues closer to home. In the middle of July, Roosevelt returned to his office one afternoon "to find not only a vast accumulation" of paperwork, as he wrote to Eleanor, who by that time had departed with the children for Campobello, "but also an interesting situation in Haiti and Santo Domingo, with a hurry call for marines from the State Department."

The "interesting situation" referred to the civil unrest that had broken out in Haiti and its neighbor on Hispaniola, Santo Domingo (now known as the Dominican Republic), which not only threatened American residents of the island, but, because the island lay athwart international trade routes, also threatened the Panama Canal, which was nearing completion. On July 13, Secretary of State William Jennings Bryan burst into FDR's office, shouting, "I've got to have a battleship! White people are being killed in Haiti and I must send a battleship there within twenty-four hours!" Roosevelt told him that would be impossible. "Our battleships are in Narragansett Bay," he explained, "and I could not get one to Haiti in less than four days, steaming at full speed. But I have a gunboat at Guantanamo and I could get her to Haiti within eight hours if you want me to." Bryan was much relieved. "That is all I wanted to know," he said, turning to leave and then stopping in the doorway and, looking back, said, "Roosevelt, after this when I talk about battleships, don't think I mean anything technical."

Roosevelt loved to cite the incident, which became one of his favorite anecdotes about the folly of so-called experts.

By the time Roosevelt was finally able to free himself and join his family at Campobello, the European unrest triggered by the assassination of the Austrian archduke had grown into a major diplomatic crisis, and the world was watching with mounting alarm and horror as a huge multi-national war became increasingly likely. When Austria declared war on Serbia on July 28, Roosevelt received an urgent message requiring him, in light of the grave international situation, to return to Washington. On his way to the train he stopped at the telegraph office in Eastport, Maine to get the latest war news, all of which was grim. In response to Austria's move, Russia, honoring her commitment to the Serbs, was mobilizing her troops, which meant Germany would come to the aid of Austria, which in turn would cause France, Russia's ally, to join the fray. Britain, tied to the continent by only vague diplomatic pacts, remained a question mark, but the assumption, which proved correct, was that she would become a belligerent soon enough. Enthralled by the exciting news, and already calculating how the U.S. Navy should respond, Roosevelt climbed aboard the southbound Bar Harbor Express and found his way to the smoking room.

As he recalled the scene years later, "The smoking room of the Express was filled with gentlemen from banking and brokerage offices in New York, most of whom were old friends of mine; and they began giving me their opinion about impending war in Europe. These eminent bankers and brokers assured me, and made it good with bets, that there wasn't enough money in all the world to carry on a European war for more than three months."

Roosevelt was astonished at the naïveté of the financial experts. Anyone who knew anything about history knew that nations at war always find the money to keep fighting. They raise taxes. They borrow. They mortgage the future. They will do anything rather than surrender. But here were Roosevelt's friends offering even-money bets that the war would be over before Christmas, bets of 2 to 1 that it would be over by Easter, bets "that it was humanly impossible—physically impossible—for a European war to last for six months—odds of 4 to 1, and so forth and so on. Well, actually I must have won those—they were small, five dollar bets—I must have made a hundred dollars. I wish I had bet a lot more. There was the best economic opinion in the world that the continuance of war was absolutely dependent on money in the bank. Well, you know what happened."

On his arrival at the Navy Department in Washington, he found the same myopic bewilderment that he had encountered on the train. He scribbled a note to Eleanor on August 1: "A complete smash up is inevitable, and there are a great many problems for us to consider. Mr. D. totally fails to grasp the situation and I am to see the President Monday A.M. to go over our own situation. . . . These are history-making days. It will be the greatest war in the world's history."

The following day, he wrote her a much longer, more detailed letter outlining his forebodings of the future and his frustrations of the moment. It shows how clearly he understood what was happening on the other side of the Atlantic.

> *At last I have time to write you a real letter. I posted a line on the train last night, and on arrival went straight to the Department, where, as I expected, I found everything asleep and apparently utterly oblivious to the fact that the most terrible drama in history was about to be enacted. . . .*
>
> *To my astonishment on reaching the Dept. nobody seemed the least bit excited about the European crisis—Mr. Daniels feeling chiefly very sad that his faith in human nature and civilization and similar idealistic nonsense was receiving such a rude shock. So I started in alone to get things ready and prepare plans*

for what ought to be done by the Navy end of things. Friday I worked all day on these lines, and actually succeeded in getting one ship north from Mexico.

These dear good people like W.J.B. and J.D. have as much conception of what a general European war means as Elliott [their four-year-old son] *has of higher mathematics. They really believe that because we are neutral we can go about our business as usual. To my horror, just for example, J.D. told the newspaper men he thought favorably of sending our fleet to Europe to bring back marooned Americans!*

Aside from the fact that tourists (female etc.) couldn't sleep in hammocks and that battleships haven't got passenger accommodations, he totally fails to grasp that this war between the other powers is going inevitably to give rise to a hundred different complications in which we shall have a direct interest. Questions of refugees, of neutrality, of commerce are even now appearing and we should unquestionably gather our fleet together and get it into the highest state of efficiency. We still have 12 battleships at Vera Cruz—their "materiel" has suffered somewhat, their "personnel" a great deal! The rest of the fleet is scattered to the four winds—they should be assembled and prepared. Some fine day the State Department will want the moral backing of a "fleet in being" and it won't be there.

All this sounds like borrowing trouble I know but it is my duty to keep the Navy in a position where no chances, even the most remote, are taken. Today we are taking chances and I nearly boil over when I see the cheery "mañana" way of doing business.

Two hours ago a telegram from Badger [Admiral Charles J. Badger, Commander of the Atlantic Fleet] *came in asking for information about the war and instructions as to neutrality. Nobody had thought it necessary to keep him in touch! And yet he has a German, a French and an English cruiser off Vera Cruz! . . .*

There seems no hope now of averting the crash. Germany has invaded France according to this afternoon's report. The best that can be expected is either a sharp, complete and quick victory by one side, a most unlikely occurrence, or a speedy realization of impending bankruptcy by all, and cessation by mutual consent, but this too is I think unlikely as history shows that money in spite of what the bankers say is not an essential to the conduct of a war by a determined nation.

Toward the end of his letter, he set aside any pretense of objectivity and made his own feelings clear:

Rather than long drawn-out struggle I hope that England will join in and with France and Russia force peace at Berlin!

CHAPTER TWENTY-TWO

I n assessing Franklin Roosevelt's early political career, it is notable how few mistakes he made, how rarely it was that he made the wrong turn or found himself up a blind alley without the means of escape. Blessed as he was with a famous name and family wealth, he had exploited his advantages at every turn, making the right friends and—equally important—the right enemies, and with astonishing ease maneuvering himself into precisely the hard-to-get job he most wanted.

Given his record for making the right decisions, it comes as something of a surprise when, on August 14, 1914, just as the European war was getting under way and the office of Assistant Secretary of the Navy was gaining in stature and importance as a result, Franklin Roosevelt chose to announce that he would be a candidate for the United States Senate in the upcoming New York Democratic primaries.

Most of the details relating to his decision to enter the primaries have been lost in the mists of history, but it seems clear that William Gibbs McAdoo, who by that time was not only Wilson's treasury secretary but also his son-in-law, was a major factor in persuading

Roosevelt to run. McAdoo was eager to weaken Tammany's hold on New York's Democrats and saw Roosevelt, with his reputation for defying Boss Murphy, as a means to that end. It is possible that FDR took McAdoo's encouragement as tacit approval for the move from Wilson, although later events suggest that such was not indeed the case.

Josephus Daniels was strongly against the run for the Senate and tried to convince his headstrong young assistant that attempting such a race at that particular juncture was inadvisable for any number of reasons, but Roosevelt brushed off the advice. What could Josephus Daniels possibly know about New York politics?

Louis Howe, Roosevelt's most trusted source of political advice, was away on vacation when Roosevelt informed him of his decision in a telegram. FDR explained that he was motivated by "an important political development." Almost assuredly, Louis Howe would have done everything in his power to convince Roosevelt not to make such a run, and Roosevelt seems to have understood that when he added blithely, "My senses have not yet left me."

Tammany's Boss Murphy was one of the first to act on the news. He still harbored a grudge against FDR for his campaign against Sheehan in the Legislature, and he saw in Roosevelt's announcement a way to even the score. He knew he would need a "good government" candidate to oppose FDR in the primary, so instead of putting forward one of his own clubhouse cronies for the Democratic nomination, he reached across the ocean and named James Gerard, Wilson's ambassador to Germany, as Tammany's candidate. Gerard had been regularly receiving favorable press notices since the start of the war as newspapers featured his diplomatic efforts to rescue stranded Americans trapped by the outbreak of hostilities.

Gerard accepted Murphy's offer, but announced that he would not be able to come back to New York to campaign because he could not leave his post at such a critical time, thus adding further luster to his stature. Murphy's move placed Roosevelt in an awkward position, competing for the nomination against a phantom opponent who was forced to remain at his post across the Atlantic, serving as Wilson's plenipotentiary in a war crisis. Murphy's strategy worked like a charm. Three weeks later, Roosevelt went down to a crushing defeat, collecting only 76,888 votes against Gerard's 210,765. Roosevelt may not have made many political mistakes, but when he did, he learned from them. In this case, his defeat taught him that he should have checked out the president's views on his candidacy, in which case he would have learned that there was no chance of getting Wilson's endorsement, even before Murphy's canny selection of Gerard made such a move impossible.

There was enough happening in the summer of 1914 to keep even a peripatetic hustler like Roosevelt fully occupied, even without the distraction of running a statewide primary campaign. On August 6, the president's wife died, leaving Wilson devastated and the White House given over to funeral arrangements. (This may have been the reason Roosevelt failed to seek advice from Wilson on his candidacy.) On August 17, Franklin Delano Roosevelt, Jr. was born at Campobello. He was the second Roosevelt child to bear the name, the first having died within a year of his birth. The island of Campobello, despite its proximity to Eastport, Maine, is in New Brunswick, and the fact that this newest Roosevelt was born in Canada gives him a peculiar distinction. He is the only one of Franklin and Eleanor's children who was thus deprived of the right to run for president, a factor that would undoubtedly have been understood by a family so steeped in politics and so keenly aware of its rules.

As the war in Europe and its potential impact on America and American policy continued to dominate Washington, Roosevelt initiated a correspondence with his boyhood idol, the retired naval theorist Admiral Alfred Thayer Mahan. Predictably, Mahan's first concern was the immediate return of the Navy ships from Mexico, in accordance with his most basic precept, the insistence that in time of danger the fleet must be united. But by August 18, Mahan was warning of an entirely different peril. Ironically, he pointed out, the European war was threatening America's ability to defend itself on the other side of the globe. Japan, Britain's ally in the Far East, had taken advantage of Germany's preoccupation with the war in Europe to threaten Germany's colonies in the Pacific. Mahan warned, "Japan, going to war with Germany, will be at liberty to take the German islands Pelew, Marianne, Caroline and Samoa. The first three flank our Mercator course to the Philippines, and it is one thing to have them in the hands of a power whose main strength is in Europe, and quite another that they should pass into the hands of one so near as Japan." Further, he pointed out, Japan's actions would directly affect America's relationship with Britain. "Let Great Britain be brought at once to face the fact that the action of her ally thus seriously affects her relationship with us, because of this military contingency."

Mahan's warning of Japanese aggression proved accurate. Japan declared war on Germany, soon after he had predicted such a move, and promptly took over Germany's Pacific island colonies at little cost in men or material. The United States—and to a lesser degree Great Britain—would pay dearly as a result, twenty-seven years later, in World War II.

Although Wilson worked continuously, and generally success-fully, to keep American involvement in the war to a minimum, the conflict was simply too big to ignore. In October, a great national debate began, led by Theodore Roosevelt and his friend Senator Henry Cabot Lodge, on America's need to prepare for possible involvement in the war. They called for a massive buildup in the defense budget to ensure that America would be strong enough to remain at peace. Opposing the call for Preparedness were William Jennings Bryan and Josephus Daniels, who suspected that any campaign to increase defense spending was simply a ruse to increase the profits of big business, and who also feared that any increase in military spending must inevitably lead to America's direct involvement in the war.

Franklin D. Roosevelt at ten years old in 1892. It was around this age that he first read *The Naval War of 1812*, by Theodore Roosevelt, a book that would greatly influence him. *Image courtesy of the Franklin D. Roosevelt Library.*

TOP: FDR, age 16, with his parents, James and Sara, in May 1899. He was in his fifth-form year at Groton and still contemplating applying to the Naval Academy at Annapolis. A year later he would enter Harvard. BOTTOM: FDR, age 24, at the helm of the *Half Moon II*, off Campobello, circa 1906. Always an avid yachtsman, he would continue recreational sailing into his presidential years. *Images courtesy of the Franklin D. Roosevelt Library.*

TOP: FDR campaigning for the New York Senate during his first run for office in 1910. Eleanor Roosevelt can be seen directly behind him. BOTTOM: FDR, age 29, at his desk Number 26 in the New York Senate in 1911, the year he led the fight against "Blue Eyed Billy" Sheehan, the Tammany candidate. *Images courtesy of the Franklin D. Roosevelt Library.*

FDR (at far right) during his tour of the Panama Canal construction site in 1912. The great size and complexity of the project would leave a lasting impression on him. *Image courtesy of the Franklin D. Roosevelt Library.*

FDR with Secretary of the Navy Josephus Daniels. Their relationship was at times contentious during their more than seven years together in the Navy Department. *Image courtesy of the Franklin D. Roosevelt Library.*

TOP: Tammany Boss Charles F. Murphy and Assistant Secretary of the Navy FDR. Long-term antagonists since the Sheehan fight, they reached an accommodation in 1917, but it was never more than a marriage of convenience for either man. BOTTOM: FDR, age 35, on a rifle range in Winthrop, Maryland. After America declared war in 1917, he repeatedly requested permission to resign his office and enlist in the military, but President Wilson and Secretary Daniels would not allow it. *Images courtesy of the Franklin D. Roosevelt Library.*

TOP: FDR, age 36, at Pauillac, France during his European tour in 1918. He is just returning from a flying inspection of the huge American military installations along the Gironde River. BOTTOM: FDR with Admiral Plunkett at St. Nazaire, France, August 17, 1918. Plunkett commanded the battery of 14" naval guns mounted on railway carriages, and promised FDR a position. *Images courtesy of the Franklin D. Roosevelt Library.*

Franklin and Eleanor Roosevelt in France, January 1919, on his return to Europe to supervise the disposal of naval stores. Behind them are the ruins of the St. Quentin Cathedral. *Image courtesy of the Franklin D. Roosevelt Library.*

Privately, Franklin Roosevelt strongly supported Uncle Ted's preparedness campaign but, in deference to Secretary Daniels's strong opposition, made no public statements to that effect.

Yet his loyalty to Daniels, always equivocal, had its limits, and when Republican Representative Augustus P. Gardner of Massachusetts, chairman of the House Military Affairs Committee and son-in-law of Senator Lodge, stood on the floor of the House charging that the nation's defenses were dangerously undersubscribed, calling for a special committee to investigate the matter, Franklin waited until Daniels was away from Washington, and then, in his temporary position as Acting Secretary of the Navy, released a lengthy memorandum prepared with the help of Admiral Fiske and other "big navy" officers supporting Gardner's charges. One of his more sensational revelations was that thirteen American battleships were out of commission because Congress had not authorized sufficient manpower levels.

He sent a copy of the memorandum to Eleanor, who was still at Hyde Park, recovering from the birth of Franklin Junior:

> *Dearest Babs,*
>
> *The enclosed is the truth and even if it gets me into trouble I am perfectly ready to stand by it. The country needs the truth about the Army and Navy instead of a lot of the soft mush about everlasting peace which so many statesmen are handing out to a gullible public.*
>
> *All is well here. The Secretary left yesterday morning. I spent most of last evening with Mr. Milburn who came down to the meeting of the Bar Association. The servants have safely arrived.*
>
> *Tomorrow I hope to play golf in the morning with John McIlhenny.*
>
> *I do hope the little Babs progresses and that Nurse does too! Lots of love and kisses.*
>
> *F*

Despite Franklin's brave words, he quickly disavowed his ringing call for a larger Navy as soon as Daniels returned, although he was careful not to disavow any of the specific charges he had made.

Throughout the autumn, as the European conflict settled into the muddy trench-warfare stalemate that would characterize it for the next four years, Roosevelt began to speak out gingerly in favor of Preparedness but tried to fashion his arguments to conform with White House policy. It was not always easy. When he came out for universal military training, he was branded a warmonger. When he called for an expanded Navy, he was accused of advocating war, which he vociferously denied. "Many of us who want to keep the peace," he declared, "believe that $250,000,000 a year for the Navy, which amounts to only one-half of one percent of our national wealth, is merely good insurance."

Wilson quickly made it clear he did not agree with his young assistant secretary's proposals. In the president's annual message to Congress in December, he came out vehemently and explicitly against both universal military training and an expanded Navy. Roosevelt could not have been cheered when the combined Congress rose almost to a man to applaud him.

When Congress sought clarification on the issue, both Daniels and Roosevelt testified before the House Naval Affairs Committee. Appearing on different days, the secretary claimed that the Navy was in excellent shape, while the assistant secretary supported his superior as best he could without actually agreeing with his assessments. Franklin Roosevelt was getting very good at equivocating.

As 1914 ended, anyone who cared to notice would have been reminded that for all the noise out of Europe, a clear and present danger continued to lurk just south of the American border. The New York *Times*, in a dispatch from Juarez, Mexico, reported that "Before leaving Chihuahua City today, Gen. [Pancho] Villa announced that he had arranged to lease the fishing beds off Magdalena Bay to the Japanese Fishing and Navigation Company."

CHAPTER TWENTY-THREE

In his first two years in Washington, Franklin Roosevelt had learned a lot about polishing his social skills, particularly his ability to charm the press. A good example of his skill at winning over and even dazzling interviewers can be found in a rapturous description of him that appeared in the Utica *Saturday Globe* of January 23, 1915: "As he stood in front of a cheerful wood fire, his arm resting on the marble mantle, a bronze bust of John Paul Jones peering over his shoulder, he was an engaging picture of young American manhood," gushed reporter Ashmun Brown, who interviewed him in his office. "Through the wide windows rays of dazzling light, reflected from the snow-clad expanse of the White House grounds across the street, caught the clean lines of his face and figure and threw them into sharp relief. They, the air of alertness they conveyed, the natural pose, were the sort of thing one sees in the work of leading American illustrators more often than in real life. The face was particularly interesting. Breeding showed there. Clearly cut features, a small, sensitive mouth, tiny lines running from nostrils to the outer lines of the lips, a broad forehead, close-cropped brown hair, frank, blue eyes, but, above all, the proud, straight, upstanding set of the head placed the man."

This admiring verbal portrait of the assistant secretary of the Navy is a far cry from the lightweight dandy described by Frances Perkins in her account of that long-ago Gramercy Park tea dance in 1911. Nor were such worshipful descriptions all that rare. Another, published in the New York *Tribune,* is almost as laudatory: "His face is long, firmly shaped and set with marks of confidence. There are faint wrinkles on a high straight forehead. Intensely blue eyes rest in light shadow. A firm, thin mouth breaks quickly to laugh, openly and freely. His voice is pitched well, goes forward without tripping. He doesn't disdain shedding his coat on a hot afternoon; shows an active quality in the way he jumps from his chair to reach the cigarettes in his coat. He is a young man, a young man with energy and definite ideas."

While good looks and an ability to charm can be important assets for any political figure, they are primarily valuable only if they help the politician accomplish his goals. In the Washington of early 1915, it was becoming increasingly difficult for Franklin Roosevelt to accomplish almost any goal, due to the sharp division within the administration relating to America's proper relationship to the European war. There were those who advocated ignoring the war entirely and adopting a strictly isolationist policy toward the combatants, and those who wanted to maintain a closer, but still hands-off, policy, favoring nei-ther side, standing ready at all times to broker peace. For those like Roosevelt, who actually favored taking sides and supporting the Allies, the problem was all the more difficult.

The question had been exacerbated when Wilson, early in the war and in spite of Secretary Bryan's pleading, decided not to back up his neutrality proclamation with effective restrictions upon the sales of American goods or the extension of American credit to the belliger-ents. Theoretically that meant that all the European powers had an equal right to trade with American firms, but in reality, because of the

British Navy's control of the seas, only the Allies could take delivery of American goods, while Germany and the other Central Powers were effectively cut off from any trade. This resulted almost immediately in an increasingly heavy economic investment in the Allies by Wall Street and leading American manufacturers. Bryan fulminated against the British blockade, which he claimed was against international law, but in this he was either naïve or mistaken. True enough, a proposal to ban blockades had been floated at a London naval conference attended by European powers plus Japan and the United States in 1909, but Britain, which had employed blockades as its principal means of warfare for centuries, refused to ratify the proposal, as did most of the other parties. The United States was one of the few to accept it, so while it might be true that blockade was against American law, it was not against international law.

Germany, in an attempt to counter the Royal Navy's control of the seas, had vastly expanded its U-boat fleet as a means of evading Britain's domination of the ocean's surface. In the early months of the war, when Britain was still establishing its blockade, German submarines limited their activities to the long-established wartime practice known as *guerre de course*, preying exclusively on unarmed Allied merchant ships in a relatively gentlemanly fashion. In accordance with international maritime law, when a patrolling U-boat encountered an enemy merchantman, it would surface nearby, and the German captain, standing in the conning tower, would declare his intention of torpedoing the merchant ship, giving the crew only enough time to lower lifeboats and abandoned the doomed vessel.

Over the years, many nations—including the United States—had employed this form of warfare, but the conventions governing *guerre de course* covered only armed surface raiders chasing their quarry across the open sea and took no account of the nature of submarines, which approached their victims by stealth. The ability of submarines to operate underwater gave them a certain advantage, but it also entailed a great disadvantage. Because they had to be built for maximum buoyancy, submarines were almost as fragile as aircraft. They had no armor plating to protect them, and they were so defenseless that theoretically a single rifle shot could puncture their ballast tanks and sink them. Their only safety lay in secrecy and surprise, and so long as the merchant vessels they preyed upon were unarmed, the submarines could safely operate under the laws governing the *guerre de course*.

The British quickly developed countermeasures to take advantage of the vulnerability of U-boats, the most dramatic of which were the Royal Navy's "Q-boats," which were heavily armed warships disguised as innocent merchantmen. When a U-boat, attracted by what looked like an easy kill, surfaced to order the ship's crew into the lifeboats, the false bulkheads on the Q-boat would be thrust aside to reveal multiple guns which would open fire and make quick work of the U-boat. By this and other stratagems, the British seemed to have contained the U-boat threat, but seven months into the war the Imperial German Government took the fight to the next level. On February 15, 1915, Berlin announced: "The waters around Great Britain, including the whole of the English Channel, are declared hereby to be included within the zone of war, and after the 18th inst., all enemy merchant vessels encountered in these waters will be destroyed, even if it may not be possible always to save their crews and passengers."

This was unrestricted submarine warfare, and the reaction in America was one of shock and anger. The idea that Germany would deliberately target unarmed civilians as well as uniformed fighting men was seen as barbaric and helped move public sentiment closer to the Allied cause, at least in those areas in the East bordering the Atlantic. Like many others in Washington, Roosevelt thought long and hard about how the new German policy might play out in regard to American interests. As it happened, the answer would not emerge until the late spring.

Early in March, Franklin and Eleanor were assigned to accompany Vice President Thomas R. Marshall and his wife to the opening of the Panama Pacific Exposition in San Francisco. It was to be a grand affair, a world's fair full of parties and ceremony, celebrating the completion of the Panama Canal. Marshall was a genial travelling companion who has come down in history principally for his oft-quoted aphorism, "What this country needs is a good five-cent cigar." When Roosevelt discovered that the office of Vice President did not have its own naval flag, he quickly remedied the situation by designing one and arranging for it to be stitched together in time to be displayed—along with the flag of the Assistant Secretary of the Navy, of course—at the fleet review.

On that occasion, Vice President Marshall was delivered alongside the flagship by the admiral's barge and clambered up the gangway, apparently unaware of the protocol involved in coming aboard a Navy vessel and totally unprepared for what was about to happen. He stepped jauntily over the rail and onto the grating—silk hat, frock coat, gloves in his left hand, pearl-handled cane in his right, a cigar stuck jauntily in his mouth. He was momentarily startled by the piercing shriek of the boatswain's pipe, followed immediately by four drum ruffles and the whole ship's company at salute, and when the band struck up "The Star Spangled Banner," Marshall realized he had to do something and do it quickly. After a moment of hesitation, he transferred the cane from right hand to left, whipped the cigar out of his mouth, and somehow managed to get his hat off. As the band came to the end of the national anthem, he started putting his hat on—once again transferring his cigar, cane, and gloves to his left hand, at which point the first gun of his salute went off with a bang, and the whole kit and caboodle flew two feet into the air.

A few days later, watching the motion-picture record of the scene, a mortified vice president turned to Roosevelt and said, "My God, if I looked like that, I will never go on board another ship as long as I live."

After leaving the Exposition and before returning east, Roosevelt continued down the coast on Navy business. While in Los Angeles, he learned that the Navy submarine F-4 had failed to surface after a dive off Pearl Harbor, with the loss of her entire crew. In a message to the stunned public, he addressed the loss, noting that, sad as it was, it was something "that must be expected in any great navy." Then, with the press standing at dockside, he arranged to board a submarine at San Pedro and make a very public dive. On resurfacing, a beaming Roosevelt told reporters that for the first time since leaving Washington, he felt "perfectly at home." He then boarded a destroyer for a storm-tossed run down to San Diego before finally catching a train east.

As he crossed the country, dispatches and local newspapers along the route told of the first occasion in which Germany's unrestricted submarine warfare policy had directly impacted the United States. A U-boat in the Irish Sea had without warning torpedoed a small British liner, the *Falaba*, killing several crewmen and passengers, including an American engineer, Leon C. Thrasher, en route to his job in West Africa. Newspapers across the country rose as one to condemn this latest act of German barbarism; in Washington, statesmen worked late into the night worrying about how to respond to the "atrocity." Eventually, much to Roosevelt's displeasure, it was decided not to send even a note of protest.

Viewed from a century's distance, with the intervening history of two cataclysmic world wars, the first of which accounted for over twenty million deaths and the second fifty-five million, it is difficult to comprehend the shock and distress brought on by the death of a single American civilian, killed while traveling on a belligerent vessel in a war zone; but in 1915, the concept of total war was still new. In a time before huge civilian casualties became commonplace, the casualties of war were still assumed to be borne pretty much exclusively by men in uniform. Noncombatants were still understood to be bystanders.

On May 1, the Germans upped the ante again, this time torpedoing an American tanker, the *Gulflight*, once again in the Irish Sea, this time with the loss of three American lives. But much worse was about to happen, with profound effect upon the Wilson cabinet.

CHAPTER TWENTY-FOUR

I n private, Franklin Roosevelt made no effort to disguise his support for the Allied cause despite the Wilson government's strictly neutral stance. He was quite open about the warm relations he maintained with many of the British and French diplomats in Washington, and in a cheerful letter to Eleanor he described dining with the British ambassador at the Metropolitan Club: "Today Sir C. Spring-Rice lunched with me. . . . Von Bernstorff [the German ambassador] was at the next table, trying to hear what we were talking about! Springy and Von B. would kill each other if they had a chance! I just *know* I shall do some awful unneutral thing before I get through!"

In the spring of 1915, the European war entered a new phase which would severely challenge the strict neutrality of the White House. On April 22, an advertisement appeared in some fifty American newspapers, including those in New York. The advertiser had specifically instructed that the ads be placed directly adjacent to the Cunard Line notice advertising the sailing of the giant steamer *Lusitania* for Liverpool:

NOTICE!

TRAVELLERS intending to embark on the Atlantic voyage
are reminded that a state of war exists between Germany
and her allies and Great Britain and her allies; that the
zone of war includes the waters adjacent to the British
Isles; that, in accordance with formal notice given by the
Imperial German Government, vessels flying the flag of
Great Britain, or any of her allies, are liable to destruction in those waters and that travelers sailing in the war
zone on ships of Great Britain or her allies do so at their
own risk.

IMPERIAL GERMAN EMBASSY
WASHINGTON, D.C. APRIL 22, 1915

The *Lusitania* sailed from New York on May 1 with 1265 passengers and a crew of 702. Virtually all the Americans holding tickets
for the voyage had received anonymous telegrams beseeching them
to cancel their bookings. Everyone recognized that the telegrams had
come from the Germans in what was perceived as a clumsy attempt to
intimidate them. The Germans, it was generally agreed, were bluffing.
Only one American cancelled.

For most of the crossing, the ship proceeded without incident. A
week after leaving New York, as she approached the Irish coast, a
blackout was imposed on board as a precaution, and the ship's forty-
eight lifeboats, more than adequate to accommodate everyone on
board, were run out on their davits, ready to be lowered should the
need arise. Then, shortly after noon on May 7, 1915, the German submarine U-20 fired a single torpedo into the *Lusitania*, ripping a hole
in her starboard bow. The original explosion was almost immediately
followed by a second explosion, which puzzled the U-boat captain,
since he had fired only one torpedo. In just eighteen minutes, the
huge 30,396-ton liner listed and sank, bow first, with the loss of 1198

souls, including 274 women and 94 children. Of the 139 Americans on board, 128 perished.

As the news of the *Lusitania* raced around the world, shock waves spread. The sinking was seen as an unparalleled act of barbarism. In the United States, newspaper headlines labeled it WANTON MURDER ON THE HIGH SEAS. Theodore Roosevelt pronounced it as "piracy on a vaster scale of murder than the old-time pirates ever practiced. . . . It seems inconceivable that we can refrain from taking action in this matter, for we owe it not only to humanity but to our own national self-respect."

President Wilson, shocked to tears, made no immediate comment and took no action, and went into virtual seclusion for three days. Then in a speech in Philadelphia he proclaimed his justification for inaction in the face of provocation. "There is such a thing as a man being too proud to fight. There is such a thing as a nation being so right that it does not need to convince others by force that it is right."

His apathetic response was met with scorn and contempt by millions, and applauded only by those determined to keep America out of the war by any means. Wilson almost immediately regretted his words and tried to take them back at a press conference the following day. Goaded by the jeers of an angry nation, he wrote a protest note to the German government, demanding that it disavow the torpedoing of the *Lusitania*, make reparations for losses incurred, and "take immediate steps to prevent the recurrence of anything so obviously subversive of the principles of warfare." His note was unanimously approved by the cabinet and, when the text was released to the public, it was overwhelmingly supported by the press.

But William Jennings Bryan, the strongly pacifist secretary of state, had only signed off on Wilson's note on the understanding that the president would take an equally strong stand against the British blockade, which Bryan claimed was just as illegal as Germany's submarine campaign. He pointed out that the *Lusitania* had been carrying contraband in the form of 4,200,000 rounds of rifle cartridges and

1,250 unarmed fragmentation shells, all designed to kill Germans, and the purpose of the Royal Navy's blockade included starving the German civilian population, which he claimed was an equally barbaric course of action.

Franklin Roosevelt was not an active participant in the deliberations arising from the *Lusitania* sinking, but there was no question where his heart lay. He was deeply committed to the Allied cause and determined that America, and its Navy in particular, should be prepared to join the fight if necessary—although he did not go as far as Uncle Ted, who wanted to declare war. While Wilson and the country awaited a response to the president's note, Franklin Roosevelt and Josephus Daniels both addressed a Navy League dinner in New York. The secretary of the Navy advocated a stay-the-course policy, in keeping with Wilson's call for a slow but orderly program of naval improvement, while the assistant secretary, constricted by his subsidiary position but determined to propound a greater urgency to naval expansion regardless, demanded—to great applause—a stronger, larger, more modern navy. The contrasting views of the two men did not go unnoticed, and an unrepentant Roosevelt may have wondered whether once again he had gone too far in catering to his "big navy" audience. As on previous occasions, Josephus Daniels once again was willing to overlook any signs of insubordination in his assistant.

On his return to Washington, Roosevelt wrote Eleanor on May 20, "Quantities of things to do at the office and dinner at the Daniels', who were cordial (!) but no reference was made to the New York episodes."

When the German response to Wilson's note finally arrived, it was notable chiefly for its pious legalisms and lack of any sense of repentance. It argued that since the *Lusitania* was carried on the Royal Navy's rolls as an auxiliary naval vessel, she was a legitimate target, and charged further that the mysterious second explosion, which had caused the ship to sink so quickly, and which had not been caused by a second torpedo, may actually have been caused by high explosives carried illegally in the ship's hold. It held the Cunard Line responsible for the American deaths.

The German response to Wilson's letter was clearly unsatisfactory, so the president prepared a second, stronger note, demanding that Germany stop its "ruthless" submarine campaign, and if it did not do so, the United States would hold Germany strictly responsible.

When the president submitted the text to his cabinet for approval, Secretary of State Bryan, noting that once again it included no condemnation of the British blockade, could not bring himself to sign it and, after much soul-searching, resigned.

William Jennings Bryan was a man of unquestioned moral authority and more than ordinary political stature, and he had been a major figure in Democratic politics for decades. His resignation made headlines across the country and generated thoughtful editorials, but it elicited only jeering catcalls from Franklin Roosevelt. "These are the hectic days all right," he wrote Eleanor. "What d' y' think of W. Jay B.? It's all too long to write about, but I can only say I'm disgusted clear through. J. D. will *not* resign!"

Over half a century later, in 1973, British investigative reporter Colin Simpson discovered that the Germans had been right. He established that nearly the whole of the *Lusitania*'s cargo was contraband and that a false manifest had been prepared to conceal the fact. Simpson later dived on the wreck and brought up some of the 10½ tons of explosives. The 1,250 cases of shrapnel were falsely franked "non explosive in bulk." Some 3,813 40-pound packages assigned to the Naval Experimental Establishment at Shoeburyness and labeled "cheese" were actually pyroxylin, a nitrocellulose explosive highly susceptible to seawater, and were almost certainly the cause of the second explosion.

CHAPTER TWENTY-FIVE

lthough Roosevelt was not privy to Wilson's inner circle, he was close to those who were, and was therefore intimately familiar with their concerns and worries as the president wrestled with the difficulties of trying to impose his will upon Germany—which the public clearly wanted him to do—while at the same time keeping America out of the war—which the public also clearly wanted him to do. On June 23, FDR returned to his office after lunching with Josephus Daniels and Secretary of Commerce William C. Redfield at the Shoreham Hotel and set down some private thoughts and observations relating to America and the war, as if to find in them some thread of logic or reason to define his own thoughts. These personal notes, which he filed away for future reference, go to the heart of his reactions to the crisis of the *Lusitania* sinking seven weeks earlier, and provide an insight into how he could understand and define opinions that he did not share, and in some cases strongly opposed:

"As we were walking over Mr. Daniels talked of the difficulty of our position: that Germany might not agree to give up her submarine warfare—that if she did not & refused to do so ever so politely, what could we do? He seemed worried & bewildered questioning without daring to suggest to himself any answers then he said—'you know one or two men in the Cabinet spend a lot of time working things out to an ultimate conclusion. For instance Garrison [Secretary of War Lindley Garrison, a leading proponent of Preparedness] has kept on speculating about what we could do or should do in case Germany does not back down—of course he has that kind of a mind, the mind of a lawyer & it makes him see a whole lot of unnecessary bogies.'"

"I asked him [Josephus Daniels] 'Do you think people would stand for raising an army?' He said 'No, it would create terrible divisions of opinion.'"

"This reminds me that Garrison told me yesterday that Daniels had said to him 'I hope I shall never live to see the day when the schools of this country are used to give any form of military training—If that happens it will be proof positive that the American form of government is a failure.'"

"And then he went on to me 'You know it was just that that made Bryan resign—the fear of the next step if Germany does not give in. It is a mistake to look too far ahead, to cross the bridges before we get to them; it is sufficient to take up each step as it comes up.'"

"My one regret is that the Cabinet has not more Garrisons—the President is not getting real information because

the Daniels[es] & Bryans prevent discussion of the future
steps because it is a disagreeable subject. I know for a fact
that the president has not had the advice of a single officer
of the Army or of the Navy on the question of what we
could do to carry out our declared policy."

Given the benefit of hindsight, what we can see in these private notes
is that FDR was grappling with Wilson's problems from Wilson's
perspective. He was attempting to teach himself how to think the
way a president has to think.

The Germans replied two weeks later to Wilson's second diplomatic
note protesting the *Lusitania* sinking. Their response continued to
be argumentative and provided none of the assurances demanded
by Wilson, so he sent a third, final note that contained serious but
ambiguous threats designed to force the Germans to wonder whether
they really wanted to risk America joining the Allies. He warned the
German Imperial Government "that repetition by the commanders
of German naval vessels of acts in contravention of . . . neutral rights
must be regarded by the Government of the United States, when they
affect American citizens, as deliberately unfriendly."

When the newspapers reported that Wilson had sent still a third
protest note, a testy Theodore Roosevelt asked his daughter Alice
mischievously if she had noticed its serial number. "I fear I have
lost track," he told her, "but I am inclined to think it is No 11,765,
Series B."

But if Uncle Ted ridiculed Wilson's attempts at diplomacy, he
might have looked with greater favor on one of the other actions the
president took that same day. In a dramatic about-face, Woodrow
Wilson committed himself to the Preparedness program he had
heretofore opposed, and formally requested his secretary of war and
his secretary of the Navy to prepare expansion programs for both the
Army and the Navy.

Franklin Roosevelt, recuperating at Campobello from an appendicitis operation, was delighted by the news. For a year, he had been one of the very few voices warning that the war would be long and brutal and advocating the need for American Preparedness. Now, at last, his message seemed to be getting through to the White House.

Woodrow Wilson's angry protests to Berlin seemed to be having no effect whatsoever. The Germans continued their campaign of unrestricted U-boat warfare. On August 19, three days after Roosevelt returned to his office from his sickbed, the British White Star liner *Arabic* was torpedoed with the loss of 44 killed, including two Americans. The ship had been bound to New York and therefore could not logically have been carrying contraband, and once again the American public was outraged. But again Wilson refused to take any action other than to fire off still another note of protest to the Germans and then sit back and wait for a response.

Maintaining any sort of diplomatic communication with Berlin was time-consuming because the British Navy, in one of its first acts in the war, had severed all of Germany's underwater cable connections with the outside world. In consequence, the German government had been forced to develop substitute methods of transatlantic communication, all of which were slow. The wait for answers from Berlin was therefore often a long one. There were now two different protests in the pipeline, the third *Lusitania* note and the new *Arabic* note. Two weeks after Wilson sent off the *Arabic* note, the German ambassador was finally able to present a response to Wilson's third *Lusitania* note. This time Wilson's veiled threats seemed to have forced Berlin to modify its stance. Bernstorff had been instructed to relay to the American government that "Liners will not be sunk by our submarines without warning and without safety of the lives of noncombatants provided that the liners do not try to escape or offer resistance."

This was a major concession on the part of the Germans and a considerable diplomatic triumph on Wilson's part, but of course the German promise rang hollow in the face of the much more recent torpedoing of the *Arabic*. It was not until a month later that Bern-storff was able to confirm in writing that Germany "regrets and disavows" the sinking of the *Arabic*, and was "prepared to pay an indemnity for the American lives which . . . have been lost." Then, in an even more significant passage, "The orders issued by His Majesty the Emperor to the commanders of the German submarines . . . have been so stringent that the recurrence of incidents similar to the *Arabic* case is considered out of the question." The White House and the nation as a whole celebrated the "*Arabic* pledge," and Wilson was hailed for his cool negotiating skill. Millions of Americans took note of the fact that once again "he has kept us out of the war."

Meanwhile Roosevelt, on his own initiative, and taking advantage of Josephus Daniels's absence from the office on holiday, used his temporary position to move the Navy significantly closer to a wartime footing by announcing the formation of a Naval Reserve which would be made up of fifty thousand men and squadrons of private power-boats, ready to be pressed into service should a national emergency arise. Such a Naval Reserve had long been one of FDR's pet ideas. He had often suggested such an organization to Daniels, and while the secretary had been agreeable, somehow the idea of a Naval Reserve had never gotten beyond the talking stage.

"Today I sprang an announcement of the national Naval Reserve, and trust J. D. will like it!" he wrote Eleanor. "It is of the utmost importance, and I have failed for a year to get him to take any action, though he has never objected to it. Now I have gone ahead and pulled the trigger myself. I suppose the bullet may bounce back on me, but it is not revolutionary or alarmist and is just common sense." When he returned from vacation, Daniels did in fact approve the step, but cautioned that it must be run democratically, not just for FDR's yachting cronies.

Both Roosevelt and Daniels were quick to note that when Wilson made public his shift to Preparedness on September 3, 1915, both the press and the public received the news coolly. Many opposed it outright. Later, in December, when Wilson outlined to Congress his program to expand both the Army and the Navy, the response was equally negative, or at least apathetic. Advocates of Preparedness complained that Wilson's plans were insufficient, while pacifists—including a significant percentage of Democratic representatives—were sure his program would lead the country closer to war. It was clear that the White House was going to have difficulty negotiating the passage of Wilson's program.

In December, Roosevelt wrote an article in *The Nation's Business* addressing the public's apathetic response. It laid out in detail what it was that the Wilson administration was committed to do in the way of Navy expansion and made the case that the considerable growth anticipated was "purely defensive." The article, "The Navy Program and What It Means," was almost certainly ghost-written by Louis Howe, but it accurately reflected what Franklin was thinking at the time. Roosevelt did not dodge the question of cost. Navies are expensive, he admitted, and the cost of the expansion program would be steep, some $500,000,000 over five years, but he presented the extra millions in the context of other expenditures. He had made the point elsewhere that "we spend more money per year for chewing gum . . . than we do to keep our Army, and more money is spent for automobile tires than it costs to run the Navy."

The article deliberately echoed the style of Uncle Ted, combining straight talk with a very personal appeal. "People are beginning to realize that naval defense does not mean merely the protection of certain harbor mouths along our Atlantic and Pacific coasts. Naval warfare from its earliest days has meant the control for defensive purposes of those portions of the ocean in which a country is immediately interested. . . . The program does not go as far as many would desire, or even as has been suggested as necessary by many experts. It is, however, the first attempt to apply ordinary business sense to this great national problem. It is, of course, for the people of the United States, through their representatives, to say how fast the extension and development shall go on. But a real beginning has for the first time been made in defining the true requirements of national safety."

While Preparedness and concerns over the U-boat situation continued to dominate talk in Washington, there were certain other gnawing anxieties that simply would not go away, as indicated in a brief New York *Times* story toward the end of 1915:

GERMAN WIRELESS IN MAGDALENA BAY?

Washington, Dec. 4: A report came to the State Department today, from a source that was not disclosed, that a German wireless station was said to be in operation in Magdalena Bay in the Mexican State of Lower California. The State Department sent the information to the Department of Justice for investigation.

As it turned out, there was nothing to the story, but it served to keep alive the American government's nervous awareness of Mexico's political fragility, and the threat it posed to the defense of the United States.

In the Roosevelts' private life, Eleanor had discovered that Lucy Mercer, who had proved to be invaluable as a social secretary, could also be counted on to fill in as a guest at dinner parties when an extra female was required. The dignitaries and naval officers at the Roosevelts' table were charmed by the attractive young woman whose youth and looks added such grace and spirit to the occasion.

CHAPTER TWENTY-SIX

Nineteen-sixteen would be a presidential election year, and, as the new year opened, that meant a time of decision for Franklin Roosevelt. Four years earlier, he had cast his lot with Woodrow Wilson, and he owed his current position to that original leap of faith. Now it was time to decide whether to stand pat and put his faith in Wilson's ability to win the November election, or to strike out in a new direction, either in New York politics or perhaps in the private sector. And behind that question lay another: if Wilson were to win reelection, could FDR expect to retain his position as assistant secretary of the Navy, or might he even hope to be rewarded with some even more important job, even a cabinet post?

And still another question: could Wilson win? Any realistic handicapping of the president's chances in November had to take into account the growing discontent within his party. The resignation of William Jennings Bryan had exposed a bitter divide within the Democrats. The millions—particularly in the West—who still revered and trusted the Great Commoner felt betrayed by Wilson. Even those who sided with the president found his shifting positions relative to the Allies and the Central Powers inconsistent and unpredictable, and his September shift into the Preparedness camp was seen as more worrisome than welcome.

There was still another factor which, while not strictly political, was likely to have significant political consequences. In December 1915, to the distress of many of his fellow citizens, the president had married Edith Galt, widow of a Washington jeweler. His remarriage, coming so soon after his first wife's death, seemed likely to cast a shadow over all of Wilson's initiatives.

And once again, there was the nagging question of Uncle Ted. Theodore Roosevelt, whose split with William Howard Taft had made Wilson's election possible in 1912, was still hugely popular, and was now making it increasingly clear that he wanted very much to run again for the White House. This time he stipulated beforehand that he would only run if he could get the backing of the Republican Party, and the consensus among most knowledgeable observers was that if TR could somehow manage to mend fences with the GOP, he would be unbeatable.

Franklin Roosevelt knew he would have to address the question of his own future at some point, but he also recognized that the unpredictable nature of the European war and America's responses to the constantly shifting state of play as it approached its third year would generate any number of opportunities and points of danger as the year progressed, and that, for the time being, the prudent expedient was to stay the course and see what happened.

Many politicians in his position, with their future in the balance, might decide to adopt a cautious, wait-and-see attitude, but Roosevelt's response was exactly the opposite—an increased boldness and self-confidence, which would make itself evident throughout the year in both his public and private lives.

That January, Roosevelt was suffering with a throat infection so severe and intractable that he barely had the energy to get through each day, let alone face the problems of his job. He was still sick when

Wilson set out on a cross-country tour to sell the public on his new plans to expand America's military forces. In St. Louis, in his final address of the tour, he defended his Preparedness campaign with an enthusiasm and eloquence that Franklin Roosevelt would have appreciated. "Have you ever let your imagination dwell upon the enormous stretch of coast from the Canal to Alaska, from the Canal to the northern corner of Maine?" Wilson asked his audience. "There is no other navy in the world that has to cover so great an area of defense as the American Navy and it ought, in my judgment, to be incomparably the greatest navy in the world."

The tour seemed to have the desired effect, and public opinion appeared to be moving Wilson's way. He returned to Washington ready to move forward on his plans for a larger and stronger Army and Navy, when he was momentarily caught off guard by the resignation of Lindley Garrison, his bellicose secretary of war. Unlike Bryan, who had resigned because he felt Wilson's policies were too warlike, Garrison, who had been a staunch supporter of military expansion from the beginning, resigned because he felt Wilson's new measures were too modest, nowhere sufficient to the need.

There was immediate speculation in the press that Roosevelt might be selected to replace Garrison, and various high-ranking Army officers and powerful members of the business community let it be known that they were very much in favor of such a move. Louis Howe, who still maintained close relations with his colleagues in the press, undoubtedly helped spread the story. But even had FDR wanted to bring about such a move—and there is no question he would have eagerly welcomed such a promotion, even if it meant leaving his beloved Navy Department—he was in no position to make it happen. By the time of Garrison's resignation, an ailing Roosevelt had decamped for Atlantic City, where his doctors hoped the sea air would improve his sore throat. There, under the watchful eye of his mother, he wrote to Eleanor on the twenty-first of February:

> *Dearest Babs—*
>
> *This "health resort" is purgatory, the place of departed spirits. It is a heavenly day and my throat is, if anything, a little redder, but what I fail to understand is how anybody can stay here more than 24 hours without wanting to murder somebody. Except for throat I feel better as to strength.*
>
> *I shall return Friday if I can stick it out that long. . . . Your affectionate but mad clear through F*

As it turned out, Roosevelt had never been in the running for secretary of war. The president eventually announced that his choice for the position was Newton D. Baker, a cautious Ohio mayor who had recently announced himself strongly opposed to the Preparedness program. The fact that Wilson had now appointed pacifists in charge of both the Army and the Navy indicates just how complicated and volatile the situation had become within the Democratic Party and how difficult it was to find a way to accommodate its contending factions.

Soon after the announcement, there was once again troubling news from the American Southwest, reminding everyone in the defense establishment that the European war was not the only threat to America's security. On March 9, Pancho Villa, the Mexican general who was at that time in a struggle with General Carranza for control of the northern states of Mexico, crossed the American border to sack the town of Columbus, New Mexico, killing nineteen Americans before he was driven off. Villa's raid was a deliberate attempt to exact revenge on Woodrow Wilson, who had helped Carranza make an end run around Villa's troops by allowing Carranza to pass through U.S. territory. Villa hoped to provoke America into war so he could exploit the turmoil, but Wilson avoided the trap. Instead of declaring war, he ordered General "Black Jack" Pershing to cross the Rio Grande with a force of 5,800 men and chase down Villa.

But public attention quickly veered back to the European war when, on March 24, a U-boat torpedoed the ferry-steamer *Sussex* in the English Channel, killing several passengers and injuring four of the twenty-four Americans on board. Once again, Americans reacted with fury. What had happened to all those German promises to abandon such tactics in the wake of the sinkings of the *Lusitania* and the *Arabic*? Once again, on April 18, 1916, Wilson sent an angry note to the German government, this one stronger than any of his previous ones. He threatened to sever diplomatic relations if Germany did not immediately abandon its present method of submarine warfare.

This was head-to-head diplomacy, demanding an unequivocal answer, and the Germans responded quickly, promising to mend their ways but insisting that the United States must make similar demands on the British to abandon their blockade, which they claimed was the sole reason for the U-boat attacks. The White House hailed the German note as the "*Sussex* triumph."

From the Germans' point of view, their response was well timed, and something of a propaganda victory. Americans did not much care one way or another about the blockade, but they were growing increasingly upset by the Royal Navy's high-handed and capricious blacklisting of certain American companies, and by the ever-lengthening list of goods that the British determined were "contraband" and therefore subject to seizure on the high seas without payment, as well as by their interference with Red Cross hospital shipments. Anti-British feelings—particularly in the large and politically influential Irish American community—was also increasing as a result of reports of the British government's brutal suppression of the Easter Rising in Dublin.

It did not go unnoticed by Roosevelt that Wilson was gaining support in American public opinion, while the Allies were losing it. Franklin Roosevelt was keenly interested in such shifts in public sentiment. Privately he had been a staunch supporter of the Allied cause from the beginning (as had Wilson), but he continued to maintain an impartial even-handedness in his public statements, in deference to the president's neutral position. Even so, in the spring of 1916 his increasing independence and self-confidence was becoming more evident. He eagerly accepted an invitation to speak once again to the Navy League in New York, despite the fact that Josephus Daniels was at that point openly boycotting the League, which he described as nothing more than a pressure group of greedy industrialists whose call for a larger Navy was motivated primarily by a desire for fat new construction contracts. Roosevelt was well aware that his superior and the League held each other in contempt but chose to pay no attention, and many both in and out of government saw his speech to the Navy League as a source of tension between the two men.

The month of May 1916 was to prove a landmark in Woodrow Wilson's tortured progress in self-education as he wrestled with his efforts to master two irreconcilable political goals—how to stay out of the most terrible and pointless war in history while simultaneously finding a way to end that war and establish some mechanism to guarantee that it would never be repeated. When he had first called for enlarging the Army and Navy in 1915, he knew it was a risky move and might be seen as taking the first significant step toward engagement in the European war. In May 1916, he deliberately took the next step, which was to define the goals and purpose of that war. It was a radical and even presumptuous move for a noncombatant to set the terms for a war that was being fought by other nations on another continent, and many Americans saw it as a step toward intervention. While Franklin Roosevelt had little if anything to do with the preparation of the speech that Wilson gave on May 27 to an influential ad hoc group called the League to Enforce Peace, he would spend the rest of his life profoundly influenced by the principles expressed in it.

The League had been put together in 1915 by former president Taft and Harvard president A. Lawrence Lowell, and aimed to establish a postwar international organization to keep the peace. Wilson made it abundantly clear that he was in accord with the League's goals. "We are participants, whether we would or not, in the life of the world," he told his two thousand listeners, and "the nations of the world must in some way band together to see that right to choose the sovereignty under which they shall live." Then, in solemn tones he declared, "the United States is willing to become a partner in any feasible association of nations formed in order to realize these objectives and make them secure against violation."

The speech was Wilson's first public attempt to define what would become his primary contribution to history—the establishment of a League of Nations.

CHAPTER TWENTY-SEVEN

E arly in June 1916, Franklin Roosevelt sat in his office doggedly working his way through a somewhat hysterical intelligence report evaluating purportedly secret Japanese political activities in Mexico and how they might relate to General Pershing's pursuit of Pancho Villa south of the Mexican border. As was often the case with compilations of raw intelligence hurriedly thrown together from various different sources, the report was written in a disjointed style, rife with innuendo and unsubstantiated rumor.

"By secret methods on or about April 21 last," it reported breathlessly, "Viscount Chinda, Japanese minister at Washington, notified [Mexico's] Secretary of Foreign Relations at Mexico City—*that Japan objected to the United States troops invading Mexico beyond Parral, Mexico, in pursuit of Villa.* Secretary Aguilar issued an order to General Louis Gutierrey, Military Commander of the Mexican troops, so directing this order as if it originated through Mexican decision." The report detailed purported close cooperation between the Mexicans under Villa and Japanese emissaries. "It was this order that caused the ambush of the United States troops when they arrived at Parral in search of Villa. . . . When the time was favorable for Villa to leave the protection of the Mayor's home, he was disguised as a Jap—his moustache, etc. removed—and under cover of the night and assisted by friendly Japs—he made his way North and safety—in Sonora."

In occasionally garbled prose, the report discussed some of "the obstacles with which the German-Jap-Villa-Carranza combination has to contend," the most significant obstacle being "the treachery of the average Mexican." In another section it described how "the Japanese spy system—under German advice" sent "skilled Japanese Navy and Army officers" to the United States disguised as "agricultural agents," purportedly to investigate American food production, but in actuality to spy on America's defenses.

Despite the almost comically shrill tenor of the report, Roosevelt read it carefully through to the end and ordered it filed for future reference. He did not necessarily believe the questionable details of sinister Oriental plots. What interested him were the repeated rumors gathered in the field suggesting cooperation between Japanese, German, and Mexican nationals which may or may not have had any basis in fact but which had been at the heart of an enduring American suspicion for years, simply because the likelihood of such an alliance was so logical. The fact that Germany and Japan were enemies in the current war, and that Mexico was a neutral party, had done little to discredit the suspicion. Everyone in Washington recognized that all it would take to create an international conspiracy would be a hastily arranged secret agreement between the three countries—or any two of them—to turn their adversarial relationship into a very powerful alliance. Only months earlier, Wilson had sent Marines into Haiti on the suspicion that German and French bankers were working in concert to collect on debts owed by the Haitian government, this despite the fact that Germany and France were locked in a war to the death. It is worth noting that within a year, every aspect of that improbable American nightmare would be confirmed.

That summer, Roosevelt was principally occupied with helping Josephus Daniels prepare the large new naval expansion bill called for by Wilson. "Our poor old Naval bill is still a bill and not a law," FDR wrote Eleanor, "but it looks as if the House would adopt the Senate increases when it comes up next Tuesday. They have agreed on a fool personnel provision that won't work as in practice it will create retirements, block promotions and do just the things it aims to prevent. They worked it out without consulting any of my board which had become expert in the figures."

Roosevelt's letters that summer express his mingled personal feelings about Josephus Daniels. At times he seems amused by his superior's deliberate ways, and at other times he expresses angry contempt at what he regards as his rustic simplemindedness and naïveté. Yet for all his condescension toward Daniels, there remains in FDR's comments a great affection, a great respect for Daniels's character and integrity. Throughout their years together in the Navy Department, their relationship continued to gravitate between sweet and sour. During the sunny times, they could exchange bits of nonsense that expressed their shared sense of humor. One example, found among Roosevelt's personal correspondence, was scribbled on a piece of official stationery labeled MEMORANDUM OFFICE OF THE ASSISTANT SECRETARY. Roosevelt, addressing his boss by his official acronym of "Secnav," wrote, "1. I beg to report (a) That I have just signed a requisition (with four copies attached) calling for the purchase of 8 Carpet Tacks. (Signed) Astnav," to which Josephus Daniels has appended, "Why such wanton extravagance? I am sure that two would suffice."

One particularly delicate congressional issue unique to the Navy Department involved the naming of vessels. Most warships were given geographic names—battleships were named for states, cruisers for cities, many lesser vessels for rivers, regions, and smaller towns—and the choice of names was a matter of vital concern for members of Congress, which in 1916 included a certain Representative J. Fred

Talbott of Maryland, who was determined to have the name of his hometown immortalized on a warship. Talbott was making life difficult for Assistant Secretary Roosevelt, who was only too happy to turn the matter over to Daniels:

> *My dear Chief:*
> *. . . In regard to the names . . . I am somewhat up a tree and am withholding the announcement . . . until I hear from you. Congressman Talbott wants the armored cruiser named Towson. I am ashamed to say that I never heard of Towson before! It turns out that it is the Congressman's county town—twenty-five hundred inhabitants—but really a suburb of Baltimore, the buildings being practically continuous between the two. I fear that we would get into a good deal of trouble if we took that name. About the only two places in Maryland that are possible, it seems to me, are Hagerstown and Frederick. We already have an Annapolis and Cumberland, and I have turned down the suggestion of certain people in the Department that she be called the Chevy Chase! I hate to go against Talbott's wishes, but suppose that the best thing to do is to do nothing for a while and I have merely told him that I would take the matter up with you. . . .*

The name eventually agreed upon was USS *Frederick*.

The work in Congress continued into some of the summer's hottest, most stifling weather. "The Sec'y is still busy with the Naval Bill," Franklin wrote Eleanor, "and I am trying though I fear in vain to eliminate a number of fool features in it and to get into it a few more really constructive items."

Late in August, Congress finally approved a bill providing for the construction of 156 vessels of all classes—including sixteen capital ships—within three years, and an increase in naval enlisted strength to 67,800 men. The total cost came to $600,000,000, the largest appropriation ever devoted to naval expansion by any country. Roosevelt could take note that within a month Wilson had become almost as hawkish as he was. Never before had America challenged Britain's position as the primary sea power, but with the passage of the naval bill Wilson told a confidant, "Let us build a navy bigger than hers and do what we please."

The summer of 1916 was also notable for bringing with it the worst ever outbreak of poliomyelitis, the mysterious and frightening viral disease that attacked the nervous system. Known to the public as "infantile paralysis" because it primarily attacked children, it struck down twenty-seven thousand victims that summer, of whom some six thousand died and thousands more were left permanently crippled.

Since the disease seemed to concentrate in cities, Roosevelt was anxious to get his family out of Washington as soon as practicable. He accompanied Eleanor and "the chicks" (now augmented by the infant John Aspinwall Roosevelt, born March 13, 1916, the final member of Franklin and Eleanor's family) to Campobello. There was a theory that the dread disease might be carried by houseflies, and Franklin spent hours swatting them there before returning to Washington. Only a few years into the future, FDR would become the world's most famous victim of polio, and there is a poignancy in the earnest letter he wrote to Eleanor on his return to Washington: "The infantile paralysis in N. Y. and vicinity is appalling. *Please* kill all the flies I left. I think it really important."

The epidemic raged long past the end of summer, and because Franklin and Eleanor were afraid to expose the children to the threat of catching the disease as a result of traveling on public transport, they did not want the children to return to Washington until FDR could commandeer a naval vessel to carry them south, which he was not able to arrange until October.

CHAPTER TWENTY-EIGHT

After the passage of the Navy Bill, FDR turned to the task of creating the Navy it authorized, only to discover that the raw materials to build and sustain such a mighty sea force were growing increasingly expensive and hard to find as the European powers chewed up billions of dollars worth of goods on an almost weekly basis. American mines and factories were working full tilt to supply the Allies, and Roosevelt and his staff had to search the world to find what they needed at reasonable prices. In 1916 alone, they purchased one and a half million pounds of shellac in Calcutta, a two-year supply of tin in Singapore, and another two-year supply of teak in Rangoon.

As the search for commodities expanded, Roosevelt discovered that there were times when he had to bend the rules to get what he wanted. Obtaining sodium nitrate was an example. Sodium nitrate was an important ingredient in the manufacture of explosives, but in the autumn of 1916 all the high-grade Chilean nitrate available in the United States was held by one company, which took advantage of its monopoly to jack up the price. Roosevelt protested angrily, but to no avail. So he sent Louis Howe, in an unofficial capacity, to look elsewhere. Howe soon discovered that the Chilean government had its own large supply of high-grade sodium nitrate, but to get it they were going to have to work under cover. Both Roosevelt and Howe were fully aware that there was a hard-and-fast rule that forbade any U.S. government agency from dealing with a foreign power except through the State Department, but Roosevelt decided to overlook such niceties. He sent Howe to the Chilean embassy with a direct appeal to purchase five million pounds of nitrates for the U.S. Navy. The Chileans recognized the unorthodox nature of the request but agreed to investigate the possibility. The request was, after all, coming from a senior American official, and it probably helped that his name happened to be Roosevelt, to boot.

A few days later, the Chilean diplomat met again with Howe, informing him that yes, his country would be pleased to furnish the requested nitrate. "But," he cautioned, "your specifications are so elaborate, we cannot guarantee—"

Howe raised his hand. "We will waive all specifications," he said gallantly. "This is not a matter for specifications, but of honor between two friendly countries. Just provide us with what you consider good nitrate."

For weeks Roosevelt and Howe waited anxiously while the nitrate was mined and shipped to Antofagasta, where a Navy collier picked it up for transport to the United States. By then, the Navy's top procurement officers had learned of the deal, and to a man they predicted disaster. The sodium nitrate, negotiated for by rank amateurs, would almost certainly prove either too volatile or too unstable, and in either case the Navy would have paid serious money for a useless commodity. When the cargo reached Norfolk, it was tested immediately, and the report was telephoned directly to Louis Howe's desk. The nitrate, it turned out, "was the finest ever shipped to the United States."

By November, many of the political questions relating to the presidential election that had been of concern at the beginning of 1916 had resolved themselves. Wilson, who had started out the year with little hope of gaining a second term, had been greatly helped by the Republican conservatives, who had once again turned down Theodore Roosevelt for the nomination, this time in favor of Charles Evans Hughes, a Supreme Court justice and one-time governor of New York, who was an eminently respectable but somewhat bland and colorless candidate. (Because Hughes was bearded, TR referred to him disparagingly as "Wilson with whiskers.") The war in Europe continued to overshadow all other issues, and Wilson had benefited at the polls with his party's rallying cry, "He kept us out of the war." Privately, Wilson was uncomfortable with the slogan. "I can't keep the country out of the war," he complained to Daniels. "They talk of me as if I were a god. Any little German lieutenant can put us into the war at any time by some calculated outrage."

On election night, the odds stood at 10-6 in favor of Hughes. Franklin joined other Democratic leaders at a large dinner party at the Biltmore Hotel in New York to await the results. The evening started off cheerfully enough, but as the returns came in it began to appear increasingly certain that Hughes was going to win decisively. Outside the Solid South, which always voted Democratic, Hughes had swept the entire Eastern seaboard with the possible exception of New Hampshire. The New York *Times* and the New York *World*, both of which newspapers had strongly supported Wilson, ceded the election to Hughes in huge headlines, calling it a "sweeping victory."

At midnight, with the first inconclusive votes from the Midwest beginning to filter in, Roosevelt and his friend, Interior Secretary Franklin K. Lane, left the Biltmore to catch the last train for Washington. Both men were aware they were likely to be out of a job in the very near future. Wilson felt strongly that the international situation was simply too volatile to safely accommodate the four-month interregnum between the election and inauguration of the new president, as called for by the Constitution. It was widely rumored that if Hughes were to win, Wilson planned to immediately name him secretary of state and then arrange for the resignations of both the president and the vice president. Under the rules of succession then in force, Hughes could then immediately assume the position of president and take control of the government. If the rumors were true, it meant that FDR might be out of a job within days. All of this would have been on his mind as he climbed into his Pullman berth that night.

What might his next steps be? If he planned to stay in politics, it meant returning to his roots in New York, where Tammany still reigned supreme. Was he willing to make peace with boss Charles F. Murphy and, if so, at what price? Or should he be thinking not of politics but of the military? As war seemed increasingly inevitable, should he be making plans to secure a commission and, if so, in what service and in what capacity? And of course, there was always the law. Should he form a new partnership, perhaps with State Department counselor Frank Polk, his Groton and Harvard colleague who would also be looking for employment outside the administration? And if it was to be the law, where would he practice? New York? Washington? Ironically, he and his family had just moved into a commodious new home at 2131 R Street NW. Would they now just as abruptly move out?

The one question that Roosevelt apparently did not consider as he surveyed his future that night was: what if Wilson won the election? But by the time his train pulled into Washington the next morning, that was the question all America was asking. As if by magic, and quite literally overnight, Hughes's commanding lead had shrunk to a much narrower majority, and as the votes continued to come in from the West, even that lead grew increasingly tenuous. "The most extraordinary day of my life," Franklin wrote excitedly to Eleanor, who was at Hyde Park. "Wilson may be elected after all. It looks hopeful at noon. The reaction from yesterday is great. All well here. . . ."

By the next day, Thursday, Wilson had moved into the lead, and FDR's next gleeful letter to Eleanor bubbled over with the statistics. "Another day of the most wild uncertainty. Returns, after conflicting, have been coming in every hour from Cal., N.M., N.D., Minn., and N.H. Without any of these Wilson seems to have 251 [electoral] votes safe, 266 necessary to choice. This P.M. it appears we have N. Dakota 5 votes safe and in California (13) we are well ahead, though there are still 200 districts to hear from. Minn. (12) looks less favorable, also N. Mexico (3), but N. Hamp. (4) is getting better and we may carry it. . . . It is warm today, real Indian Summer. I have any amount of work to do and J.D. is too damn slow for words—his failure to decide the few big things holds me up all down the line."

On Friday, when the final votes were in, it was the thirteen electoral votes of California that provided the margin of victory, and Wilson won by 277 to 254. With the election over, Wilson's focus quickly returned to the war in Europe and his self-appointed role as peacemaker. On December 18, he sent a note to all the belligerents requesting them to "state their views as to the terms on which the war might be concluded . . . in order that we may learn how near the haven of peace may be," but his attempts at mediation met a cool reception in the capitals of Europe.

Roosevelt, with his instinct for getting at the heart of the matter, now saw that the only hope of an Allied victory depended on America coming into the war. As the year ended, he found himself moving from a support of military preparedness to a position favoring military intervention. "We've got to get into this war!" became his new mantra. "I sincerely hope not!" Daniels would respond with feeling.

Nineteen-sixteen saw one other significant event in Franklin Roosevelt's life—perhaps one of the most important: the beginning of his love affair with Lucy Mercer.

Elliott Roosevelt, Franklin's oldest son, has left us a striking verbal portrait of his father at this period in his life. "Men and women alike were impressed by the sheer physical magnetism of Father. On meeting anyone, the first impression he gave was of abounding energy and virility. He would leap over a rail rather than open a gate, run rather than walk. The coach at the early-morning exercise classes which Father attended with a young group of other government officials said he was muscled like an athlete. Old ladies maneuvered to have him take them to dinner. Young women sensed the innate sexuality of the self-confident assistant secretary, who liked to work at his desk in shirt sleeves."

Such a man would by his nature seek ways to employ his energies both at work and play. He golfed and sailed and played poker late into the night when the opportunity arose. And because he was tied up all summer working on the naval appropriations bill, and was only able to manage a brief trip to Campobello in early August, it meant that he was alone in Washington for the better part of three months that summer. And because Washington is built on a swamp and in the summer could be unbearably hot and uncomfortable in an age long before air conditioning, it was something of a godsend to own an open car that one could drive off into the surrounding countryside in search of a cool breeze or even a cooler beach.

And then there was Lucy Mercer, someone closely involved with the Roosevelt family, a familiar figure, equally alone in the sweltering city. Well-bred, charming, very attractive, with a warm sense of humor, ready to laugh at Franklin's jokes, and impressed, as most people were, by his intelligence and drive.

When did the two fall in love? They were careful to leave no clues, so there is only conjecture, but for those who have looked longest and hardest at the question, the consensus seems to be that their romance first flowered in the summer of 1916.

Lucy had been hired by Eleanor in the late fall of 1913, and in those early days we can assume that Franklin originally saw her as a member of the household staff—someone on a par with a governess or nurse, perhaps. His perception of her would have changed considerably when, in addition to her secretarial duties, she was asked on occasion to become a guest at the Roosevelt dinner table when an extra female was needed. At such times she was a de facto equal, and an equal she remained when she once again reverted to her role as Eleanor's social secretary.

Each would have sensed the growing attraction, and we can safely assume that each would have suppressed any desire to encourage it. They were both principled people, mindful of propriety, and intelligent enough to recognize the potentially dangerous path that might lie ahead. But history, and daily newspapers and family trees, are filled with accounts of prudent, principled lovers who have flouted the conventional mores in order to fulfill their needs, and Franklin and Lucy were among the number who joined their ranks that summer.

Ever since the story of their love affair began to emerge after Franklin's death, the question has inevitably arisen as to its nature. Was it platonic? Conjugal? The most obvious answer is that the question is irrelevant. They lived during an age, and within a society, in which their romance, had it become public, would have been scandalous, even had it been platonic. Joseph Alsop, the prominent journalist and a distant relative of FDR who came from precisely the same social environment, stated unequivocally that in his opinion the affair could not possibly have been intimate. But it is probably naïve to think the two lovers would have been able to limit their relationship to the platonic. As we know from copious evidence, both of them recognized the romance as the great love of their lives. Franklin's strong libido, his determination to have what he wanted, the compelling urgency of his nature, all make the assumption of a platonic relationship difficult to sustain. Corinne Robinson, Eleanor's cousin, who was aware of the affair, thought it had a "profound effect on Franklin. It is difficult to describe, but to me it seemed to release something in him. . . . Up to the time that Lucy Mercer came into Franklin's life, he seemed to look at human relationships coolly, calmly and without depth. He viewed his family dispassionately and enjoyed them, but he had in my opinion a loveless quality as if he were incapable of emotion."

Was Franklin Roosevelt expressing a greater sense of self-confidence by engaging in a love affair with Lucy Mercer, or was it the other way around, and the love affair was an expression of his growing self-confidence that had been generated by other causes? Whatever the case, Corinne Robinson's thoughtful observation of Roosevelt's deepening character shows clearly that he was continuing to grow away from the shallow, awkward state senator-elect at the Gramercy Park tea dance, and toward the deeply thoughtful and compassionate leader who would lead his country, and then the world, out of the twin nightmares of the Great Depression and World War II.

CHAPTER TWENTY-NINE

I t was dawn on a morning in late January 1917, and Franklin Roosevelt was having an absolutely wonderful time. He was standing on the bridge of the United States destroyer *Wainwright*, dressed in top hat and morning coat. Above him fluttered the flag of the Assistant Secretary of the Navy, and before him lay the entire Atlantic fleet at anchor, awaiting his inspection: ninety-two warships drawn up in two parallel lines that stretched halfway to the horizon. The place was Port-au-Prince, Haiti, and the warm Caribbean sun was already making his heavy formal wear uncomfortable, but Roosevelt was enjoying himself too much to care. As the *Wainwright* made her way grandly through the massive display of seapower, each vessel in turn boomed out the seventeen-gun salute FDR so delighted in.

Early in January, when Josephus Daniels had offered to send him on an inspection trip to Haiti and the Dominican Republic, Roosevelt had jumped at the opportunity. The warmth of the Caribbean sun was a powerful inducement for such a trip in the midst of a wintry Washington, and an opportunity to get away from the frustrating indecisiveness of the Wilson White House was still a further attraction, but it was the political and military aspects of the trip that primarily intrigued him.

From the founding days of the Republic, the Caribbean had been a contentious sea of troubles for the nascent United States. Located right at the nation's doorstep, it presented a number of problems and headaches. It was dotted with islands controlled by European powers, each one a handy base for potentially troublesome naval operations. Dutch, British, French and Spanish planters governed the economy of the area, often assisted by pirates preying on merchant shippers trying to do business there.

The twentieth century had brought new problems. In 1906, when the Dominican Republic defaulted on its debts, Germany, which held a large number of Dominican bonds, threatened to invade. President Theodore Roosevelt hastily reinterpreted the Monroe Doctrine and sent the Marines into Santo Domingo before the Germans could make good their threat. More recently, the continuing civil instability and frequent revolutions in the Dominican Republic and Haiti, its neighbor on the island of Hispaniola, Woodrow Wilson had once again sent in the Marines.

And now Washington had something new to worry about—the Panama Canal. The Canal, so vital to the mobility of the U.S. Navy, could easily be compromised should an unfriendly power find a way to establish its presence in the Caribbean. The protection of the Canal was the main reason the Atlantic Fleet spent so much time at its base at Guantanamo.

Roosevelt made sure his inspection trip would be designed as much for recreation as it was for carrying out government business, and headed south on board a Navy destroyer on January 21, accompanied by his old college chum Livingston Davis, as well as by Major General George Barnett, Commandant of the Marines, and John A. McIlhenny, chairman of the U.S. Civil Service Commission. After a stopover in Cuba to sample the daiquiris and the nightlife, the group had steamed east to Haiti to begin the official part of the trip. After the fleet review, they spent several days exploring the interior, traveling on horseback through the back country, accompanied by 50 Marines and 150 Haitian militia.

Then it was on to the Dominican Republic, which occupies the eastern half of the island. Here they were greeted with appropriately elaborate ceremonies by the local Marine contingent stationed at Santiago.

On the evening of their arrival, as the party was enjoying an outdoor dinner hosted by the local Marine commandant and his wife, Roosevelt's orderly entered the courtyard and handed him a cryptic message from the secretary of the Navy which had just been received over the field radio set. Roosevelt recognized the code. It was a simple but effective one he shared with Josephus Daniels and Louis Howe for confidential communications, based on the word positions in a pocket dictionary that all three men carried. Roosevelt left the table to decode the message, and was instantly excited when he was able to make out the plain text: "Because of political situation please return to Washington at once," it read. "I am sending ship to meet you and party at Puerto Plata tomorrow evening."

The message actually told him little, but implied a great deal, and when he returned to the table he could not disguise his excitement. He told the others that he was being recalled because of "political conditions." His hostess, the commandant's wife, said, jokingly, "What can 'political conditions' mean? It must be that Charles Evans Hughes has led a revolution against President Wilson." FDR laughed. "My dear lady, you have been in the tropics too long!"

What *had* happened? he wondered. How had the political situation changed? Was the country on the brink of war? Was it actually *at* war? Roosevelt, an acknowledged hawk, was impatient to find out. He and his party cut short their inspection tour and immediately began making arrangements to get to the coast the next day.

The voyage north on board the Navy collier *Neptune* was tense and filled with speculation. Roosevelt and his companions had learned by radio prior to departure that Count von Bernstorff, the German ambassador in Washington, had been handed his passports and was on his way home, but there had been no further news. Did the ambassador's dismissal indicate the breaking of relations with Germany? It seemed likely. It also seemed probable that the United States and Germany were already at war, but there was no way to know if such were the case or not. The *Neptune* was sailing under strict wartime conditions, which meant her guns were manned around the clock, there were no lights at night, and the ship maintained strict radio silence. As she made her way north through the Caicos Island Passage, lookouts were posted with orders to keep watch for any signs of U-boats, while the passengers nervously discussed the possible ramifications of what little information they had.

Finally, on February 8, the *Neptune* made her way through the Virginia Capes and into Hampton Roads. When she landed her passengers at Fortress Monroe, they were nonplussed to discover that the Army colonel in command seemed utterly surprised by their concern. No, he told them, the United States was not at war, no special preparations had been called for, and there were no orders from Washington to stand by.

"Late that afternoon we were back in Washington," Roosevelt recalled later. "I dashed to the Navy Department and found the same thing . . . no excitement, no preparations, no orders to the fleet at Guantánamo to return to their home yards on the East Coast."

If Franklin Roosevelt, who modeled himself so closely on his Uncle Ted, and who yearned for a world of adventure and decisive action, was disappointed by the relaxed and unhurried atmosphere he found on his return to Washington, he need not have been overly concerned. War was in the air. In the early weeks of 1917, the world was changing significantly, and it would continue to change even more in the weeks ahead. The war that TR had been stridently calling for since the sinking of the *Lusitania* in 1915, and which FDR had quietly supported, would soon enough become a reality.

That decision had already been made in Berlin.

CHAPTER THIRTY

B y the end of 1916, it was apparent to all the belligerents, Allies and Central Powers alike, that their war had settled into an increasingly violent and bloody stalemate. Hundreds of thousands of troops on both sides were being sacrificed and untold billions of treasure wasted in a hopeless struggle. Three enormous battles—Verdun and the Somme in the west and Brusilov's Offense in the east—had been fought for little or no gain, and at sea a single encounter off the Jutland Peninsula between the Royal Navy and the German High Seas Fleet had changed nothing.

The Allies were running out of money. The Central Powers were running out of food. In London and Paris, the hope lay in somehow getting America to come to the rescue. In Berlin, the aim was more concrete: to break the stranglehold of the British blockade. For over a year, since the crisis over the sinking of the *Lusitania*, Germany had voluntarily limited the use of the U-boat, her most effective naval weapon, solely out of the fear that continuing the unrestricted submarine campaign would bring America into the war. But Germany had continued building more submarines, and with the new year the admirals, backed enthusiastically by the Kaiser, prepared to return to their earlier practice of unrestricted warfare regardless of the possible threat of American intervention. The high command estimated that the new campaign would force Britain to sue for peace within six months, and they were no longer concerned that the U-boats might bring America into the war. They estimated—quite accurately, as it turned out—that it would take America at least eighteen months to fully mobilize her huge industrial potential and put her on a wartime footing, by which time the Allies would have long since capitulated.

It was agreed that the planned return to unrestricted submarine warfare would be implemented on February 1, 1917. To maximize its effect, the German ambassador in Washington was instructed not to inform President Wilson of the new strategy until the last day of January. At the same time, the German foreign minister, Arthur Zimmermann, was instructed to explore the possibility of an alliance with Mexico, which could provide Germany with a Western Hemisphere base of operations, and would in any case serve as an important distraction to the United States, forcing her to deal with an enemy much closer to home.

As ordered, Count von Bernstorff delivered the unwelcome news to the president on January 31; and just three days later, the merchantman *Housatonic* became the first American victim of the revived policy. A furious Wilson ordered the German ambassador sent home, but took no other immediate action. Only Congress had the power to declare war, and he was not yet ready to ask it to go that far. The president was willing to pursue certain steps that were clearly defensive in nature, most notably the arming of American merchant ships so they could protect themselves against U-boat attacks. The shipowners were clamoring for such guns, and while the White House was eager to supply them—along with Navy gun crews to man them—there was a significant constitutional problem that stood in the way. By law, the government could neither sell nor give naval guns to the shipowners without congressional approval, and there was a small group of strongly anti-war senators that was determined to filibuster such a move.

Roosevelt was eager to find a way around the problem, and on the day after his return from the Caribbean he took the train to New York to discuss it with the shipowners. Out of those meetings he came up with what looked like a simple way around the need for congressional approval, which he outlined in a memo to Josephus Daniels on February 10:

"After my investigations in New York yesterday, it is clear that American ships cannot get guns suitable for arming themselves except from the government, and I believe the position of the American Line is well taken—that they cannot square it with their conscience to let their passenger ships leave New York without some protection, either convoyed or armed. . . . I have talked to Admiral Earle and find that we have no authority to sell serviceable ordnance material [but under] the law, however, guns may be *loaned* provided a suitable bond be given." Since the Navy would not surrender ownership of the guns, there was no need for congressional action. The matter could be taken care of with an executive order from the president.

Twenty-three years later, this deceptively simple solution would be the genesis of one of FDR's most far-reaching innovations in the early part of World War II, the proposal that led to the Lend-Lease Act.

As the crisis over the U-boats deepened and the likelihood of war increased, Roosevelt became a dynamo of activity. His skill at cutting red tape became almost legendary within the Navy Department. By then, everyone knew about his success with the Chilean nitrate deal; but in the three weeks following his return from the Caribbean, he far surpassed that record, placing orders for millions of dollars of war goods—guns, ammunition, depth charges, and other equipment—before Congress had even appropriated the money. "From February 6 to March 4," he claimed proudly in 1920, "we in the Navy committed acts for which we could be, and may be yet sent to jail for 999 years. We spent millions of dollars, which we did not have—forty millions on one contract for guns alone to be placed on ships to fight subs. We had only 100 ships and a 1,000 were needed. . . . We went to those whom we had seen in advance and told them to enlarge their plants and send us the bills."

Ever mindful of Admiral Mahan's principles, FDR was also worried about the scattered Navy. "I was Acting Secretary of the Navy and it was the first week in March," he would recall. "I went to see the President and I said. 'President Wilson, may I request your permission to bring the Fleet back from Guantanamo, to send it to the Navy Yards and have it cleaned and fitted out for war and be ready to take part in the War if we get in?' And the President said, 'I am very sorry, Mr. Roosevelt, I cannot allow it.' But I pleaded and he gave me no reason and said, 'No, I do not wish it brought north.' So, belonging to the Navy, I said, 'Aye, aye, sir,' and started to leave the room. He stopped me at the door and said, 'Come back.' He said, 'I am going to tell you something I cannot tell to the public. I owe you an explanation. I don't want to do anything . . . by way of war preparations that would allow the definitive historian in later days to say that the United States had committed an unfriendly act against the Central Powers.'" Wilson told FDR he wanted history "to show that war had been forced upon us deliberately by Germany."

Roosevelt could take what comfort he could from the president's statement, which made it clear that Wilson had had an important change of heart. He was no longer thinking about avoiding the war, but only about how to arrange America's entry into it.

Meanwhile, the British government had come across evidence that would make any American attempts to remain neutral virtually impossible. On January 16, 1917, British intelligence had intercepted a coded cable from the German Foreign Office and had sent it immediately to the British Naval Intelligence team in Room 40 at the Admiralty for decryption. It was from the German foreign secretary, Arthur Zimmermann, and was addressed to the German embassy in Washington, with instructions that it be forwarded to the German ambassador in Mexico City. In short order, the British had decoded enough of the message to recognize that it was diplomatic dynamite of such transcendent international importance that it could provide the means of bringing the United States into the war. Feverishly they set about completing the decryption, and by February 19 they had the complete text, in which Zimmermann instructed his ambassador in Mexico City to seek an alliance with the Mexican government as well as with Japan, and offering to provide material aid in helping Mexico regain territory it had lost in its war with America in 1848.

In clear, unequivocal terms it laid out a proposal for precisely the alliance that America's military leaders had been worried about for years, and which had been elevated to a major worry ever since the Magdalena Bay issue had surfaced in 1912. On February 23, British foreign minister Balfour met with the American ambassador in London, Walter Hines Page, and presented him with the original cyphertext, the decoded message in German, and the English translation:

> *We intend to begin on the first of February unrestricted submarine warfare. We shall endeavor in spite of this to keep the United States of America neutral. In the event of this not succeeding, we make Mexico a proposal of alliance on the following basis: make war together, make peace together, generous financial support and an understanding on our part that Mexico is to reconquer the lost territory in Texas, New Mexico, and Arizona. The settlement in detail is left to you. You will inform the [Mexican] President of the above most secretly as soon as the outbreak of war with the United States of America is certain and add the suggestion that he should, on his own initiative, invite Japan to immediate adherence and at the same time mediate between Japan and ourselves. Please call the President's attention to the fact that the ruthless employment of our submarines now offers*

the prospect of compelling England in a few months to make peace. Signed, ZIMMERMANN.

Here it was all in one ominous package: Germany, Japan, and Mexico in league against the United States. The stunned ambassador immediately notified the White House.

At first, there were suspicions in Washington that the Zimmermann telegram might be a clever forgery designed by the British to bring America into the war; but once its authenticity was confirmed, Wilson released the text to the public, where it created a predictable uproar. There were angry editorials from coast to coast and cries for war from every constituency, and if Wilson had been looking for an excuse to go to war, he now had it. But despite his own fury at the Germans, Wilson refused to act.

Wilson's ineffectual and timid lack of forceful response to the Zimmermann telegram angered and infuriated Roosevelt. Even FDR's suggestion for arming American merchant ships by loaning naval guns to the shipping lines had been ignored. Instead, Wilson had allowed the issue to founder in the Senate, where as predicted, four senators who opposed the move were filibustering against it. Roosevelt's diary on March 9 expresses his frustrations. "White House statement that W. has power to arm and *inference* that he will use it. JD says he will by Monday. Why doesn't the president say so without equivocation?"

Wilson was actually moving faster than Roosevelt realized. Recent steps taken by the Imperial German government had convinced him that it was dominated by iron-willed Junker militarists who would not be satisfied by a victory over the Allies, but would see it only as an encouragement to further adventurism. He now believed that Germany must be stopped, even if it meant America going to war. He could no longer hide behind the fact that he had just won reelection on the claim that "he kept us out of war."

On the afternoon of March 20, 1917, after three more American merchant ships had been sunk with heavy loss of life, Wilson convened his cabinet to deliberate the issue of war or peace. After laying out the options, he solemnly asked each member in turn what he would recommend. All of them, even Josephus Daniels, with tears brimming in his eyes, called for war.

Two other factors may have helped the agonized president come to a decision. One was the fact that only days before, the Czar of Russia had been overthrown in a liberal revolution by a faction led by Alexandr Kerensky. The argument that the Allies represented the democratic nations of Europe had always been questionable as long as the despotic Czar held power in Russia, but the ascension of a new government, based on democratic principles, made it much easier for Wilson to support the Allied cause.

The other factor—and the one that would have particularly appealed to Wilson's strong ego—was the recognition that only by entering the war would the president have a major voice in the peace treaty that would eventually end it. Wilson was determined that the war should be brought to a close in a "peace without victory," as he had proclaimed in his inaugural address only weeks earlier, and he was convinced that only he had the vision and the influence to bring about such a treaty. On March 21, the day following the fateful cabinet meeting, he called Congress into an extraordinary session to be held on April 2, "to receive a communication concerning grave matters of national policy."

Both Eleanor and Franklin were thrilled by the president's change of heart. The president was to address both houses of Congress, and it seemed everyone in Washington wanted to be there. FDR, as assistant secretary of the Navy, was guaranteed a seat with Josephus Daniels and the rest of the Cabinet directly below the Speaker's dais; but Eleanor, who was equally anxious to attend, had no official status, and it was only after considerable string-pulling and horse-trading that Franklin was able to obtain a place for her in the visitors' gallery.

Together, they were chauffeured through the drizzle to the Capitol early in the evening of April 2, and found their way to their respective seats. The chamber was crowded and expectant, and responded enthusiastically to the president when he arrived. All were aware of the importance of his speech, and most were supportive. The president, unsmiling, laid out the arguments against the German provocations, and made the case that "the world must be made safe for democracy."

The Roosevelts, along with almost the entire Congress, interrupted the speech time and again with cheers and applause. Prominent statesmen wept. Wilson closed by calling for a declaration of war against Germany, and the Congress rose almost as one to applaud him as he departed, still unsmiling. Franklin D. Roosevelt, standing by the steps, nodding to acquaintances and waiting in the crowd for his wife, was deeply stirred. Once again, President Wilson had come around to *his* point of view.

CHAPTER THIRTY-ONE

O
n April 6, Congress passed a resolution for war and Wilson immediately signed it. Swept up in the excitement of the moment, Franklin and Eleanor hurried over to Alice Roosevelt Longworth's mansion to welcome Uncle Ted, who had just arrived in Washington to pursue his latest project, recruiting a volunteer Army division, a larger version of the Rough Riders regiment that had catapulted him to fame.

As soon as they arrived at the Longworth's, Theodore rushed up to Franklin and, grasping him by the shoulders, insisted, "You must resign! You must get into uniform at once!" This was of course exactly what the younger man most wanted to do, but he explained that he was getting no encouragement whatsoever from either Josephus Daniels or Woodrow Wilson, both of whom insisted that their highly effective assistant secretary of the Navy stay precisely where he was.

It is also probably true that much as Franklin wanted to join the military, he was also beginning to recognize that his current civilian job carried with it far more power and authority over naval matters than he could ever hope to obtain as a commissioned officer. It was clear that the long and grueling European war that America had just entered into was a very different sort of conflict than the brief, toy-soldier war with Spain that Theodore had so skillfully stage-managed two decades earlier. It was a war of conscripts rather than volunteers, a war governed by railway schedules and bond issues rather than brave deeds and rallying cries. While it would undoubtedly be good for his future political prospects to end up in uniform at some point, FDR had every reason to believe that for the time being he could do more to win the war from his office in Washington.

Uncle Ted described his plans for raising his own personal infantry division and hurrying off to France and glory. In anticipation of America's entry into the war, Theodore had been corresponding since February with Secretary of War Baker, outlining his plans, but had received no encouragement from that corner. Now he asked Franklin to arrange a personal meeting with Baker, and FDR was able to set one up for the following day. Baker was respectful and solicitous, but remained vague and noncommittal, and Theodore realized that if he wanted his next great adventure to become a reality, he would have to humble himself as never before in his public life: with Franklin's help, he arranged a meeting with Woodrow Wilson.

It must have been an interesting confrontation, the meeting of the two men Franklin Roosevelt most admired, both of them fervent Progressives, but of such radically different personalities and preju-dices, and possessed of such profoundly deep antagonisms, that the gulf between the loud, pugnacious adventurer and the cold, stiff-necked Puritan idealist was probably unbridgeable. Even though Theodore Roosevelt had left the White House eight years earlier, at age fifty-nine he was still two years younger than Wilson. But he had aged significantly since his disastrous trip up the Amazon, where he had lost the sight of one eye and incurred permanent dis-abilities from tropical diseases. Wilson listened without comment to his predecessor's plan. TR estimated he could raise a volunteer division of twenty-five thousand men in a few weeks, then train them with the help of General Leonard Wood, and transport them to Europe before the end of the summer. The president cautioned that the war in Europe was no "Charge of the Light Brigade," but promised to consider the matter and bring it to the attention of the Army authorities.

After Theodore left, Wilson's private secretary, Joseph Tumulty, asked the president for his impression of Theodore Roosevelt.

"He is a great boy," Wilson replied thoughtfully. "There is a sweetness about him that is very compelling. One can't resist the man."

But when Wilson described TR's plan to General John Pershing, who was to lead the American Expeditionary Force, Pershing dismissed it out of hand. The last thing he needed was a rogue division roaming across Europe on its own, commanded by an independent glory-seeker determined to win new laurels. Wilson recognized that it would be imprudent to turn down the ex-president immediately. Theodore Roosevelt was still immensely popular, and millions would have enthusiastically approved his leading his own division. Wilson waited until the end of May before rejecting TR's proposal.

"It would be very agreeable to me to pay Mr. Roosevelt this compliment, and the Allies the compliment, of sending an ex-president," he announced, "but this is not the time for compliments or for any action not calculated to contribute to the immediate success of the war. The business now in hand is undramatic, practical, and of scientific definiteness and precision."

FDR was furious. "We ought to have sent TR over with a hundred thousand men," he complained bitterly to Daniels.

It was one thing for Congress to declare war on the Central Powers, but it was another thing entirely for the Navy Department to figure out how to wage that war. In those first confused weeks of April 1917, while the Americans awaited the arrival of British and French naval delegations who would presumably help the Americans coordinate their activities with the Allies, most of the admirals in Washington were busy getting their dreadnoughts and cruisers back from Guantanamo and readying them for action.

Meanwhile, Franklin Roosevelt and Admiral Frederick R. Harris, Chief of the Bureau of Yards and Docks, were studying the feasibility of something that would eventually come to be known as the North Sea Barrage, which would prove to be Roosevelt's most important contribution to the war effort.

Ever since Germany's return to unrestricted U-boat warfare in February, the number of merchant ships torpedoed and sunk had increased significantly. The Allies were doing their best to keep their losses secret, but it was becoming increasingly clear to observers in Washington that the losses must be precipitous. Roosevelt and Harris were exploring a way to counter the U-boat menace. Their idea was neither new nor particularly original. Many other officials, both military and civilian, had looked at a map of the North Atlantic and wondered if there wasn't some way to bottle up the German submarines in their home ports at Ostend and Zeebrugge, Belgium, northeast of the Straits of Dover in the English Channel, in such a way as to make it impossible for them to get to the killing fields west of Britain, in that part of the North Atlantic known as the Western Approaches, where most of the merchant ships were being sunk. Woodrow Wilson, on several occasions, had expressed to Josephus Daniels his surprise at the failure of the Admiralty to use its great naval superiority to somehow stop the U-boats. "Why don't the British shut up the hornets in their nests?" he asked. The Royal Navy was "hunting hornets all over the farm and leaving the nest alone."

Roosevelt proposed to solve the problem by blocking the U-boats' routes out of the North Sea. This would entail building a huge underwater barrier made up of minefields, nets, and other underwater obstacles stretching from Scotland east to Norway in the north, and a similar barrier across the Straits of Dover in the south. If successful, these two barriers, watched over by a fleet of patrol vessels, would bottle up the U-boats in their home ports and effectively neutralize them.

The idea, which was deceptively simple in theory, would depend on the practicality of its execution, which was problematic at best. Admiral Harris, who understood the enormous scope of the plan far better than Roosevelt, and who was familiar with the effectiveness of various anti-submarine devices, drew up a tentative project plan and an estimate of its costs, which were immense. When he studied the huge expenses involved, he was ready to drop the project then and there, but Roosevelt was undeterred. He had witnessed Uncle Ted's Panama Canal, and knew that, given the money and the will, great dreams could be turned into reality. He had the dream, and the United States Navy would supply the money.

FDR took the plans to the Navy's Bureau of Ordnance, where Commander S. P. Fullinwider, in charge of the mines section, was working on a similar idea. Fullinwider explained that his biggest problem had been the lack of an appropriate sea mine. Given the difficult conditions of the North Sea, with its strong currents, its great depth, its high tides, and its frequent storms, no one had ever developed a suitable explosive device that would remain operative long enough to do any good. Fullinwider had already put his people to work on the problem, so far without success.

On April 15, Roosevelt called a conference to consider the plans for the North Sea Barrier that he and Admiral Harris had worked up. Included in the meeting were Josephus Daniels, Admiral Harris, Chief of Naval Operations Admiral William S. Benson, as well as Chief of Ordnance Rear Admiral Ralph Earle and various technical specialists. Daniels was immediately excited by the potential of the project, and hurried next door to the White House to get Wilson's endorsement. The following day, with "the President's hearty approval," he sent a cable to Rear Admiral William S. Sims, the chief American naval officer in London. "Is it not practicable to block German coast efficiently and completely, thus making practically impossible the egress or ingress of submarines?" he asked. "The steps attempted or accomplished in that direction are to be reported at once." Sims's reply was discouraging. He cabled back that when he had broached the subject to the Admiralty, he was told that the British had considered the possibility of such a barrier earlier in the war, but had rejected it in part because it would be too expensive, and equally important, because the British had not been able to develop a mine that could stand up to the harsh conditions of the North Sea. Sims's negative response cooled the interest of Secretary Daniels and Admiral Benson, but Roosevelt refused to accept the Royal Navy's findings. He remained convinced he could overcome any inherent difficulty. All he needed was the right people and the right technology.

It was only when the various British naval missions began arriving in Washington in the following weeks, to establish a working relationship between the two navies, that Americans learned the shocking truth about the U-boat problem. To their astonishment and distress they learned that the U-boats were even more effective than they had feared, and were sinking one in every four oceangoing vessels clearing British ports. More ominous still, only some ten percent of the lost tonnage was being replaced. In April 1917, the month America entered the war, almost 900,000 tons of allied and neutral shipping was lost by enemy action, the vast bulk of it to the submarines. Admiral Jellicoe, First Sea Lord, described it as nothing less than "the greatest danger ever to face the Empire." The British were reduced to a few weeks' supply of grain and only ten days' stock of sugar. But the most serious shortage was that of oil. The Grand Fleet was so short of oil that its ships were forced to operate at half speed and any further constriction in the oil supply would cripple the antisubmarine effort. The British public had been kept in the dark about this dire situation, and the even greater secret that the Admiralty was not even sure how to solve the problem.

Desperate to find some solution to the U-boat crisis, the British had decided to try convoying, using destroyers to guard their merchant ships. Originally they had rejected convoying because it would have resulted in congested harbors, making it impracticable to assemble the convoys, but they hoped to circumvent the problem by arranging for the various vessels to rendezvous in some secret location on the open sea, where destroyers and other antisubmarine vessels would be on hand to guard them. Once assembled, the convoy, with its guardian destroyers, could move off to its final destination. While this was a promising shift in strategy, it meant there was suddenly a desperate need for destroyers to do the guarding.

The British had almost three hundred destroyers in their navy, but many could not be spared for convoy duty. They hoped the Americans could make up the difference. The United States Fleet included about seventy destroyers, most of which were needed to protect their capital ships. The admirals in Washington suggested they might be able to spare a squadron of six destroyers for guarding merchant convoys. When the British protested, the Americans explained they needed to complete their ambitious program of dreadnought construction they had embarked on in 1916. The British countered that the Allies had more than enough heavy warships in the British and French navies. What was needed now were destroyers, which could be built quickly and cheaply. They were perhaps the only means of counteracting the submarine menace. Only after long days of discussion did the British come to understand the American insistence on the larger ships, which arose from the U.S. Navy's deeply ingrained fear of a future two-ocean war against Germany and Japan. It was precisely that fear, spelled out in chilling detail in the Zimmermann telegram, that had brought the United States into the war.

Roosevelt, who was not willing to put his trust in the convoy system—he still strongly favored his North Sea Barrier—made a private suggestion to Colonel Edward M. House, Wilson's personal confidant. Perhaps the Americans could be persuaded to postpone their dreadnought program and concentrate on building destroyers if, following the successful end of the war in Europe, Britain would be willing to lend the United States sufficient battleships to provide for American security until such time as her own ships were ready. It was an interesting idea, and might have solved an important issue of American defense policy, but Wilson turned it down, because such an agreement would have to be secret, and he was convinced that such secret agreements between nations were the curse of European diplomacy and in fact, the direct cause of the war then raging.

As the two navies dickered, the mounting number of merchant ship sinkings made it clear that an immediate countermeasure was required, and eventually the British insistence on adopting the convoy system prevailed. The United States reluctantly agreed to suspend its dreadnought program in favor of a massive construction program to build 250 destroyers.

By the middle of May 1917, the convoy system was already being put into operation. The Royal Navy predicted it would solve the problem, but Roosevelt, for one, remained skeptical and never abandoned his determination to build an anti-submarine barrier across the North Sea. In the coming months he would meet stiff opposition, primarily from the Royal Navy, which did not take kindly to the Americans' temerity in questioning British naval authority, but in the long run he would get his way. It would be FDR's first major triumph in the halls of power, a harbinger of the skillful infighter who would in time emerge.

Roosevelt knew it was a sound idea, but he understood from the start that his plan had one major drawback—no one had come up with a sea mine sufficient to the needs of the proposed barrier, and, without such a mine, the plan was nothing more than a theoretical exercise.

CHAPTER THIRTY-TWO

O ne day late in May, fate intervened in the busy life of Assistant Secretary Roosevelt and moved his concept for a North Sea Barrier one step closer to reality. Shortly after noon, he looked up from his desk and saw a man standing before him who he later described as looking "just like one of the thousand[s] of crank inventors who pestered the Navy Department. . . . Most of them sported whiskers and carried black bags. And so annoying had they become that a retired Admiral with nice manners had been detailed to shunt them away from the active naval officers. One day one of them got through the guard. My secretary was out to lunch and he just walked in."

The man introduced himself as Ralph C. Browne, of Salem, Massachusetts. "I wanted to tell him to get out but I ended up with asking him what I could do for him. Well, he pulled out some sticks and proposed the same old idea that hundreds of others had of laying floating poles on the ocean from which submarine nets could be lowered. The only trouble was that any decent sea would knock it to pieces immediately. Then he showed me a peculiar looking affair with antenna-like attachments. 'When a sub hits the cable, they go off all at once,' he said.

"'Fine,' I thought. 'This is just what we have been looking for.'"

Roosevelt sent Browne over to see Commander Fullinwider at the Bureau of Ordnance with a note saying that he appeared to have "something interesting." Fullinwider and his assistant examined the model the inventor had brought with him, which he called the Browne Submerged Gun. The Navy men showed no interest in the gun itself, but the novel firing device at once caught their attention. It was made up of a copper antenna suspended from a buoy, which contained an electrical relay mechanism. If a submarine were to touch the antenna, the contact of metal closed the circuit and automatically fired the gun. Fullinwider thought that if the firing mechanism could be adapted to sea mines, it would solve one of his biggest problems. But Browne objected. He insisted that the key part of his invention was the gun, not the firing mechanism, and that it would not work on a mine. Fullinwider finally persuaded him to let the Navy try, and on June eighteenth a first crude model was tested at the submarine base at New London. On July tenth a new, more sophisticated model was tested with such success that the Bureau of Ordnance reported that it now had the makings of a new mine suitable for use in the North Sea. The Chief of Naval Operations took note. This achievement removed most of the remaining skepticism in the Navy Department, but the problem of manufacturing the enormous quantity of mines necessary, and of transporting and deploying them, remained imposing. Roosevelt began looking for an answer.

America's entry into the war was not only changing Roosevelt's job, it was changing the whole city of Washington. The sleepy Southern town was being transformed by a dynamic new energy, a new sense of urgency, and Eleanor and Franklin were both caught up in the change.

The war had brought with it a relaxation of the strict social code that Eleanor had been forced to live by. No longer was it quite so imperative to paper the town each week with calling cards, to remember quite so many birthdays and anniversaries, to make note of so many promotions and transfers. With the arrival of so many foreign missions, made up of officials on their own who needed to be welcomed and entertained, hostesses were hard pressed to find enough extra females for the luncheons and dinners they were called upon to give.

All of which meant that Eleanor had less need of Lucy Mercer as a social secretary, but a greater need of her as a dinner guest. On April 24, 1917, Eleanor arranged a small luncheon at which Lucy was invited as the extra woman, and the following Sunday she hosted a somewhat larger dinner party for Navy officers, and again Lucy was at the table. One of the other guests that evening was Eleanor's cousin Alice Roosevelt Longworth, one of Washington's most prominent gossips.

Alice, unhappily married herself, and with no particular fondness for her cousin Eleanor, had recently noticed a certain tension that seemed to be growing up between her and Franklin. Intrigued by the possibility of scandal, she began looking for corroborative evidence. One of the stories she began circulating that summer concerned the evening that the Roosevelts took their house guests, Warren Delano Robbins and his wife Irene, to a dance at the Chevy Chase Club. Around midnight, Eleanor excused herself and took a taxi home. The other three did not return to the R Street house until around four in the morning, and when they got there they were astonished to find Eleanor sitting forlornly outside on the doormat. She explained that she had lost her key. Franklin asked why she had not awakened the servants or taken a cab back to the club. Eleanor, in a pathetic voice, said that she did not like to bother people if she could possibly avoid it, and as for returning to the dance, "I knew you were all having such a glorious time and I didn't want to spoil the fun." The psychological term "passive-aggressive behavior" had not yet gained currency in that day, but everyone could recognize it when they saw it, and Irene Robbins, recalling that night, remembered thinking she would not "have blamed Franklin if he had slapped Eleanor hard."

As usual, summer arrived early and stifling in Washington, and Franklin Roosevelt was quick to use the perquisites of his office to escape the oppressive heat. On the weekend of June 16, he requisitioned the 124-foot government-owned yacht *Sylph*, which had been TR's favorite when he was president, and put together a small party made up of friends and family, including Lucy Mercer, who was invited presumably as company for Nigel Law, a young man from the British embassy who had recently become a close friend of Franklin's.

According to at least one account of that weekend, something transpired on board the *Sylph*—some troubling suggestion to Eleanor that there was a relationship between her husband and Lucy that she had not been aware of previously—that caused her to abruptly terminate Lucy's employment later that week.

Perhaps that account is correct, but subsequent events suggest it was just as likely that the decision to terminate Lucy's employment was made jointly by both Eleanor and Franklin—most likely with the involvement of Lucy herself—and simply reflected the changes that were taking place in Washington and in the Roosevelts' circumstances. Eleanor felt less need for a social secretary, and perhaps at the same time was feeling the pinch of wartime inflation. But both Roosevelts would have known that Lucy relied heavily on the money she got from Eleanor, and it was probably Franklin who came up with a solution—which was to keep Lucy on, but to cut her duties and salary significantly, and arrange for her to make up the lost income by joining the Navy Women's Corps. Whatever the circumstances, on June 29, 1917, Lucy Mercer was sworn in as a Yeoman's Third Class (F) at the Washington Navy Yard, and was promptly assigned to the office of the Assistant Secretary of the Navy.

The love affair between Franklin Roosevelt and Lucy Mercer is probably one of the most important, if shadowy, events in the life of this very important man. It marks one of the rare occasions when this otherwise circumspect individual, with a seasoned poker player's instinct for risk assessment, allowed himself to take a huge gamble and surrender to a passionate adventure. Whether the adventure began in 1916, as some speculate, there is no question that Lucy's move to the Navy Department in 1917 would have been critical to the development of their relationship. It must have been a remarkable experience for Lucy to find herself in Franklin's office, privy to the daily business at the heart of a great nation at war. She would have already been quite familiar with his private opinions of many of the people she was now meeting for the first time—Josephus Daniels, Louis Howe, Admiral Benson, and the others—from Franklin's casual and unguarded comments at his R Street home: and his often candid, and occasionally contemptuous, comments on his co-workers now became a new kind of secret the two lovers could share.

Eleanor was reluctant to leave for Campobello that summer, possibly because she feared for her marriage, but by the middle of July she could put it off no longer and departed with the children, leaving Franklin in Washington. It was there, on the morning of July 17, that he was startled to read in the New York *Times* a story about how rich families were dealing with wartime difficulties. Under the headline HOW TO SAVE IN BIG HOMES, he read: "The food saving program adopted at the home of Franklin D. Roosevelt, Assistant Secretary of the Navy, has been . . . a model for other large households. Mrs. Roosevelt . . . said that there were seven in the family, and that ten servants were employed. Each servant has signed a pledge card and there are daily conferences. Mrs. Roosevelt does the buying, the cooks see that there is no food wasted, the laundress is sparing in the use of soap, each servant has a watchful eye for evidence of shortcomings on the part of the others; and all are encouraged to make helpful suggestions in the use of 'left overs.' No bacon is used in the Roosevelt home; corn bread is served once a day. The consumption of laundry soap has been cut in half. Meat is served but once daily, and all 'left overs' are utilized. Menu rules allow two courses for luncheon and three for dinner. Everybody eats fish at least once a week. 'Making the ten servants help me do my savings has not only been possible but highly profitable,' said Mrs. Roosevelt . . . 'prices have risen, but my bills are no larger.'"

As a politician with a keen awareness of his public image, Roosevelt would have cringed at the picture of the entire staff in his office discussing the assistant secretary's family and its ten servants bravely making do with fish at least once a week as they struggled along with "left overs" while doggedly saving soap. Somewhat shaken, but maintaining a jocular mood, he dashed off a good-natured but pointed note to Campobello:

> *All I can say is that your latest newspaper campaign is a corker and I'm proud to be the husband of the Originator, Discoverer and Inventor of the New Household Economy for Millionaires! Please have a photo taken showing the family, the ten cooperating servants, the scraps saved from the table and the handbook. I will have it published in the Sunday Times.*
>
> *Honestly, you have leaped into public fame, all Washington is talking of the Roosevelt plan and I begin to get telegrams of congratulation and requests for further details from Pittsburgh, New Orleans, San Francisco and other neighboring cities.*

Eleanor's embarrassed response exhibited appropriate contrition: "I do think it was horrid of that woman to use my name in that way and I feel dreadful about it because so much is not true and yet some of it I did say. I never will be caught again that's sure and I'd like to crawl away for shame."

Alice Longworth remained in Washington through the summer, and kept a cousinly eye on the comings and goings of Franklin and Lucy, as well as the young man from the British Embassy, Nigel Law, who so often seemed to accompany them. The three were seen to spend considerable time together on board the *Sylph* and elsewhere, where Nigel played the part of Lucy's escort as a cover for Franklin. Alice would undoubtedly have understood the subterfuge.

One day Franklin received a telephone call from Alice. "I saw you twenty miles out in the country," she said. "You didn't see me. Your hands were on the wheel, but your eyes were on that perfectly lovely lady." Franklin answered blithely, "*Isn't* she perfectly lovely." Apparently he felt he could trust Alice.

CHAPTER THIRTY-THREE

The summer of 1917, for all its pleasantly romantic aspects, was in large part a summer of frustration and discontent for Franklin Roosevelt. The main reason for his unhappiness was the man sitting in the next-door office, Josephus Daniels. FDR's relationship with his superior, ranging from warm cordiality one day to haughty contempt and distrust the next, was acceptable during peacetime; but now that America was at war, now that lives were at risk, now that decisions—or the lack of them—resulted in real consequences of blood and money, Roosevelt was no longer willing to forgive what he saw as defects in Daniels that in his opinion amounted to something close to criminal negligence.

Daniels's greatest sin in Roosevelt's eyes was procrastination. He appeared to have no sense of urgency in the running of the Navy Department. In an angry, ten-page private memo now in the FDR Library at Hyde Park, the assistant secretary described how Daniels's mismanagement had created serious problems when America's entry into the war had made it necessary to double the Navy's personnel. In the months leading up to April 1917, Daniels was told "hundreds of times" that the Navy would have to expand from 70,000 to 150,000 in a very brief time—a month or two at the most—and it was crucial that preparations be made for that event. "The Surgeon General begged for reserve tents, hospital supplies, etc. etc. [T]he Bureau of Navigation begged for additional training camp sites. The Bureau of Supplies and Accounts begged for additional clothing. It was not until *well along in March* of this year that they were able to obtain the authorization to spend the money to get these things even though the money was appropriated. The result has been a disgrace to the country. The conditions at the four regular training camps—Newport, Norfolk, Great Lakes and San Francisco—have been such that contagious disease of every form, spinal meningitis to measles, has taken a large toll of men. The hospitals have been overcrowded and the actual training of the men has been put on a far less efficient basis. This is due not only to the delay of the past, but to the impossibility of getting a decision yes or no immediately."

FDR poured out his frustrations, citing one case after another of delay caused by what he saw as Daniels's confusion and procrastination. In an ironic comment on Daniels's negotiations over munitions contracts, he wrote: "it is absolutely true that the secretary has saved the government much money by dickering with steel plants, shipbuilding companies etc. etc., but it is an absolute fact that the savings caused by these long preliminary negotiations has been eaten up many times by the fact that when war actually came on April 7th the government had to jump in and purchase millions of dollars worth of supplies at higher figures in order to make up for the deficiencies."

Nor was Daniels the only one to blame. Roosevelt was equally scathing of Admiral William Benson, who Daniels had specifically selected to be Chief of Naval Operations, and who "proceeds cautiously and slowly from day to day with little questions of dispatching gunboats around the West Indies, with pleasant chats with American and foreign officers, who also come to talk about a hundred different subjects, and every matter of real moment is delayed from 24 hours to 24 weeks. . . . The whole question resolves itself down to this: in the Secretary's office the least that can be said is that there is constant delay and lack of decision— so much, in fact, that the actual naval operations in this country by the United States have been seriously threatened. The delay of two months, which has already occurred, has, in all probability, meant the loss of many thousands of tons of merchant shipping. The same delay . . . if it is carried to its logical conclusion . . . may mean . . . the actual winning of the war by the enemies of the United States."

The memo, undated, unaddressed, and unsigned, stands as mute and angry evidence of FDR's determination to move things forward, and his frustration at being stymied. Of course, the fact that the memo is undated, unaddressed, and unsigned also makes it clear that he understood that in the world of Washington bureaucracy, there was always a need for discretion.

But not all of FDR's problems originated in Washington. High on his list of frustrations were his dealings with the British Admiralty and its stubborn opposition to his pet project, the North Sea Barrier. While Roosevelt was busy encouraging the development and testing of an appropriate sea mine, and setting up a program to manufacture and deploy it should it prove satisfactory, the Admiralty was doing its best to scuttle the whole idea. Typical of the Royal Navy's diffident reaction to the barrier was the politely worded but dismissive letter from Rear Admiral Dudley R. de Chair:

12 July 1917

My dear Roosevelt,
You will remember that before I left Washington you handed me a memorandum on the submarine situation, dated May

24th, in which you advocated a scheme for placing a barrier between Scotland and Norway in order to prevent the egress of enemy submarines. Your memo was put before the Board of Admiralty and they are of the opinion that though the placing of such a net is practicable the difficulties attending its maintenance, and the prevention of submarines from passing through it or over it are so great as to render it of secondary value compared to the present methods of dealing with the submarine menace.

I find that such a barrier has already been tried in the Channel but has not been satisfactory.

After the Ordnance people had developed a promising design for a North Sea mine and tested it successfully off New London, Admiral Benson, in Washington, cabled Admiral Sims, the chief U.S. Navy officer in London:

18 August 1917

Bureau of Ordnance has developed mine, which [it] is hoped may have decisive influence upon operations against submarine. Utmost secrecy considered necessary. Request that officer representing Admiralty, clothed with power to decide, be sent here to inspect and thoroughly test mine. If found satisfactory arrange for cooperation in mine operation.

The Admiralty did indeed detail officers to examine the new mine, and they were impressed, but the Admiralty remained unmoved and still doubted the effectiveness of the barrage.

On September 25, Admiral Sims explained in another cable the Admiralty's patronizing disdain of the American plan:

. . . it is hardly possible to do anything efficient in the way of manufacturing or laying mines without taking full advantage

of all of the experience which has been gained on this side in actual warfare. It is by reason of the very bitter experience which the English and French have had in this particular respect that they are so reluctant to accept a mine which is believed by those having no war experience to be superior to theirs instead of going ahead with the manufacture of a mine which has been tried out in actual experience until it has proved satisfactory. . . . This is a good scheme if it works but a very expensive one if it does not. . . .

Through all this transatlantic chatter, President Wilson looked on with growing irritation. If Britannia ruled the waves, as everybody seemed to believe, why had the Royal Navy been so conspicuously ineffective throughout the war? Not only had it failed for three years to solve the U-boat problem, but for all its vaunted power it had not been able to bring the German fleet to action, other than in the one inconclusive instance at Jutland. "Every time we have suggested anything to the British Admiralty," Wilson complained to a group of American naval officers, "the reply has come back that virtually amounted to this, that it had never been done that way, and I felt like saying, 'Well, nothing was ever done so systematically as nothing is being done now.'"

Roosevelt had insisted from the start that time was of the essence in laying the barrier and finally, on October 3, he gave up waiting for approval from the Admiralty and put in an order for 100,000 of the new firing devices. Within weeks, five hundred contractors and subcontractors were at work manufacturing various parts. Only then, in late October, was Sims finally able to confirm, "Admiralty has approved mine barrier."

In celebration, FDR addressed a triumphant memorandum on the subject to Daniels, which in places is notable for its discourteous and even rude tone and shows an almost childish determination to claim full credit for the project:

Washington, October 29, 1917

MEMORANDUM FOR THE SECRETARY

Subject: Proposed measures to close English Channel and North Sea against submarines by mine barrage.

1. This is, of course, nothing more nor less than a resurrection of my proposition, which, with all earnestness possible, I called to the attention of the President, the Secretary of the Navy, the Chief of Operations, the General Board, Admiral Sims (and through him the British Admiralty), Admiral de Chair (and through him also the British Admiralty) and Admiral Chocheprat (and through him the French Ministry of Marine) during the months of May and June past.

2. While I have never claimed that the proposed plan was an infallible one, and while, quite properly, I have never attempted to lay down the exact location or the exact type of mines, etc., to be used in the barrage, I did state, and still state, that every consideration of common sense requires that the attempt be made, first in the English Channel and then in the North Sea.

3. But above all, starting when the Balfour and Viviani Missions were here in May, I reiterated the need for haste. I know how unseemly it is to seem to say "I told you so," but it is a literal fact that, while the British Admiralty may be blamed in part, our own Navy Department is at least largely responsible for failing to consider this proposition seriously during all of these months—May, June, July,

August, September and October—which have gone over the dam beyond recall.

4. Now, this is the milk in the cocoanut: The powers that be seem at last willing to take up this proposition seriously. Unless we are willing to throw up our hands and say it is too late, we must admit that the same need for immediate haste exists today as existed last May. We have done altogether too much amiable "consideration" of this matter. If it is to be carried out at all it must be carried out with a different spirit from any of the operations up to now. It will require prompt decision all along the line and an immediate carrying out of the procurement of the material—mines and ships.

5. To accomplish the above it should be placed in the hands of one man on our part and one man on the part of the British. These two men should receive orders from their governments, not as to details, but simply orders to carry out the plan. *And most important of all, these men should have all the authority requisite to do this.* This is a bigger matter than sending destroyers abroad or a division of battleships, or building a bunch of new destroyers—it is vital to the winning of the war. Its success cannot be guaranteed. No military or naval operation can be guaranteed. But if it works it will be the biggest single factor in winning the war. I have seen something during the past four and a half years of how our present Navy Department organization works and it so happens that I am also fairly familiar with the way the British Admiralty works. If the suggested plan is carried out solely under the present organizations its chance of success will, in my judgment, be seriously diminished. You need somebody with imagination and authority to make the try.

6. I know you will not mind my sending a copy of this to the President, as I have discussed it with him several times.

FDR's memo, in which he takes the lion's share of the credit for the project, may have been more than a little self-serving, but it was also probably true. As Admiral Harris observed years later, "If Roosevelt had not been there the North Sea Barrage would never have been laid down."

But Roosevelt's sense of triumph was not to be unalloyed. Lucy's work at the Navy Department was going well. As someone with a good sense of style, she was probably distressed by the shapeless and ungraceful uniform she was required to wear as a yeomanette, but the job kept her close to Franklin, and that would have been what mattered. She was soon promoted to yeomanette second class, with a performance rating of 4.0. But four months after her naval career began, it suddenly came to an abrupt end, and she was discharged by "Special Order of Secretary of the Navy," with no reason given. It seems likely that Josephus Daniels had heard something about his assistant secretary and the lady in question and had decided to take matters into his own hands.

CHAPTER THIRTY-FOUR

Roosevelt had grown up with an innate admiration for business and businessmen, but he had discovered during his years in the Navy Department that businessmen could sometimes play rough, and when that happened the only appropriate response was to play even rougher. One such confrontation arose when the State Department asked him to deal with a dispute between the government of Argentina and the huge Fore River Shipyard in Quincy, Massachusetts.

Roosevelt had been instrumental in arranging for the shipyard to build two battleships for Argentina, but when construction was completed and the Argentine Navy came to collect their new ships, the shipyard refused to release them until they had been paid for in full. The Argentines, referring to the original contract, suggested a deferral of payment, but the shipyard, pointing to the same contract, was adamant. No money, no battleships.

The U.S. State Department feared a potential international incident. With America now at war, State was particularly keen on avoiding any unnecessary foreign confrontations. The problem was handed over to

Franklin Roosevelt, who had helped broker the deal, and who dealt regularly with the Fore River Shipyard regarding U.S. Navy requirements. He was friendly with the shipyard's assistant manager, a tough Harvard-educated Boston Irishman named Joseph P. Kennedy. The paths of these two young men would continue to cross in the years ahead, and the fact that Kennedy, along with Roosevelt, would rise to prominence in the Democratic Party—first as a member of FDR's administration and later as father of John F. Kennedy—gives a unique resonance to their faceoff over the Argentine battleships.

In the normal course of business, the two men got along well, so when Kennedy came into FDR's office to discuss the Argentine battleships, it is likely that they both were confident they could settle the problem quickly. Roosevelt explained the State Department's worry about an international incident, but Kennedy was not sympathetic. His shipyard, part of Charles M. Schwab's mighty Bethlehem Steel Company, wanted its money, and that was that. End of discussion. "But the State Department will collect the money for you," Roosevelt pleaded. Kennedy refused.

Roosevelt tried to reason with him, pointing out that if the two of them could not agree on a way to release the battleships, the U.S. Navy would simply take them by force and turn them over to the Argentines. Kennedy thought that highly unlikely. He would not budge. The two men parted amicably, but with no resolution to their problem.

Later, Kennedy reported the substance of the meeting to Charles Schwab, describing Roosevelt as "a smiling four-flusher." Schwab laughed and told Kennedy, "We'll call this youngster's bluff."

It was only a few days later that Kennedy learned just how profoundly he had misjudged the soft-spoken FDR, when he looked out his office window and saw four tugboats steaming into the shipyard, each crowded with armed Marines. Without so much as a court order to justify their actions, the Marines clambered onto the dock, took command of the two battleships, cast off their lines, and towed them into the harbor, where they turned them over to waiting Argentine crews.

Years later, Kennedy would admit that "Roosevelt was the hardest trader I'd ever run up against."

The urgent imperatives brought on by the war led very quickly to a certain kind of bureaucratic ruthlessness, and Roosevelt discovered that he was very good at it. Even before the United States officially entered the war, he had established a reputation as something of a pirate when it came to amassing strategic war materiel. He liked to tell the story of the day, soon after the declaration of war, when he was summoned to the White House and was confronted by both President Wilson and Army Chief of Staff Major General Hugh Scott. The president looked at Roosevelt—with a twinkle in his eye, according to Roosevelt—and said, "Mr. Secretary, I'm very sorry, but you have cornered the market for supplies. You'll have to divide up with the Army."

As American business geared up for wartime manufacturing, the need for such banditry increased. When the Navy agreed in May 1917 to set aside its ambitious program for building dreadnoughts in favor of its even more ambitious program for building 250 destroyers, it opened up immense gaps in the manufacturing process that threatened to play hob with delivery schedules. It quickly developed that the first of the new destroyers would soon be ready to go to sea, except for the fact that they still lacked certain shafting and other essential details. There were no plants in existence which could turn out the required shafts, so Roosevelt, pressed for time, picked out the Erie Forge Company at Erie, Pennsylvania, and offered to build a plant for the company, to be paid for later by the company or else kept by the Navy Department. The plant was put up in record-breaking time. As the plant neared completion, it required a particular kind of motor generator. Roosevelt and Howe scoured the market in search of one, but there were none to be found. They approached the General Electric Company and were told that yes, that company had just completed a similar generator for another customer which was still in the process of being delivered, but they could not begin building a new one in less than three months.

Roosevelt and Howe arranged for a bright young man, armed with a blank naval commandeering order, to poke around the railroad yards in search of the generator. In a long freight train parked on a siding at Philadelphia, he came across a promising object consigned simply to "General Electric, New York." It proved to be the generator. He slapped the commandeering order on it, and ordered the car cut out of the train. Within two hours it was on its way to Erie. Some time later, the Navy Department received a letter from an official of the Statler Hotel Company in New York City, explaining good-naturedly that the Navy probably didn't know it, but it had delayed the opening of the Hotel Pennsylvania for three months.

Once it became clear to Roosevelt that his superiors were not going to let him resign his office in order to get into uniform, he put aside his disappointment and determined to make the best of the situation. There was more than enough work to keep him busy in Washington, he knew, but amid all the urgency and shifting priorities and general hurly-burly of a Navy Department suddenly immersed in the greatest war in history, there was also a more provincial problem which he knew required his attention: he needed to mend fences with Boss Charles F. Murphy of Tammany Hall.

His resistance to Murphy back in the fight over Sheehan had been the making of Roosevelt's reputation as a champion of clean government. It had also undoubtedly helped him come to the attention of Woodrow Wilson, and thereby contributed to being named assistant secretary of the Navy. But there had been other occasions more recently when the enmity between FDR and Murphy had hurt him politically. In 1914, when he had tried to run for the Senate, Murphy had swatted him down like a house fly, and made him something of a laughing stock. More recently, on Election Day 1916, when it looked like Wilson might lose and Roosevelt might soon be out of a job, he had come to realize how valuable it might have been to be in Boss Murphy's good graces. From Roosevelt's perspective, it made sense to try to come to some sort of understanding with Murphy at a time when there was no immediately pressing need to do so.

Of course, there was always the possibility that a rapprochement with Tammany might reflect poorly on Roosevelt's good government credentials, but if handled properly that need not be a problem. Besides, what good would his reputation do him if Murphy saw to it that he never got another nomination?

So in the spring of 1917, negotiations were opened between the squire of Hyde Park and the Grand Sachem of Tammany, and in due course an accommodation was reached, and the peace between two very different kinds of Democrats, one an aristocrat and proud of it and the other a commoner and equally proud of it, was finally confirmed by a photograph taken at a political rally on July 4, 1917. It shows two unsmiling pols, looking uncomfortable and standing stiffly side by side, mute testimony to one of the basic truths of American democracy: political power grows out of the grass roots, and the politician who ignores that fact does so at his peril. Within a year, Roosevelt's accommodation with Boss Murphy would start to pay dividends.

Much of Roosevelt's time was now taken up with pressing ahead with the North Sea Barrier program—or, as it was now being referred to, the North Sea Barrage, a more satisfyingly aggressive title. It was a massive operation requiring a huge workforce and factories on both sides of the Atlantic. The individual parts that made up the mines—the housings, antennae, electrical elements, explosives, safety devices, and such—were all contracted for through bids to hundreds of suppliers. A new subassembly plant of twenty-two different buildings was constructed at St. Juliens Creek, Virginia, near Norfolk, to receive, assemble, load, and ship a thousand mine cases a day. For greater safety and efficiency, the plant incorporated the global assembly-line system recently perfected by Henry Ford to build automobiles.

The new factory began operating in March 1918, by which time the Navy had assembled a special fleet of twenty-four lake cargo carriers dedicated specifically to the North Sea Barrage program, which began sailing from Norfolk at the rate of two or three every week. The mines were landed on the west coast of Scotland to avoid the greater danger of U-boats in the North Sea, and transported overland to the two final assembly points at Inverness and Invergordon. Here, a locally recruited work force of 2,200 men completed the final assembly of the mines and loaded them on the minelayers. The Americans would eventually lay some 56,000 mines, while British vessels would lay 16,300 more. The cost would eventually be huge—eighty million dollars. But it was less, as Roosevelt liked to point out, than the cost of a single day of the war as a whole.

While the fighting in 1917 did not turn out to be quite as bloody as 1916, the year ended on a sobering note. In November, the Kerensky government in Russia, which Wilson had welcomed in March because it toppled the old Czarist monarchy, was in its turn toppled by the Bolsheviks, under the leadership of Vladimir I. Lenin. On taking power, Lenin issued a call to all the belligerent powers to lay down their arms and negotiate a peace, and pledged to publish the secret treaties entered into by the Czar's government, treaties that the Bolsheviks now declared null and void. It was generally recognized that it was exactly such secret covenants, secretly arrived at, that had unintentionally brought about the war currently raging across Europe, and the Allies were acutely aware that their starchy new co-belligerent, Woodrow Wilson, who was already suspicious of British, French, and Italian war aims, wanted to outlaw such private agreements in the future.

In response to the Bolshevik revelations, Wilson, in a speech to Congress on January 8, 1918, included a list of fourteen points that he was determined should govern international relations in the postwar years. The first five points were general in nature, calling for "open covenants . . . openly arrived at," freedom of the seas, removal of trade barriers, disarmament, and national self-determination. The next eight were specific, dealing with such matters as evacuation of Russian and Belgian territory, the future of Poland, and the return of Alsace-Lorraine to France. The final point called for "a general association of nations," or what would in time become known as the League of Nations.

Like everyone else in a position of power in Washington, Franklin Roosevelt was fully conversant with Wilson's program and its purpose, but he was too busy with his own responsibilities to pay much attention, and may well have ignored the president's promise on February 11, 1918, that there "shall be no annexations, no contributions, no punitive damages" at war's end. This provision, so diametrically at odds with the plans of the Allies for punitive damages from the Kaiser's government, would shape the politics of the peace table and beyond and would determine Roosevelt's political philosophy for the rest of his life.

On March 3, 1918, while FDR was attending to the myriad details involved in the North Sea Barrage, the new Bolshevik government in Russia signed the Treaty of Brest-Litovsk, which formally ended the war on Germany's eastern front and promised to make the rest of the war much more difficult for the Allies. It made possible the massive transfer of German troops from Russia to the west, greatly strengthening Germany's ability to fight, and at the same time put the Ukraine into the hands of the Central Powers to serve as a granary, thereby offsetting the effects of the Allied blockade. Just two weeks later, on March 21, General Erich Ludendorff, supreme commander of the German armed forces, launched the first of a series of massive assaults on the British and French lines intended to overwhelm them before America's growing strength became effective on the battlefield.

Roosevelt was still determined at some point to get into uniform and into the fight; but, faced with the opposition of Wilson and Daniels, who insisted that he remain at his post, he looked around restlessly for some way to enlarge his role in the war. By the spring of 1918, his work on the North Sea Barrage was completed, and he decided it was time for him to get across the Atlantic to where the action was, even if he had to do it in his civilian capacity. In a plaintive memo to his superior, he laid out his argument for a European tour.

Washington, April 5, 1918

My dear Mr. Daniels:

Following our several talks recently, and as you suggest, I am putting down a rough list of the various activities of the Navy on the other side. As you know, most of the requisitions for materials, and you might say the business and legal part of the Naval operations in Europe, come over my desk. Their volume has assumed such proportions and such a diversity that it is next to impossible for those over here without a close knowledge of affairs over there to form an intelligent opinion upon which to base appropriate action. All the Navy shore stations, whether in Ireland, England, France or Gibraltar, are theoretically under Admiral Sims, and the cables in regard to these stations are reaching a very large daily total. It is obvious from an inspection of these daily cables that while of course Admiral Sims has been magnificent in the way he has handled the work, it would be a great help to him to have me go over there for a short time to help him coordinate the business end of his work. Admiral Benson entirely approves, and Admiral Sims himself has written that he would be only too glad if I could go over.

I hesitate to speak about the personal side of it, but many of the returning officers have been good enough to say that it would help our Naval officers and men on the other side if I could look in on them and see their work at first hand.

But aside from this I feel the business efficiency of the forces and especially of the shore stations could be benefited. And there

have been a good many cases in the cables of late that made
me feel that things could be improved from the administrative
standpoint.

If the President approves, there is no particular reason why I
could not go now just as well as later. I could perfectly well catch
the cruiser that leaves on Sunday.
Very sincerely yours,
Franklin D. Roosevelt

Before he had a chance to persuade Daniels to act on his memorandum, Roosevelt was presented with a highly tempting political
opportunity from an unlikely source: Charles F. Murphy of Tammany
Hall sent a personal emissary to Washington to offer him the Democratic nomination for governor of New York. It was the first dividend
from the agreement the two adversaries had reached the previous
July. Under ordinary circumstances such an important offer would
have been welcomed as an exciting opportunity, particularly since the
governorship was a key step in the career plan he had so confidently
defined even before he had entered politics.

But tempting as Murphy's offer was, Roosevelt was reluctant to
accept it. His political instincts told him that it simply would not look
right if he campaigned for governor while the war still raged, and the
general consensus was that the latter would continue for a long time to
come. In that spring of 1918, virtually no one believed that the Allies
could possibly win by the end of the year. At best, everyone expected
that the war would grind on at least through 1919. If he were to desert
his post in the Navy Department to make the run for governor, it
would be seen either as overblown egotism, or, even worse, an admission that his job as assistant secretary was not all that important.

Then in mid-June, President Wilson increased the pressure on
Roosevelt by asking Daniels to "tell Roosevelt he ought not to decline
to run for Governor, if it is tendered to him." But Roosevelt remained
reluctant.

When Roosevelt finally convinced Josephus Daniels that he could not be induced to run for governor despite the urging of Woodrow Wilson himself, Daniels relented and authorized the inspection trip to Europe for which Roosevelt had so long campaigned. The trip, which would last two months, would turn out to be everything FDR could have hoped for, a personal triumph he would remember fondly for the rest of his life. It would include meetings with virtually all the leading political and military leaders running the war, as well as a close-up view of the war itself. On July 9, he set sail in the USS *Dyer*, one of the Navy's brand-new destroyers, accompanied by Captain Edward McCauley, his naval aide, and a Marine sergeant orderly. The rest of his small personal staff were to follow three days later on board the relatively luxurious *Olympia*, a British Admiralty transport.

CHAPTER THIRTY-FIVE

Roosevelt arrived at Portsmouth, on the south coast of England, on July 21, and was met by a solicitous group of Royal Navy admirals who treated him as an honored guest and drove him up to London in a Rolls-Royce. He was delighted by all the attention, but, as he wrote later, "Personally I think it is because they wanted to report as to whether I was house-broken or not."

Thus began a week in which every waking moment seemed to be crowded with significant events. Over the next few days, he had several long confidential and fruitful conferences with Sir Eric Geddes, the First Lord of the Admiralty, and Admiral of the Fleet Sir Rosslyn Wemyss, the First Sea Lord, during which he learned that a new antisubmarine-net barrier had been designed for closing the English Channel to U-boats; that six million tons of shipping a month was being convoyed by British escort vessels, which was twenty-four times the amount convoyed by all other Allied navies, including that of the United States; and that certain large British fighting ships were being fitted out as "airplane ships," with clear decks for the takeoff and landing of wheeled aircraft (the U.S. Navy had experimented with aircraft carriers as early as 1910). He spent three highly interesting and educative days with Geddes in an inspection trip to Queenstown, Ireland, headquarters of an Anglo-American naval command that would supply more than ninety percent of the escorts for 360 convoys during the war. Overall, he was highly impressed by the magnitude and ingenuity of the British naval effort.

Returning to England from Queenstown, he made further inspections of British and American installations and attended more conferences with British and American officers at the Admiralty and at the U.S. Navy headquarters in London. He learned of a disagreement between the American Admiral William Sims and the British Admiral David Beatty, regarding the laying of the North Sea mine barrage. Beatty, who had led the Royal Navy at Jutland, disliked the barrage intensely and insisted that extensive gaps be left in it for the passage of British ships. Sims, now fully converted to the North Sea project, insisted that the line of mines run unbroken from Scotland to Norway. Roosevelt cabled Washington, urging the Navy Department to firmly support Sims.

He spent the weekend of July 27 as guest of his old friends the Waldorf Astors at Cliveden, their grand country estate outside London. Early Monday morning, July 29, he motored to London to begin the most memorable two days of his stay in England—indeed, two of the most memorable days of his life. He was delighted and flattered by his private audience with King George V at Buckingham Palace. "The king has a nice smile and a very open, quick and cordial way of greeting one," he wrote Eleanor. "He is not as short as I had expected, and I think his face is stronger than photographs make it appear." When Roosevelt mentioned "something about having been to school in Germany and having seen their preparations for the first stages of the war machine," the king said that he too had gone to school in Germany for a year, and then, "with a twinkle in his eye," adding, in reference to his cousin the Kaiser, "you know, I have a number of relations in Germany, but I can tell you frankly that in all my life I have never seen a German gentleman." The king told Franklin that he had just had a nice letter from Uncle Ted, which led him to speak with much sympathy about the loss of Quentin Roosevelt, TR's youngest son, who had died when his airplane was shot down at the front. "This type of interview is supposed to last only 15 minutes," Roosevelt noted proudly, "but it was nearly three quarters of an hour before the king made a move."

There followed a luncheon given for him and Geddes by the Anglo-American luncheon club, at which both he and Geddes spoke; then, in the afternoon, a visit to London's principal YMCA, where he spoke "to a great gathering of American soldiers, with a sprinkling of Canadians, Anzacs and our blue jackets." That evening, he attended, as a prominent guest, "one of the famous Gray Inn's dinners, a really historic occasion in honor of the war ministers," at which he heard Lord Curzon speak "most wonderfully for an hour," and, after listening to responses to Curzon by a Canadian and by General Jan Smuts of South Africa, was himself unexpectedly called upon to speak, "to my horror."

It was at this dinner that Roosevelt first met Winston Churchill, newly appointed Minister of Munitions. It was not a cordial encounter. Churchill was patronizing and dismissive of Roosevelt, probably as a result of drink. Years later, in 1939, Roosevelt would tell Joseph P. Kennedy: "I have always disliked [Churchill] since the time I went to England in 1918. He acted like a stinker at a dinner I attended, lording it over all of us. . . ." In a subsequent conversation with Kennedy, he added that Churchill had been "one of the few men in public life who was rude to me."

The next day, at a luncheon given him at the American Embassy, he had a "very good time" with Prime Minister David Lloyd George, who is "just like his pictures; thick set; not very tall; rather a large head; and rather long hair; but what impressed me more than anything else was his tremendous vitality."

Throughout that week in London, the British treated Roosevelt at every turn as a very important person. He was given direct access to all the most significant members of government and society, and was treated as an honored guest everywhere. The fact that his name was Roosevelt undoubtedly weighed heavily in his favor, and was at least as significant as his secondary position in the American Navy Department, but what may have been just as important to the British was the fact that he was indeed "house-broken." He had Old World manners, a sense of values with which they could identify, and a degree of finesse that only a handful of American political figures could match.

On Wednesday morning, July 31, he and his party traveled to the coast and at noon arrived at the Dover headquarters of Admiral Sir Roger Keyes, commandant of the naval district through which the great bulk of troops and materiel were pouring from the British Isles into Belgium and France. After lunch with Sir Roger and Lady Keyes, he boarded a new British destroyer. "As I came over the side my flag was broken out at the main," he reported proudly, "the first time this sort of thing has ever happened on a British ship," and made the two-hour run to Dunkirk, during which he and his party witnessed a special demonstration of Britain's new "artificial fog," laid by high-speed P-boats (patrol boats, similar to destroyers).

As they approached Dunkirk during the last ten miles of their crossing, they passed through an Allied minefield, "with which I had something to do in the summer of 1917," Roosevelt reported smugly, and which had proved to be highly effective. "Sir Roger Keyes told me that he did not think more than five submarines had passed through the channel since January 1."

At Dunkirk he had his first direct view of the actual fighting war. For three years, the town had been bombed virtually every night that flying was possible. It also lay within long-range shelling distance of the front, and regularly took fire from the German artillery. That night he slept in a château outside Calais, which had been heavily damaged by bombs. By evening of the following day, August 1, he was luxuriously housed in the Hotel Crillon, in Paris, as a guest of the French government.

His reception in Paris was in every way a repeat of the triumphant welcome he had received from the British. On his first full day in the city, he managed to squeeze in interviews with the minister of foreign affairs, as well as President Raymond Poincaré and the fiery Premier Georges Clemenceau, who "almost ran forward to meet me and shook hands as if he meant it; grabbed me by the arm and walked me over to his desk and sat me down about two inches away. He is only 77 years old and people say he is getting younger every day." He then attended a luncheon at the Élysée Palace in honor of Herbert Hoover, who had recently arrived in Europe to organize food distribution. That evening, they attended a special American program at the Folies Bergère.

The next day being Saturday, he took time off from official duties to catch up on various family members residing in Paris. "I went for Aunt Dora at noon and with her went out to Neuilly to see Cousin Hortense Howland, then back to pick up Cousin Charlie Forbes Gaston." After lunch, he called on Marechal Joseph Joffre at the École Militaire. "We had a delightful and intimate talk about the days in May 1917 when our decision to send a really great army to Europe hung in the balance. . . . I think he felt, and rightly so, that only a small part of the million and a quarter Americans now in France would be here had it not been for his mission at the outbreak of the war."

Then it was tea with more Americans, including his Cousin Archie—Archibald Bulloch Roosevelt, Theodore's third son—who was serving as a captain in the 26th Infantry Division and had established a "splendid record," as Franklin reported with a tinge of envy.

The next morning, Roosevelt and his eight-man entourage piled into two cars to visit the front. The date was August 4, the start of France's fifth year of war, and as they traveled out of Paris they passed scenes of carnage everywhere. At Château-Thierry, where the U.S. Marines had distinguished themselves, they tramped through what had been known as the Bois de Belleau until the French changed the name to the Bois de la Brigade de Marine in honor of the heroic fight they had put up.

On the following day, Roosevelt inspected a battalion of the Fifth Regiment of Marines. "The majority were in the khaki of the army, their own olive drab having been worn out long ago. The replacement troops were eagerly recognizable by the olive drab. It gave one a pretty good idea of the heavy casualties which had taken place in the last fighting near Soissons." The Marines had suffered about forty percent casualties at Belleau Wood and another twenty percent soon after, at Soissons.

Roosevelt commented that the Marines in the army khaki could scarcely be distinguished from the Army troops. Marine General John A. Lejeune said he wanted his men to wear the Marine Corps' globe and anchor symbol on their collars to distinguish them, but that he lacked the authority to give such an order. Roosevelt immediately understood the important morale boost such an order would give the men, and enthusiastically concurred: "I told him I would assume responsibility and then and there issued an order that this device be worn in recognition of the splendid work of the Marine Brigade."

Before returning to Paris, the group motored on to Verdun, scene of one of the bloodiest engagements of the war where, in a battle that raged from February to December 1916, over 300,000 French and German soldiers were killed, and where at least another half million were wounded. The fighting ended in a stalemate, with each army in control of the same territory it had held at the start. Roosevelt and his party proceeded across the River Meuse to the famous battlefield. They were supplied with helmets and gas masks, since German artillery still contested the area. On their way, they passed huge cemeteries that reached to the horizon, "thousands and thousands of graves tightly packed together . . . only a few hundred yards short of the actual fighting line." The battlefield itself "didn't look like a battlefield, for there was little or nothing to see . . . there were no gashes on these hills, no trenches, no tree trunks, no heaps of ruins . . . this earth had been churned by shells, and churned again . . . trench systems and forts and roads have been swallowed up in a brown chaos."

The French colonel who was their guide pointed out where the village of Fleury had once stood. "Not even a brick on the tumbled earth could verify his statement." When the awed Americans stopped to take pictures, the colonel hurried them along. He had noticed German observation balloons to the north, which would have undoubtedly have spotted them, and he warned that they would soon be the target of German artillery. Sure enough, moments later they heard "the long whining whistle of a shell . . . followed by the dull boom and puff of smoke of the explosion" at the point they had just left.

Franklin Roosevelt's tour of the front lines in August 1918 is central to any understanding of him as a future war leader. He was shaken by the high casualty figures of the Marine Corps and by the grim horror of the butchered landscape and the almost endless rows of graves at Verdun. It was the only time in his life that he experienced modern war at first hand, and the memory of it left a deep and profound impression that would influence his thinking about war forever. In 1936, as president, he shared his feelings with the public in a famous speech at Chautauqua:

> I have seen war . . . I have seen blood running from the wounded. I have seen men coughing out their gassed lungs. I have seen the dead in the mud. I have seen cities destroyed. I have seen two hundred limping, exhausted men come out of line—the survivors of a regiment of one thousand that went forward forty-eight hours before. I have seen children starving. I have seen the agony of mothers and wives. I hate war.

The tour of the front would have generated other consequences as well. The ugly, pointless horror of the battlefield stood in stark contrast to the romantic concept which had always been central to Theodore Roosevelt's philosophy, that war was somehow a noble enterprise. In the days following FDR's tour of the front, it would have been natural for him to reflect on the fact that if America had declared war after the *Lusitania* sinking, as TR had demanded and FDR had secretly wanted, many of those graves would have likely been filled with American doughboys. Would America's earlier involvement in such a frightful, meat-grinding land war have been an appropriate response to a single U-boat attack on an ocean liner of a belligerent power? Whether Franklin was conscious of it or not, the visit to Verdun would permanently redefine his unquestioned admiration for Uncle Ted.

CHAPTER THIRTY-SIX

After returning to Paris, and following an extended detour to Italy, where he was again fêted as a senior statesman and had an opportunity to catch up with an old New York political friend, Congressman Fiorello LaGuardia, serving as a captain in the Army Air Corps, Roosevelt resumed his inspection tour of France.

At the bustling port of Bordeaux, the American presence was everywhere. The U.S. Army was in command of all the docks, which extended up the banks of the Gironde for almost two miles. The wharves were crowded with ships, traveling cranes, railroad tracks, freight cars, and storehouses, handling the colossal influx of materiel pouring in on a daily basis to feed and equip the nearly two million uniformed Americans in France. At Pauillac, near the mouth of the Gironde, he inspected the huge air station built and manned by the American Navy. When he learned that the unassembled aircraft shipped over from America had proved unfit to fly, he fired off a blistering cable to Washington reporting "present conditions are scandalous." At Bassens, another busy American station about five miles from Bordeaux, he ran into more old friends, Mr. and Mrs. Vincent Astor, and he spent the night at their home.

Then it was down the Loire to Saint-Nazaire, where FDR was particularly eager to inspect the five U.S. naval guns which had recently arrived from the States, and which were in the process of being mounted on railroad cars. These huge 14-inch guns were the heaviest mobile artillery being used by the Allies. Each gun was sixty feet long, weighed ninety tons, and hurled fourteen-hundred-pound projectiles as far as twenty-five miles. They were sea-going guns, originally designed for battlecruisers; but when it became clear that American battlecruisers were not going to play much of a part in the war, someone suggested that the guns be mounted on railway cars for use on land. Roosevelt had seized on the idea and immediately became its chief proponent. It was his enthusiasm that had been responsible for the acceptance of the extraordinary proposal.

The Baldwin Locomotive Works had built the specially designed mounts and carriages in record time. Each gun had its own railroad train, made up of a regular Baldwin locomotive and its tender; the huge gun car; three construction cars, one fitted with a crane and another with material for the emplacement of the gun; two ammunition cars; a workshop; a fuel car; three berthing cars for the crew's living quarters; a kitchen car; and a car for the officers in charge. All crew members were Navy personnel, and each car had "USN" stenciled on its side. An American flag flew from the top of the gun car.

All five guns were under the command of Rear Admiral Charles P. Plunkett. Roosevelt and his naval aide, Captain Edward McCauley, were waiting for Plunkett outside the headquarters building, when they saw him approaching, dressed in a U.S. Army khaki uniform, like the Marines they had seen at the front. He wore two stars on each shoulder, indicating the rank of either a major general or a rear admiral.

As Plunkett came within hearing distance, Roosevelt turned to McCauley with a wink and asked loftily, "Captain McCauley, who is this major general?"

"Mr. Secretary, this is Admiral Plunkett, commanding the Naval Battery guns," McCauley answered.

"Admiral," Roosevelt said sternly, "you are out of uniform."

Plunkett, a tough, hardnosed veteran, was momentarily nonplussed by Roosevelt's reprimand, and began to explain why it was impossible for him or his men to wear the easily soiled whites or the heavy navy blue uniform for what was essentially railroad work, and how he had petitioned Washington for permission to wear khakis but had received no response. A smiling Roosevelt assured the admiral that he had only been joking, and immediately gave him the necessary authority for the change in uniform. In return, he asked Plunkett for an equally unorthodox favor.

He explained to the admiral that he was determined to get into uniform as soon as he returned to America and he wished to do so as a Navy officer. But he also wished to serve at the front, and in this war few U.S. Navy officers were seeing action of any kind except convoy duty. Plunkett and his men, however, were going to the front, and Roosevelt asked if he could join them. Plunkett thought about it for a moment and countered with request of his own: since Roosevelt spoke French, could he provide Plunkett with enough swear words to force a French train into a siding when the admiral needed to move his guns forward? Roosevelt laughed, and then "with certain imaginative genius . . . handed him a line of French swear words, real and imaginary, which impressed him greatly," whereupon Plunkett promised to take Roosevelt on as a lieutenant commander.

Over the following week, Roosevelt kept up the same whirlwind pace, going north to Belgium—or at least to the 235 square miles of Belgium still in Allied hands—where he was presented to the Belgian king. In the same week he managed to survive two air raids and several German artillery bombardments, to witness from land a sea fight between destroyers and a U-boat just off the beach, and to hold long talks with the British Field Marshal Douglas Haig, the French Marshal Ferdinand Foch, and the American General John J. Pershing. Then it was time to get back to England and his own pet project, the North Sea Barrage.

The Roosevelt party, traveling in a special train furnished by the Royal Navy, traveled north overnight, and arrived at Invergordon on the east coast of Scotland on the morning of August 30. It was one of the two American advance bases that had been set up to lay the thousands of sea mines—manufactured in the United States and assembled in Scotland—that would form the barrage, stretching in a fifteen-mile-wide swath across the 240 miles of the North Sea from the Orkney Islands to Norway. The operation was being carried out by a fleet of American minelayers that had been specially equipped to handle the attenuated electrical mines. The actual laying of the Barrage had started in June 1918, and most of it had been completed by the time of Roosevelt's inspection.

As soon as their train arrived, Roosevelt and his team were ushered on board the USS *Roanoke,* one of the converted minelayers, and taken out for a demonstration of mine-laying techniques. The squadron of minelayers, protected by an escort of cruisers and destroyers, and traveling at top speed, could drop off the mines at the rate of one every twelve or fifteen seconds, and in the course of thirteen expeditions of two days each, the Americans laid 56,600 mines over the 240-mile width of open sea.

The mines, each with an anchor to hold it in place and a buoy to keep the antenna vertical, took their places automatically as the unit hit the water and lay at 300-foot intervals in three tiers, the first at a depth of 45 feet, the second at 160 feet, and the third at 240 feet. As more of these three-tiered rows were put down, the Barrage was built to a thickness of many miles, requiring from one to three hours for a submarine to traverse it. Each mine contained 300 pounds of TNT, set to explode whenever metal brushed against the wire antenna suspended between its buoy and the mine. Before the close of the war, 22 million pounds of TNT and 50 million feet of wire cable went into the manufacture of this barrier of high explosives. After the war, Admiral Sims would look back on the North Sea Barrage in wonder. "Nothing like it had ever been attempted before," Sims wrote. "The combined operation involved a mass of detail which the lay mind can hardly comprehend."

By any measure, Roosevelt's European trip had been an unalloyed triumph. Over a period of two months, he had seen and heard, experienced and accomplished, everything he could have wished for. He had seen the devastation of war and been close enough to the action to undergo air raids and be fired upon by enemy artillery. He had dealt with every issue involving the U.S. Navy in Europe, from the strategic relationships with the Royal Navy to the deployment of U.S. destroyers at Queenstown, and from the serious production problems at the Navy aircraft assembly base at Pauillac to the morale issues of U.S. Marines dressed in Army khaki. And to top it off, he had seen the completion of his most prized project, the North Sea Barrage, and had even secured, through Admiral Plunkett, a place at the front as a commissioned officer of the United States Navy.

Throughout his long weeks of travel, he had been accorded every formal honor, including state dinners, official briefings, and private meetings with every Allied leader, political, military, and royal. It was this last achievement that is probably the most telling achievement of his trip—that he was treated more as a head of state than an assistant secretary of the Navy—for it suggests just how important the Roosevelt name was in 1918, and how closely Franklin was perceived as an embodiment of Theodore, a younger, equally authoritative, spiritual reincarnation of the former president.

But there was a price that Roosevelt had paid for such a triumph. He had pushed himself relentlessly from the time of his arrival, meeting a schedule of state and social obligations that overwhelmed everyone else in his party, and his body, always susceptible to illness and minor breakdowns, had at last succumbed to exhaustion. Bound for home at last, he fell ill with double pneumonia and collapsed into bed in his stateroom on board the *Leviathan* and barely left it for the entire voyage. When the ship finally docked in Hoboken, he was still gravely ill, and Eleanor and his mother, forewarned of his condition, met the ship with a hired ambulance. He was carried ashore on a stretcher and transported as quickly as possible to his mother's house in Manhattan, because his own house next door had been rented out while he and Eleanor lived in Washington.

Soon after his return, he was gratified by a brief but heartfelt note from Sagamore Hill:

> *Dear Franklin,*
> *We are deeply concerned about your sickness, and trust you will*
> *soon be well. We are very proud of you. With love,*
> *Aff. Yours Theodore Roosevelt*

A few days after his arrival, Eleanor was dutifully unpacking his extensive luggage, which contained everything from elaborate formal wear to fishing gear, along with official papers and correspondence. Among the latter she came upon a group of letters addressed in a familiar hand. With a shock, she realized they were love letters from Lucy Mercer. As she read the letters, "the bottom dropped out of my particular world," she told biographer Joseph Lash many years later, "and I faced myself, my surroundings, my world, honestly for the first time."

What happened next remains something of a mystery to this day. We know that Eleanor confronted Franklin and offered him his freedom if he wished to continue the relationship with Lucy, but should he—for the sake of the children—wish to keep the family together, he must never see her again. Franklin's mother was far less lenient in her reaction. She told him that if he chose to desert his wife and five children, she would never forgive him, would never give him another dollar, and he would never inherit Springwood, the Hyde Park home he so loved.

Louis Howe was consulted, and he made the painful but obvious observation that a divorce would be the end of his political career.

After considerable soul-searching, Franklin agreed to give up Lucy and try to rebuild his marriage with Eleanor. What is generally overlooked is the fact that he did not immediately agree to Eleanor's terms, lenient as they were. It took him a long time. One might assume that Franklin Roosevelt, so profoundly ambitious, so keenly aware of his position in life and so determined to take full advantage of it, would have very quickly seen that his relationship with Lucy Mercer, no matter how gratifying it might be, simply had to be sacrificed to his future White House aspirations. But in fact there was no quick decision. It was a long, wrenching process, and clearly Franklin must have agonized over the prospect of losing Lucy.

Eleanor had to return to Washington to put the children into school, while Franklin went north to Hyde Park to recuperate. Weeks later, in the middle of October, with the decision to give up Lucy somehow made, Franklin and Eleanor returned together to Washington and a strained future.

We are left to wonder: what if they had decided to divorce? What if he had chosen Lucy and, with her, the end of his political career? Rarely, if ever, has a domestic decision between two private people held such profound consequences for the future of so many billions of people the world over.

CHAPTER THIRTY-SEVEN

E ven after his return to Washington, Roosevelt was too weak to resume his duties. His exhaustion from his European trip, combined with the lingering effects of his pneumonia, now supplanted by the Spanish flu, along with the emotional storm over his personal life, was enough to keep him bedridden until the end of the month. By that time, events had so piled up in his absence as to make meaningless all his well-laid plans for the future.

His first move upon his return to the office was to meet with Josephus Daniels, tell him about his agreement with Admiral Plunkett, and repeat his plea to resign his job and join the Navy as a commissioned officer. Daniels was finally willing to grant Roosevelt's wish, and gave him permission to present his case to Wilson himself.

"I went to see the President," Roosevelt recalled later, "and the President told me that in his judgment I was too late—that he had received the first suggestion of an armistice from Prince Max of Baden, and that he hoped the war would be over very soon."

This was a stunning turn of events. Only weeks earlier, Roosevelt had been in Europe talking directly with all the top political and military commanders, and every one of them expected the war to last at least another year. What had brought about this sudden change? It was common knowledge that German troops had suffered *some* setbacks, but nothing all *that* serious. The German Army was still fighting on foreign soil, which clearly implied that they were still the aggressor, bringing the fight to their enemies.

But the German General Staff understood what was hidden from the rest of the world—the increased political unrest at home, the shortage of supplies, the serious problems facing the country and its war machine—and they realized that Germany no longer had a chance for victory. It was months before the full story would come out, but when it did, most accounts traced the turnabout in Germany's fortunes to the evening of September 28, 1918, when General Quartermaster Ludendorff, the de facto dictator of Germany, lost all control of himself in a meeting with his staff. Overcome with nervous exhaustion, he fell to the floor, foaming at the mouth and shouting curses at all those who would betray the fatherland through their cowardice and stupidity.

Later that night, after recovering himself, he met with Paul von Hindenburg, Chief of the General Staff, and told him that in his opinion Germany had lost the war and even a military stalemate was no longer possible. Germany must sue for peace immediately, while the country still retained the appearance of being able to keep fighting. Hindenburg agreed.

Prince Max of Baden, a liberal, was hastily named German chancellor and foreign minister. Within hours, he put together a peace proposal; but, rather than address it to the Allies, as the generals had specified, he addressed it, on October 6, 1918, specifically to the President of the United States. The British and French, Prince Max reasoned, would almost certainly demand crushing terms, while Woodrow Wilson had gone out of his way to make clear he wanted a "peace without victory."

In his note to the president, the chancellor called for "the immediate conclusion of an armistice on land, water, and in the air" in order "to avoid further bloodshed," and he accepted "as a basis for the peace negotiations the program set forth by the President . . . in his message to Congress on January 8, 1918." Thus were Wilson's Fourteen Points introduced into the peace process by the losing side.

It was a brilliant strategic move by Prince Max. He knew that Germany must eventually come to terms with the British, French, and Italians who had suffered so much from Germany and would have every reason to seek revenge and compensation for their great losses; but by initiating the proposal with the idealistic Wilson, he could be sure that Germany would at least have the assurance that the Americans would have a leading role in the negotiations.

Wilson was energized by Prince Max's message and saw it as an opportunity to shape the international world to his own design. His response was to treat it as a private, personal communication, which he initially kept secret from the Allies and even from his own military leaders. Through his secretary of state, he addressed himself directly to the chancellor and sought clarification of terms for an armistice.

A few days later, on October 10, news came of two particularly brutal U-boat torpedoings in which more than eight hundred died, many of them women and children. Wilson was furious and sent off an angry message to the German chancellor. Prince Max, terrified that he might have lost his last chance to give Wilson the decisive role in the armistice negotiations, hastily apologized, and on October 20 announced the end of unrestricted submarine warfare. Three days later, Wilson at last officially disclosed to the Allies what he had been up to.

The Allied leaders had been unofficially aware of what was happening, and by the time Wilson's personal agent, Colonel Edward House, arrived in France to work directly with the British and French on details of an armistice agreement, he quickly discovered that they had already decided on what they considered appropriate terms for an armistice, and were not going to accept their American colleague's diplomatic efforts without significant changes. Bickering broke out immediately between the Europeans and the Americans. The main stumbling block was Woodrow Wilson's determination to make sure that his Fourteen Points would form the basis for the peace and the postwar world to come. Clemenceau would comment that Wilson's Fourteen Points were being presented to the Allies as if they were Fourteen Commandments, which seemed to him a little excessive, since the Good Lord had made do with ten.

Woodrow Wilson had overplayed his hand, and Franklin Roosevelt, picking up rumors from his office in the Navy Department and from dinner-table gossip in Washington society, watched and learned with a sense of detached interest. Here was a president who, in addition to leading his country, wanted to use his office to lead the world. Here was a man who kept a copy of Kipling's "If—" on his desk and who was determined to live up to its deceptively simple code. He had demonstrated many times that he trusted himself when all men doubted him. Now it was time to see if he could live up to Kipling's corollary and "make allowance for their doubting too." The whole world would soon be asking that question of the cool, self-confident idealist, and none would be assessing him more keenly, or at a closer range, than his assistant secretary of the Navy.

Then on October 25, almost three weeks after the first tentative feelers from Prince Max, Woodrow Wilson chose to release a statement to the American public that was at best foolhardy, and at worst almost criminally inappropriate. It concerned the upcoming congressional election in November. At a time when it was vital to bring the country together, he chose to send a deliberately divisive political message. The elections, he said, "occur in the most critical period our country has ever faced, or is likely to face in our time. If you have approved of my leadership and wish me to continue to be your unembarrassed spokesman in affairs at home and abroad, I earnestly beg that you will express yourself unmistakably to that effect by returning a Democratic majority to both the Senate and House of Representatives . . . the difficulties and delicacies of our present task are of a sort that makes it imperatively necessary that the nation would give its undivided support to the Government under a unified leadership, and that a Republican Congress would divide the leadership. . . . The return of a Republican majority to either House of Congress would, moreover, certainly be interpreted on the other side of the water as a repudiation of my leadership."

The public reaction to the statement was a firestorm of anger. Even those independent voters leaning toward the Democrats were outraged by the clear implication that the Republicans were somehow unpatriotic and untrustworthy. That the man who made this claim had been reelected in 1916 because "he kept us out of the war," only to lead the country into that very war within weeks of his second inaugural, was seen as brazenly manipulative and duplicitous. Eleven days later, on Election Day, with the armistice still only a vague future possibility, the American public resoundingly voted the Republican Party into control of both houses of Congress. In consequence, as Wilson had predicted, the world leaders now saw him as a seriously weakened head of state. Theodore Roosevelt, who had been angered and at the same time delighted by Wilson's gaffe, issued a statement that "our allies and our enemies and Mr. Wilson himself should all understand that Mr. Wilson has no authority to speak for the American people at this time," he stated. "His leadership has just been dramatically repudiated by them. . . . Mr. Wilson and his Fourteen Points and his four supplementary points and his five complementary points and all his utterances every which way have ceased to have any shadow of a right to be accepted as expressive of the will of the American people."

Franklin Roosevelt continued to watch. And learn.

CHAPTER THIRTY-EIGHT

At last, on November 11, 1918, a week after the American election, the Armistice took effect and the guns fell silent. With the war suddenly over, and his marriage still shaky, Franklin Roosevelt was in need of something to do, and he very quickly decided that what he needed was to get back to Europe, where he could supervise the disposal of the mountains of supplies and equipment the Navy had built up overseas in the months since America entered the war. Someone had to decide what to do with all that Navy property, he explained to Josephus Daniels: railroad stock, guns and ammunition, aircraft and automobiles, temporary installations like hospitals, and permanent installations like radio towers. What should be shipped home and what otherwise disposed of? Someone had to make the decisions, to cut the deals. Every agreement, every contract made by the military had been entered into under urgent, hurry-up, life-and-death wartime conditions, and on his previous trip he had seen something of the waste and inefficiency such urgency always generates. And Roosevelt was intensely aware that as a result of the November elections, the control of both houses of Congress would soon pass to the

Republicans, who would be eager to investigate anything that could be presented as wasteful practices on the part of Wilson's Democratic administration.

Daniels was reluctant to send Roosevelt back to Europe. He was quite content to let Admiral Sims and the Navy people already on the scene in Europe handle the situation. Roosevelt most emphatically disagreed, and his battle with Daniels on the issue provides an interesting insight into the continually fluctuating nature of the relationship between these two very different men.

When Admiral Benson, the Chief of Naval Operations who had recently joined Sims in London, cabled Daniels asking for directions on the Navy demobilization process, FDR wrote Daniels that "the demobilization can and should begin at once" and asked, "Are you going to leave it solely in the hands of Admiral Sims and the Naval Officers who have built it up? I am absolutely certain that a civilian is needed in charge. . . ." Of course, the most appropriate civilian was the assistant secretary himself.

When Daniels peremptorily turned down his plea to go back to Europe, Roosevelt waited a week and tried again, this time with a notably more petulant and exasperated tone: "The crux of the whole matter is this—Are you going to let the Navy people on the other side handle this business matter with their present officers, or are you going to put it in the hands of business people? . . . You know that I have just as high a regard for Sims . . . and the other officers as you have. . . . And you know, as I do, that the training of these officers, Line or Staff, does not fit them for what is nine tenths a civilian job, the disposal of material, the settling of thousands of legal questions, and the handling of these matters with French, English and Italian civilian officials. No Paymaster that you can send over has enough right or authority to act as American commissioner in collaboration with English and French Cabinet officers."

At the end of this second letter he added something very close to a warning: "I feel so strongly about this, because in my knowledge of the situation, that I have put my views in this letter in a way which is perhaps too strong. The reason I do so is because I want your administration of the Navy to continue without scandal or criticism. . . ."

Finally, when Daniels continued to stonewall him, Roosevelt took off the gloves, and in a handwritten note from his sick bed, where he was recovering from still another respiratory relapse, he laid down a delicately phrased but nonetheless clear threat to protect himself in case the messy nature of the Navy's European demobilization program fell under the scrutiny of the new Republican Congress: "This matter is in my judgment so vital, and is one with which I am personally so familiar[,] that in it I must keep my own record clear. Therefore I must with the greatest respect insist either on appropriate action being taken, or on my position being made so clear to the public that I may never be considered to have acquiesced in what I feel to be a failure to handle the problem rightly."

It was probably this final threat to publicly disassociate himself from Daniels that touched a nerve. In any case, the secretary finally agreed that Roosevelt should go to Europe once again. He quickly arranged to sail from New York on board the USS *George Washington* on January 2, 1919. But he would not be going alone. On this trip he would, by authority of the secretary of the Navy, be accompanied by his wife Eleanor. It is likely that Josephus Daniels wanted someone he could trust to keep his assistant in line.

FDR could not have expected his return to Europe to make quite the splash that he had made the previous summer. The circumstances were inherently different. On his first trip, he had been one of the highest-ranking members of the American administration to visit the war zone, and was perceived as an important representative of the Allies' vital new partner. But on this second trip he had competition. President Woodrow Wilson himself was already in Europe, the object of rapturous public receptions wherever he went. His presence completely overshadowed FDR's significance. Huge cheering crowds in Paris and London testified to the extraordinary public popularity of the president, no matter what Europe's leaders might think of him. Even as Franklin and Eleanor boarded the *George Washington* in New York, Wilson was on the train to Rome, where the huge crowds would be repeated still again. He had crossed the Atlantic to personally participate in the negotiations for the Peace Treaty in Paris. At his insistence, embedded in that treaty would be the Covenant of the League of Nations, which he was convinced would guarantee that never again would there be a war as frightful and ruinous as the one just concluded.

Three days out of New York, news came via the ship's radio of the sudden and unexpected death of the man who had played such an outsized role in the lives of both Franklin and Eleanor. Theodore Roosevelt, aged sixty, had gone to sleep on January 5 and died of a coronary thrombosis at four o'clock in the morning, without waking. Josephus Daniels immediately radioed a telegram of sympathy, and Roosevelt responded that the news had come as "in every way a great shock, for we heard just before leaving that he was better—and he was after all not old."

FDR's return to Europe was considerably less exhausting than that of the previous summer. His mission was formidable, but thanks mainly to Commander John M. Hancock of the Naval Supply Corps, who accompanied him and did most of the mountainous paperwork, FDR was left free to move around Europe at his own pace, visiting friends and relatives and sharing rumors about the secret Peace Treaty negotiations in Paris.

There was more news of the North Sea Barrage, all of it gratifying. Admiral Sims estimated that in its brief existence it had destroyed at least four U-boats and possibly twice that number. Other estimates ran as high as twenty-three U-boats sunk or damaged. Perhaps even more satisfying was the admiral's account of the influence of the North Sea Barrage on German morale. As Sims would describe it, "Stories of this barrage were circulated all over Germany; sailors who had been in contact with it related the experience to their fellows, and the

result was extremely demoralizing to the German submarine flotilla.
. . . The North Sea Barrage was probably a contributory cause of the
mutiny which demoralized the German fleet in the fall of 1918. . . .
The Germans saw the barrage not only as it was in the fall of 1918,
but as it would have been a few months or a year hence. . . . In time we
could have planted this area so densely with explosives that it would
have been madness for any submarine ever to attempt a passage."

The Peace Treaty discussions in Paris continued, and while they
remained shrouded in secrecy, it became increasingly clear as the weeks
passed that the negotiators were running into problems. Wilson's
shining idealism found little support from the Allied leaders, who
were determined to gain some recompense for their huge losses from
their defeated enemy. Instances of a falling-out among the victors
made headlines. When Secretary Daniels testified before Congress
that America planned to increase the size of its navy significantly,
the news brought on angry protests in Britain, both at the Admiralty
and among the general public. As a matter of national policy, Britain
had traditionally maintained the world's largest navy since the days
of Lord Nelson or even earlier, and the American move to build a
sea force equal to or even superior to the Royal Navy was seen as an
unfriendly act. When FDR was approached by the *Daily Mail* for
a comment, he was eager to explain the American position. "The
United States has no intention of challenging anybody's supremacy,"
he said reassuringly. "Our building program has nothing whatever in
contemplation except the creation of a first-rate fleet commensurate
with the needs of a country that has 6,000 miles and more of coastline on two seaboards which are linked by a strip of canal that one
airplane could put out of action.

"If Britain's security as an insular Power depends upon a powerful
navy, as it manifestly must, the defensive necessities of America, with
her vast ocean front, are no less palpable. There is not a sane person in
the United States who thinks of constructing a Fleet for the purpose
of disputing Britain's position at sea. I have no hesitation whatsoever

in describing such notions as utterly baseless." What the Admiralty might have taken from this apparently disarming statement, it would at best have been cold comfort.

At one point FDR traveled into Germany on a side trip, where he found an opportunity to practice a little amateur foreign policy. He was eager to visit the great Rhineland fortress of Ehrenbreitstein, which he remembered from his summer visits to Germany as a boy. The fortress was now occupied by American troops, but Roosevelt was distressed to see that the flagpole atop the fortress was bare. Where was the triumphant American flag? he demanded of the local commander, who explained that it had been decided not to display the Stars and Stripes out of respect for German sensibilities. The answer did not mollify Roosevelt. On his return to Paris, he made it a point to raise the issue with General Pershing, who was now supervising the return home of the American Expeditionary Force. Roosevelt warned Pershing that it was a grave error not to fly the flag over the fortress. "The German people ought to know for all time that Ehrenbreitstein flew the American flag during the occupation," he insisted. Pershing agreed, and promised "it will be hoisted within the hour." The flag did not come down again until the last American troops left Germany.

Throughout the Roosevelts' time in Europe that winter, the main subject of conversation was the Covenant of the League of Nations. Wilson had insisted that the leaders must agree on the organization of the League before they decided on the terms of the Peace Treaty itself. It was Wilson's idea that the two documents would reinforce each other, that the Peace Treaty would support the League and that the League Covenant would guarantee the peace.

Franklin and Eleanor had no idea how the negotiations were progressing until the night before their return to the United States, when a draft of the Covenant was released to the public. They studied it carefully, and discussed it with each other and with the other passengers on board the *George Washington*, which was to take them home.

While Roosevelt considered the Covenant a highly worthy attempt to find a formula for peace, he had already decided that it was distinctly experimental.

Also sailing on the *George Washington* was the author of the Covenant, President Wilson himself, who for the most part remained aloof in his stateroom throughout the voyage. At one point, Franklin and Eleanor were invited to a private luncheon with the president and his wife. Roosevelt thought Wilson looked tired, but on the subject of the League he expressed himself emphatically. "The United States must go in," Wilson said earnestly, "or it will break the heart of the world, for she is the only nation that all feel is disinterested and all trust."

CHAPTER THIRTY-NINE

W ilson was determined to get precisely the League of Nations he had negotiated for in the draft Covenant he was bringing home, and the cheering crowds that greeted him in Boston and later in Washington gave evidence that large parts of the public enthusiastically supported him. But the publication of the draft Covenant had generated a strong wave of opposition among the Republicans in Congress, led by Wilson's old nemesis, Senator Henry Cabot Lodge of Massachusetts. The senator's essential complaint concerned the issue of national sovereignty. Lodge was willing to concede that the world had changed, and that nations would have to find some way to work together to maintain peace; but how much would Wilson's new League impinge on America's freedom to pursue its own national interests?

The opposition of Senator Lodge created a problem for Wilson. The Senate would have to ratify the Covenant, and he needed all the support there that he could get. He made a token attempt to win the approval of Congress by inviting Lodge and other members of the Senate and House Foreign Affairs Committees to a dinner at the White House to discuss the proposed agreement. Lodge announced afterwards that the dinner had been "pleasant," but emphasized that in his opinion the president had appeared singularly ill-informed on specific details of the Covenant. Later, on the floor of the Senate, he denounced the Covenant "in the form now proposed," and suggested that a peace treaty with Germany should be negotiated and signed before considering the Covenant of the League of Nations.

Wilson refused to even discuss such a possibility, and early in March returned to Europe for further negotiations, more determined than ever to stick to his guns. But when he arrived in Paris, he discovered the other leaders at the conference table had been talking to their own constituents, and they had also been reading Lodge's statements, and they were encouraged to note that the senator's opinion of the Covenant closely echoed their own. In addition, a new factor had entered the political calculations of the European leaders, one that would strongly influence their determination to get the Peace Treaty *they* wanted, rather than the one Wilson wanted. In one country after another in the postwar world of 1919, the shadow of Lenin and his Bolshevik revolution was emerging as a powerful social and economic force, and frightened ministers were anxious to curb this new threat. "Europe is on fire," Wilson said sadly; "I can't add fuel to the flames!"

Sensing weakness in the President, the Allies now escalated their opposition to his idealism, demanding peace terms deliberately calculated to humiliate Germany along with ruinous reparations designed to ruin her economy. By the end of March, the conference was deadlocked. In desperation, and in order to save his precious Covenant, Wilson agreed to one demand after another—Italy's annexation of the Tyrol, a "Polish corridor" running directly through Prussia, Japanese exploitation of the Shantung Peninsula. Very quickly, Woodrow Wilson's Fourteen Points and his shining dream of a "peace without victors" collapsed in a shambles. Wilson, sick with anxiety and at the end of his tether, suffered a complete breakdown that may well have been a stroke, although it was not so diagnosed at the time. For a while he was bedridden, the side of his face numb and one eye twitching uncontrollably.

Meanwhile, back in America, far from the conference table, Franklin Roosevelt was having a grand time, busily preparing the Navy for a glorious new adventure. Josephus Daniels was in Paris with Wilson, and FDR, enjoying his temporary elevation to Acting Secretary, was riding in the open cockpit of the immense NC-2T flying boat, hurtling along at ninety miles an hour over New York harbor in early April, heading for the Narrows. The sky was gray, the wind was cold, and he was squeezed in behind two Navy pilots, but he was having the time of his life. Off to his left, four thousand feet below, Brooklyn was spread out all the way to Jamaica Bay, and he was able to pick out landmarks—Prospect Park, the Brooklyn Bridge, and Ebbets Field, with its baseball diamond newly spruced up for the coming season.

This was the part of his job he enjoyed above all others, where he could experience the cutting edge of naval power, where the new technologies would shape not only the future Navy, but the whole world of tomorrow. Airpower, still in its infancy, was already showing enormous promise. The British, he knew, were projecting flights to Constantinople and India in order to pioneer new global air routes, with the aim of dominating the air as they did the sea, and FDR was determined to challenge them at every step. For almost two years now, he had closely followed the development of the Navy's giant NC flying boats, and the men in charge of the project had come to rely on his ability to cut through the red tape that had been critical to their success.

The NCs—there were four of them, the world's largest aircraft— had originally been designed by Glenn Curtiss for long range anti-submarine patrol, but the war had come to an end before they could be put into operation. Now the Navy was preparing them for a far more ambitious goal—if all went according to plan, these monstrous four-engine, wood-and-fabric giants, each manned by a six-man crew, would become the first aircraft to fly across the Atlantic.

They would have plenty of competition for the honor. In London, the *Daily Mail* had put up a prize of ten thousand pounds for the first pilot to make it across the Atlantic nonstop, and any number of daredevils, crackpots, and visionaries had dreams of winning. The NCs would not be competing for the prize, since they planned a two-stage flight, but the honor of being the first across the ocean was still a top Navy priority.

The race for glory began three weeks after FDR's flight over Brooklyn. On May 8, the NC-1, NC-3, and NC-4 took off from the Naval Air Station at Rockaway on Long Island, bound for Trepassey, Newfoundland. The fourth NC flying boat, NC-2, the one FDR had flown in, would not participate in the transatlantic attempt due to last-minute design problems.

Once the three crews had assembled at Trepassey, they were held up for a week waiting for favorable weather. Finally, on the evening of Friday, May 16, they received clearance to take off. Their initial goal was the Azores, the mid-Atlantic Portuguese islands, seventeen hours distant. After reaching cruising altitude, the planes broke from formation to avoid the risk of collision, and the night passed without incident. To help guide them, the Navy had deployed a chain of twenty-one destroyers along the route at fifty-mile intervals. At dawn, the NC-3, having lost its bearings, made what the commanding officer expected to be a brief landing in the ocean in order to get a navigational sighting before taking off again, but the impact of landing on rough seas damaged the fragile craft and she was not able to take off. The crew was in no particular danger. The body of the craft was in fact a hull, and the accident had simply turned a flying boat into a floating boat. She could still navigate, powered by her four aircraft propellers.

Elsewhere in the Atlantic, the NC-1 had also made a brief landing to check her bearings, only to discover that the Atlantic's twelve-foot-high waves made it impossible for her to return to the air.

The remaining aircraft, the NC-4, remained aloft and managed to reach the Azores on schedule. But once there, bad weather held her to her moorings for three days, during which time the crew learned that all the men of the NC-1 had been rescued by a Greek freighter, and that the NC-3, using her four propellers, had made her way into the Azorean harbor of Ponta Delgado on May 19 under her own power.

The NC-4 eventually took off on the second and final leg of her flight on May 27 and landed at Lisbon that night, eleven days after leaving Newfoundland. Lieutenant Commander A. C. Read, the navigator and commanding officer, remembered the moment proudly. "No mattered what happened—even if we crashed on landing—the transatlantic flight, the first one in the history of the world, was an accomplished fact."

The achievement of the NC-4 made banner headlines world-wide, but its fame was fleeting. A fortnight later, two British airmen, John Alcock and Arthur Whitten Brown, flying a modified twin-engine Vickers Vimy RAF bomber, were able to take off from Newfoundland and in a single, nonstop flight land in Ireland the next morning. Their pluck and daring, accomplished without benefit of radio or a chain of destroyers, instantly captured the imagination of the world, and the more complicated American feat was quickly forgotten.

But as the Navy—and Franklin Roosevelt—never tired of pointing out, the NC-4 was first across.

Franklin Roosevelt was not by nature an impetuous person. He liked to think things through before committing himself, to weigh his options and calibrate his responses to any given opportunity before throwing himself boldly into the fray. So his casual, almost nonchalant response to an invitation to address the Democratic National

Committee in Chicago on May 29, 1919 has to be considered some-what unusual. For someone who had national political ambitions, it was an exceptional venue for a speech, where he would reach many influential party leaders. But there is no evidence that he thought his speech would be all that important to his career, and in fact he did not even start preparing his remarks until after he arrived in Chicago. The scheduled keynote speaker was to be the newly appointed attorney general, Mitchell Palmer, who at the time was making headlines battling a wave of radical terrorists. He was likely to get much more press attention than any other speaker, which may account for Roosevelt's offhand preparation for what turned out to be a very important speech.

It was a rousing speech, a stinging attack on the Republican Party, a speech of someone who understood not only the morality of political philosophy, but the mechanics of getting out the vote, and the party leaders from across the country, already intent on the 1920 elections, took note. He pointed out that historically there were progressive ele-ments in both major parties, which made for a certain blurring of the lines between the two, but that in recent years the Republicans had so purged themselves of the progressive influence that "by next year it will be clear to the American people that the Republican Party is the conservative party of the United States, and that the Democratic Party is the progressive or liberal party."

He closed with a ringing affirmation of his party's policies. "So we are approaching the campaign of 1920—approaching it with broad principles settled in advance; conservatism, special privilege, par-tisanship, destruction on the one hand—liberalism, common sense idealism, constructiveness, progress, on the other."

Roosevelt's speech was met with an outpouring of enthusiastic applause, and completely overshadowed that of the attorney general. The Chicago *Tribune* ran a front-page headline: PALMER LOSES PLACE IN SUN TO ROOSEVELT. History has marked it as his first great speech, and it would have important ramifications for him.

★ ★ ★

By the summer of 1919, the Versailles Treaty had been agreed to and signed. As Wilson had demanded, it included the Covenant of the League of Nations as Article One. With high hopes, Wilson returned with it from Europe and submitted it to the Senate for ratification. Predictably, Senator Lodge wanted modifications, and equally predictably, Wilson stonewalled. It quickly became clear that the Republican-controlled Senate was determined to have its way, and the angry and exhausted Wilson decided to bypass Congress and appeal directly to the public. He would mount a massive cross-country speaking tour to sell the Covenant to the nation, creating such a wave of support that the Republicans would be forced to ratify the Treaty without revision. He knew he had not fully regained his strength from his collapse in April, but his determination to force the ratification of the Treaty had taken on a messianic edge. As he told his secretary, "in the presence of the great tragedy which now faces the world no decent man can count his own personal fortunes in the reckoning." Against the strenuous pleading of his doctor and his wife, Wilson embarked on his campaign, and over the next three weeks set out on an exhausting campaign covering eight thousand miles, speaking in twenty-nine cities and at unnumbered train stops.

On September 25, a few hours after addressing a huge audience in Pueblo, Colorado, he collapsed on board his special train with a second, more severe stroke that immobilized his left side and forced him to cancel the rest of his tour. His loyal inner circle, made up of his doctor, his secretary, and his wife, closed ranks around him. For the remaining year and a half of his term of office, he would remain in virtual seclusion, a permanent invalid guarded and protected by an unelected triumvirate who would fiercely keep secret the fact that on most days of the week, the President of the United States was no longer fit to hold office.

Since Wilson would not allow the rather modest amendments to the Covenant called for by Lodge, the Senate refused to ratify it, and the United States became the only major power that was not signatory to the League of Nations.

How did Franklin Roosevelt view the sad collapse of the man he had so eagerly sought out in Trenton in 1911? He continued to admire Wilson, and to draw inspiration from him. Doubtless he sympathized with Wilson's idealism; but did he, like many others, wonder why the president so assiduously avoided any compromise in support of those ideals? Why, for instance, did Wilson refuse any effort to find common ground with Senator Lodge?

The president considered Henry Cabot Lodge the ultimate enemy, and treated him as such. But Roosevelt would have wondered about that. He knew Lodge. They were not friends—they were too far apart in age and worldview for that—but Lodge had been very close to Uncle Ted, and as far as FDR was concerned, Lodge was an elder statesman worthy of respect and even admiration. Wilson and Lodge were of different parties, to be sure, but their differences over the League were not all that significant. Both recognized the need for the League, and both were concerned about the issues of national sovereignty that were part of its concept. But where Lodge—and Roosevelt—both saw room for compromise, Wilson saw none.

There is no question that Roosevelt drew many lessons from Wilson's tragic failure with the League of Nations. One has only to study the way that President Roosevelt, twenty five years later, nurtured and brought about the creation of the United Nations—the successor to the League—with his carefully orchestrated campaign to "win the peace as well as the war."

CHAPTER FORTY

O n January 10, 1920, Mrs. Bertie Hamlin of Washington and Hyde Park, an old friend of the Roosevelts, wrote in her diary, "As I was walking along R Street . . . I met Franklin Roosevelt—he has had his tonsils out and has been ill too—he looks rather poorly for him. He had two of his boys and a dog with him, and we walked along together. Several of the children have had or are having chickenpox—James is to have his appendix out—Eleanor was getting out 2000 invitations for Navy teas. He said he did not expect to run for the Senate—that even if he wanted it or could get it—he thought it was stupid."

Mrs. Hamlin's diary entry reflects a significant shift in Franklin Roosevelt's thinking as the new decade opened. He no longer had much interest in a legislative position, even one as prestigious as a United States Senator. It seemed that after his years in the Navy Department, he had discovered that he was more comfortable as an executive, and preferred administering laws to enacting them.

Later that same day, Louis B. Wehle, general counsel of the War Finance Corporation and an old friend from Harvard, came to FDR's office with an intriguing idea. He proposed that the Democrats, at their national convention in San Francisco in July, should nominate Herbert Hoover of California for president and Franklin Roosevelt of New York for vice president. Wehle told Roosevelt that he had tried out his idea on several influential Democrats, who had enthusiastically endorsed it. Everyone knew that the political currents were running in favor of the Republicans that year, but perhaps a Hoover-Roosevelt ticket might turn the tide. Hoover, whose humanitarian efforts in Europe had saved literally millions from starvation, was an international hero and would make a particularly attractive candidate. The only question was that no one—including Hoover—seemed to know whether he was a Republican or a Democrat.

Roosevelt, like almost every American, admired Hoover, but he was skeptical of Wehle's proposal. Eventually, in March, Hoover settled the issue by announcing that he was a Republican.

There had been speculation about Roosevelt's potential future, both in political circles and in the press. As early as May 22, 1919, the New York *Sun* ran an editorial proclaiming, "If it were the job of the *Sun* to suggest to the Democratic Party the man who . . . might prove a standard bearer to be reckoned with by the opposition party in 1920, it would name Franklin D. Roosevelt, the brilliant young assistant secretary of the Navy." But the *Sun* was one of the most conservative papers in the nation, and no one, least of all Franklin Delano Roosevelt, took its suggestion all that seriously. It "is very delightful," he wrote in a letter, "but one of the largest jokes on record."

Meanwhile, Admiral William S. Sims, who had led the Navy in Europe during the war, and at various times had been both FDR's antagonist and his ally, was by 1920 back in his position as president of the Naval War College in Newport, Rhode Island, and was preparing an unwelcome surprise. He had written a book about his experiences in the war, and had come to the conclusion that the Navy had been badly mismanaged, particularly in the months leading up to America's entry into the war and in the first few months of the war itself. As

1920 opened, he sent a lengthy, vindictive memorandum to Josephus Daniels in which he charged that the fault for the Navy's failings lay not with the Navy itself, but with the incompetence and lethargy of the civilian in charge, namely Josephus Daniels himself. Sims claimed that the Secretary's shortcomings had led to the loss of 500,000 lives, 2,500,000 tons of shipping, and a waste of $15 billion.

When Sims made these sensational charges public, Roosevelt's initial position was to loyally side with Daniels. In a January 23, 1920 letter to his friend Livingston Davis, he wrote of Sims, "It does seem a pity, does it not, that really fine, interesting men seem so often to lose their heads completely. The net result of all this will be, of course, to hurt the Navy, including Sims. . . . The hurting of a Secretary or an Assistant Secretary, who, after all are but birds of passage, is very incidental and very unimportant, but the Navy has gone for nearly 150 years, and we hope, will always go on; therefore its reputation is of importance."

The Republicans who controlled Congress immediately made plans to investigate Admiral Sims's scandalous charges; when it occurred to Roosevelt that he might get caught in the crossfire and be subject to the same smears being levied at Daniels, he immediately reversed himself and gave a speech that cruelly damned his superior. He agreed with Sims that the Navy should have done much more in the way of preparation in the months leading up to the war. The New York *Times*, in its extensive coverage of the speech, reported that Roosevelt "said there was no program thought out, and that he [Roosevelt] prepared one which called for aggressive action.

"'I was opposed by the President, who said that he did not want to commit any overt act of war, but who added that he was following a definite course in an effort to avert a war.

"'Two months after war was declared,' continued Mr. Roosevelt, 'I saw that the Navy was still unprepared and I spent 40 millions for guns before Congress gave me or anyone permission to spend any money.'"

The speech was blatantly disloyal. Roosevelt regretted it almost immediately and issued an "explanation" that more or less denied that he had said anything like what appeared in the newspapers. But his attacks on Daniels and the president were so self-serving and traitorous that Daniels seriously considered forcing him to resign, an act that would almost certainly have destroyed Roosevelt's political career. Daniels changed his mind on learning that Mrs. Wilson had developed a bitter hatred of FDR, and decided against taking any action. Instead, he wrote in his diary on February 21: "FDR persona non grata with W. Better to let speech pass."

The one political position that Roosevelt most coveted in 1920 was the chance to become governor of New York. But he had missed his opportunity in 1918 when Wilson—and Boss Murphy—had urged him to run. By 1920, the governorship was not to be had. Al Smith, a Tammany stalwart, was sitting in the Governor's mansion in Albany and was almost certain to run again, unless he decided to try for the Senate seat that Mrs. Hamlin had mentioned in her diary, which did not seem at all likely.

What became increasingly clear throughout the spring of 1920 was that the speech he had so casually pulled together for the Democratic National Committee meeting the previous May was still reverberating among the party faithful throughout the country. In the political gossip and rumors bandied about in the run-up to the Democratic Convention, scheduled for June 28 in San Francisco, his name figured prominently, and he had reason to hope he had a chance to be on the national ticket.

There were three leading contenders for presidential nomination: Mitchell Palmer, the attorney general; William Gibbs McAdoo, Wilson's son-in-law and until recently his treasury secretary; and Governor James M. Cox of Ohio, a Progressive who was the candidate of the city bosses, including Tammany's Charles F. Murphy.

As a prominent member of the party, FDR was a member of the New York delegation to the convention, and he spent the four-day train trip to the West Coast currying favor and mending fences with as many fellow Democrats as he could find.

By the time the convention opened at the end of June, the Republicans had already picked a bland nonentity, Senator Warren G. Harding of Ohio, to be their presidential candidate. Harding was a conservative choice, with none of the progressive fire that Theodore Roosevelt had brought to the GOP, and there was a sense of hope among the delegates that Harding's nomination could give the Democratic ticket a greater chance of success despite the rising Republican tide in the nation.

Frances Perkins, who had been a skeptical witness to FDR's earliest political efforts, was at San Francisco, and was clearly impressed by his presence at the convention. "Franklin Roosevelt was in the thick of it," she remembered. "Tall, strong, handsome, and popular, he was one of the stars of the show. I recall how he displayed his athletic ability by vaulting over a row of chairs to get to the platform in a hurry."

As so often with the Democrats, the balloting for president went on for days, but finally, on the forty-fourth ballot, the exhausted delegates managed to nominate Governor Cox. The candidate was asleep in Dayton when he was awakened at dawn by a telephone call from his floor manager, Edmond H. Moore, who gave him the news and asked for his preference for vice president. In his autobiography, Cox recalled: "I told him I had given the matter some thought and that my choice would be Franklin D. Roosevelt of New York. Moore inquired, 'Do you know him?' I did not. In fact, so far as I knew, I had never seen him; but I explained to Mr. Moore that he met the geographical requirement, that he was recognized as an Independent and that Roosevelt was a well-known name." Moore got in touch with Murphy to get Tammany's opinion on FDR. Murphy declared, "I don't like Roosevelt. He is not well known in the country, but, Ed, this is the first time a Democratic nominee for the presidency has shown me courtesy. That's why I would vote for the devil himself if Cox wanted me to. Tell him we will nominate Roosevelt on the first ballot as soon as we assemble."

As good as his word, Murphy saw to it that Roosevelt's name was placed in nomination, and, after the other three nominees withdrew their names, Roosevelt was nominated for vice president by acclamation. Congratulations showered in from around the country, including a particularly warm one from Herbert Hoover: "The fact that I do not belong to your political tribe does not deter me from offering my personal congratulations to an old friend. I am glad to see you in the game in such a prominent place, and, although I will not be charged with traitorship by wishing you success, I nevertheless consider it a contribution to the good of the country that you have been nominated and it will bring the merit of a great public servant to the front. If you are elected, you will do the job properly."

A somewhat less effusive telegram came in from Woodrow Wilson: "Please accept my warm congratulation and good wishes."

Soon after the convention, on Sunday, July 18, 1920, the two nominees met in Washington to pay their respects to the president. At the White House, they were asked to wait fifteen minutes while Mr. Wilson prepared to receive them. Eventually they were ushered out of doors onto the south portico, bright with the summer sun. There, huddled in a wheelchair, with a shawl draped over his paralyzed left arm and his chin sunk into his chest, sat Woodrow Wilson, a figure of despair and defeat. "He is a very sick man," Cox said compassionately, as he stepped forward and greeted the president warmly. Only then did Wilson look up. With half his face immobilized, he attempted a smile. Then, in a weak whisper, he said, "Thank you for coming. I am very glad you came."

Roosevelt, who had worked closely with Wilson but had not seen him for almost a year, was shocked by his utter weakness. He saw tears standing in Cox's eyes. Cox said, "Mr. President, I have always admired the fight you made for the League." The president tried to draw himself up. "Mr. Cox," he whispered, "that fight can still be won!" Cox said, "Mr. President, we are going to be a million percent with you, and your administration, and that means the League of Nations." The president looked up again and, in a voice scarcely audible, said, "I am very grateful." His slack-jawed head fell back on his chest. The meeting was over.

It was a time for the candidates to map out their campaign, and a time for Franklin Roosevelt to bid farewell to the patient, long-suffering superior he had alternately admired and disdained. Roosevelt's letter of resignation to Josephus Daniels very deliberately glosses over the often-stormy relations that characterized so much of their seven years together. It says less about their true relationship than it does of the willingness of both of them to paper over their very real differences. In a handwritten letter, FDR wrote:

> *My dear Chief:*
> *This is not goodbye—that will always be impossible after these years of the closest association—and no words I write will make you know better than you know now how much our association has meant. All my life I shall look back,—not only on the work of the place—but mostly on the wonderful way in which you and I have gone through these nearly eight years together. You have taught me so wisely and kept my feet on the ground when I was about to skyrocket—and in it all there has never been a real dispute or antagonism or distrust.*
>
> *Hence, in part, at least, I will share in the reward, which you will get true credit for in history. I am very proud—but more than that I am very happy to have been able to help.*
>
> *We will I know keep up this association in the years to come—and please let me keep on coming to you to get your*

fine inspiration of real idealism and right living and good Americanism.

So au revoir *for a little while. You have always the*

Affectionate regards of

Franklin D. Roosevelt

There is a dissembling tone to the letter that might strike some as hypocritical. But Roosevelt was no hypocrite. He almost certainly couched the letter in sugary half-truths simply because that is what Daniels would have wanted and expected. He was playing to his audience.

What is probably more significant is that it is a letter that Theodore Roosevelt could never have brought himself to write.

CHAPTER FORTY-ONE

F ranklin Roosevelt, standing on the front steps of his beloved Springwood in Hyde Park, looked out at the huge crowd of five thousand people who had come to share with him this very important moment in his life—the formal notification of his nomination to be the Democratic Party's vice presidential candidate. He was thirty-eight years old, and doubtless he took pride in the fact that he had reached this particular milestone at an age three years younger than Uncle Ted.

He and Eleanor had attended Cox's notification the day before in Dayton, and had returned home in time for his own. Inside the house, Senator Joseph T. Robinson of Arkansas had just finished taking care of the formalities in the library, and now Roosevelt had come out into the noontime sun to make his acceptance speech.

The day was August 9, 1920, stiflingly humid as the Hudson Valley almost always is at that time of year, but the crowd appeared unaffected by the heat, delighted to be present and to help celebrate a local boy who had made good.

Nor was the crowd made up solely of neighbors. There were important people in his audience, people who had come a long way to share this moment: Josephus Daniels, up from Washington to cheer on his assistant, William Gibbs McAdoo, who had lost the presidential nomination to Cox but remained a prominent figure in the party, and Governor Al Smith, his old Tammany colleague from Albany. His mother sat proudly at his side, and Eleanor and the two oldest children were off to his right. Even Sara's older brother, Warren Delano III, had put aside his Republican convictions for this one day to celebrate his nephew's entry into national elective politics.

And they had all come to see *him*. That was important to Roosevelt. For once, he was not an outsider looking in, nor even an honored guest. He was the sole reason for these ceremonies, for this crowd, for all these people who had rearranged their lives that they might be here.

He had worked long and hard on his speech. He would try not to disappoint them.

> *I accept the nomination for the office of Vice President with humbleness, and with a deep wish to give to our beloved country the best that is in me.—No one could receive a higher privilege or opportunity than to be thus associated with men and ideals which I am confident will soon receive the support of the majority of our citizens.*

He was standing less than a hundred feet from the spot where, as a boy more than twenty-five years earlier, he first read *The Naval War of 1812*, and where he had absorbed so much of Cousin Ted's vision, his sense of urgency, his world view. What a remarkable amount of living and learning he had crowded into the years since! Those first tentative steps away from home at Groton (where his eldest son James was about to enter in a few weeks), his slow but determined mastery of his social awkwardness there and at Harvard and Columbia Law, his marriage, which bound him so directly to the Oyster Bay Roosevelts and Uncle Ted, his simplistic but astonishingly accurate career plan, which again served to tie him spiritually to Theodore, his entry into politics and his unexpected rise to prominence as a result of the Sheehan battle, his alliance with Louis Howe, part wizard Merlin, part loyal Sancho Panza.

> *Two great problems will confront the next administration; our relations with the world and the pressing need of organized progress at home. . . . We must either shut our eyes . . . close our ports, build an impregnable wall of costly armaments, and live, as the Orient used to live, a hermit nation, dreaming of the past; or we must open our eyes and see that modern civilization has become so complex and the lives of civilized men so interwoven with the lives of other men in other countries as to make it impossible to be in this world and not of it.*
>
> *As for our home problem, we have been awakened by this war into a startled realization of the archaic shortcomings of our governmental machinery and of the need for the kind of reorganization which only a clear thinking businessman, experienced in the technicalities of governmental procedure, can carry out.*

There was his embrace of Wilson's dynamic idealism, and his subsequent single-minded campaign to secure the post of assistant secretary of the Navy, and how the Navy, which had first stirred his interest in the larger world of government, had shaped his understanding of that government; how Josephus Daniels, who could be so maddeningly obtuse at times, had taught him how to deal with those who would try to impose their will on the public good for their own profit; how, in the confused years leading up to America's entry into the war, he had seen the need for America to prepare for that eventuality and how it had taken Wilson a year to recognize that need; how it was through his own vision and determination that the North Sea Barrage was brought into being.

Let us be definite. We have passed through a great war,—an armed conflict which called forth every effort on the part of the whole population.—The war was won by Republicans as well as by Democrats. . . . It would, therefore, not only serve little purpose,—but would conform ill to our high standards if any person should in the heat of political rivalry seek to manufacture political advantage out of a nationally conducted struggle.

He had learned to see war as a desperate enterprise that rarely solved the crisis that brought it on, and how it was imperative to find some means of controlling humanity's tendency toward conflict.

To this end the Democratic Party offers a treaty of peace, which to make it a real treaty for a real peace MUST include a League of Nations; because this peace treaty, if our best and bravest are not to have died in vain, must be no thinly disguised armistice devised by cynical statesmen to mask their preparations for a renewal of greed-inspired conquests later on.

Roosevelt had absorbed a hands-on education, an education like no other, where he had seen his cousinly idol go too far in the pursuit of Nobility and Honor, and his president not go far enough in his pursuit of very different ideals with the same names. He had come to understand the need for strength, and had learned where it lay and how it could be mobilized. He had learned that there would always be critical problems, that when they arose they must be faced, and willy-nilly there would be ways to solve them.

America's opportunity is at hand. We can lead the world by a great example, we can prove this nation a living, growing thing, with policies that are adequate to new conditions. In a thousand ways this is our hour of test.

For all his brave words, 1920 would not be Franklin D. Roosevelt's year. America would reject the Democratic ticket in favor of Harding and Coolidge. The country would be content to relapse into the comfort of old and familiar ways. But such would not always be the case. Franklin Roosevelt's time would come. And when it came, he would be ready.

EPILOGUE

I t was late in the afternoon of October 11, 1939, barely a
month after President Roosevelt had been awakened to learn
that Hitler had invaded Poland and ignited World War II.
The president had spent most of the time since then beginning
the restructuring of the federal government to meet the crisis and
working feverishly with a recalcitrant Congress to repeal the arms
embargo of the Neutrality Act so that America could supply Britain
and France with war materiel.

There was a discreet knock on the Oval Office door, and the president's aide, General Edwin M. Watson, ushered in a familiar face, Dr.
Alexander Sachs, a vice president of the Wall Street giant Lehman
Brothers. Sachs had been an important adviser to the president from
the early days of the New Deal. He was a polymath who had taught
at Princeton and was learned in a number of disciplines, including
economics, jurisprudence, and some of the more esoteric realms of
science. Roosevelt was aware that Sachs had been trying to meet with
him for several weeks, but he had put him off because of the urgency
of dealing with the war.

"Alex, what are you up to?" the president asked, greeting him genially.

Sachs, a serious, formal man, sat down somewhat nervously and opened his briefcase, which included a file folder with several papers and some scholarly journals. He told the president that he had come to Washington to deliver a letter from Albert Einstein. Roosevelt was intrigued. He had met the famous Einstein, but in no sense could he say he knew him. Sachs then explained that before discussing the letter, he wanted to open his presentation with a historical anecdote. He told a story about Robert Fulton, a young American inventor in Paris, who wrote a letter to Napoleon claiming that he could build the emperor a fleet of warships powered by steam that required no sails, which could cross the channel in a few hours and attack England, regardless of the weather. Napoleon was unimpressed. "Ships without sails? Away with your visionists!"

Roosevelt nodded good-naturedly. He understood that the point of the story was to show how a national leader might fail to understand an important invention that could win a war. Perhaps sensing Sachs's continuing uneasiness, FDR scribbled a note and gave it to an aide, who promptly returned with a prized bottle of Napoleon brandy that had been in the Roosevelt family for years. The president opened it, poured two glasses, and gave one to Sachs, and the two men toasted each other.

Sachs then took out an 800-word typed document that he had written himself, which, he explained, paraphrased the letter from Einstein and, he hoped, made it less technical and more understandable. He then began to read aloud his description of a potential new energy source derived from uranium, that could be used to power industry, revolutionize the practice of medicine, and create "bombs of hitherto unenvisioned potency and scope."

Roosevelt had some difficulty following the complicated explanation, but what he could understand was that this nuclear power, whatever that might be, was important enough for Albert Einstein to think that the president should be made aware of it, and that he had gone to the trouble of recruiting Alexander Sachs, a man who FDR knew well and trusted, to carry the message.

Sachs could see the president's attention wandering. He took out the Einstein letter and read the opening and closing paragraphs, which noted that German physicists were already investigating nuclear power.

That caught Roosevelt's attention.

Encouraged, Sachs reached again into his briefcase and, pulling out a scholarly journal, read aloud the closing paragraph of a 1936 lecture on nuclear power by the English chemist, physicist, and spectroscopist Francis Aston:

> "Personally I think there is no doubt that sub-atomic energy is available all around us, and that one day man will release and control its almost infinite power. We cannot prevent him from doing so and can only hope that he will not use it exclusively in blowing up his next door neighbor."

Now Roosevelt understood fully. He leaned forward cheerfully. "Alex, what you are after is to see that the Nazis don't blow us up."

"Precisely, Mr. President."

Roosevelt called in General Watson and gestured toward Sachs and the various papers surrounding him. "This requires action," he said decisively. In that simple gesture, he began the process that would eventually produce the weapon that would finally end World War II six years later.

ACKNOWLEDGEMENTS

F ranklin Delano Roosevelt lived one of the most eventful lives of anyone of his times, and left behind a remarkably detailed accounting of his life and achievements in the form of the thousands of personal letters, manuscripts, documents, speeches, magazine articles, photographs, and official correspondence now housed in the Franklin Delano Roosevelt Library at Hyde Park. My own research on Roosevelt's life, and how it related to the U.S. Navy, began there, and I am indebted to the staff members of the library, who were invariably helpful and often went out of their way to find material I did not even know I needed. I am equally indebted to the many writers who have come before me, and whose works helped shape my own understanding and interpretation of FDR and his times. Chief among these I include:

Alsop, Joseph. *FDR: A Centenary Remembrance.* New York, 1982.
Ashburn, Frank D. *Peabody of Groton: A Portrait.* New York, 1944.
Bullitt, Orville H. (ed.). *For The President, Personal And Secret.* New York, 1972.

Burns, James MacGregor. *Roosevelt: The Lion and the Fox*. New York, 1956.

Burns, James MacGregor. *Roosevelt: The Soldier of Freedom*. New York, 1970.

Burns, James MacGregor, and Susan Dunn. *The Three Roosevelts: Patrician Leaders Who Transformed America*. New York, 2001.

Churchill, Allen. *The Roosevelts: American Aristocrats*. New York, 1965.

Cross, Robert F. *Sailor in the White House*. Annapolis, 2003.

Davis, Kenneth S. *FDR: The Beckoning of Destiny*. New York, 1971.

Dows, Olin. *Franklin Roosevelt at Hyde Park*. New York, 1949.

Evans, Harold. *The American Century*. New York, 1998.

Fenster, Julie M. *FDR's Shadow: Louis Howe, the Force that Shaped Franklin and Eleanor Roosevelt*. New York, 2009.

Freidel, Frank. *Franklin D. Roosevelt: The Apprenticeship*. Boston, 1952.

Freidel, Frank. *Franklin D. Roosevelt: The Ordeal*. Boston, 1954.

Kilpatrick, Carroll (ed.). *Roosevelt & Daniels*. Chapel Hill, 1952.

Larrabee, Eric. *Commander in Chief: Franklin Delano Roosevelt, His Lieutenants & Their War*. New York, 1987.

Lash, Joseph P. *Eleanor and Franklin*. New York, 1971.

Lindley, Ernest K. *Franklin D. Roosevelt: A Career in Progressive Democracy*. Indianapolis, 1931.

Marolda, Edward J. (ed.). *FDR and the U.S. Navy*. New York, 1998.

Perkins, Frances. *The Roosevelt I Knew*. New York, 1946.

Persico, Joseph E. *Franklin & Lucy*. New York, 2008.

Roosevelt, Elliott (ed.). *F.D.R.: His Personal Letters, Early Years*. New York, 1947.

Roosevelt, Elliott (ed.). *F.D.R.: His Personal Letters 1905-1928*. New York, 1948.

Roosevelt, Theodore. *The Naval War of 1812*. Annapolis, 1987.

Rosenau, James N. (ed.). *The Roosevelt Treasury*. New York, 1951.

Simpson, Michael. *Anglo-American Naval Relations 1917-1919*. London, 1991.

Smith, Richard K. *First Across!: The U.S. Navy's Transatlantic Flight of 1919*. Annapolis, 1973.

Sprout, Harold and Margaret. *The Rise of American Naval Power 1776-1918*. Annapolis, 1990.

Symonds, Craig. *Historical Atlas of the U.S. Navy*. Annapolis, 1995.

Tuchman, Barbara W. *The Zimmermann Telegram*. New York, 1985.

Ward, Geoffrey C. *Before the Trumpet: Young Franklin Roosevelt*. New York, 1985.

Ward, Geoffrey C. *A First Class Temperament: The Emergence of Franklin Roosevelt*. New York, 1989.

Willis, Resa. *FDR and Lucy: Lovers and Friends*. New York, 2004.

A book is often more of a collaborative effort than is generally understood, and there is no way this particular book could have seen the light of day had it not been for two particularly important midwives: first, my agent, Al Zuckerman, who had the original idea that eventually evolved into the present work; and second, my publisher and editor, Claiborne Hancock, who guided me through a sometimes troubling birthing process with wisdom, patience, enthusiasm, and good humor. In addition, I would like to express my thanks to Phil Gaskill, whose awesome erudition in such diverse disciplines as naval nomenclature and baseball history was extremely helpful, and Maria Fernandez, whose design skills show up on every page. To my closest collaborator, my wife Belinda, I can finally offer a future in which every dinner hour will not necessarily be given over to a discussion of Woodrow Wilson's assistant secretary of the Navy.

INDEX